MOORE

OF

CORUNNA

MOORE

OF

CORUNNA

ROGER PARKINSON

HART DAVIS, MACGIBBON LONDON

Granada Publishing Limited
First published in Great Britain 1976 by Hart-Davis, MacGibbon Ltd
Frogmore, St Albans, Hertfordshire AL2 2NF and
3 Upper James Street, London W1R 4BP

Copyright © 1976 by Roger Parkinson

ISBN 0 246 10755 3
Printed in Great Britain by
Butler & Tanner Ltd, Frome and London

CONTENTS

List of Maps   vi
Introduction   vii

1	Damned Rebels	1
2	Chaos in Corsica	16
3	Home in Disgrace	40
4	Yellow Jack and Black Bogs	62
5	Wounds of War	89
6	Egypt and Honours	108
7	Sicily and Sweden	139
8	Advance into Spain	162
9	Retreat	182
10	Field of His Fame	203

Acknowledgements   239
Select Bibliography   240
Index   242

LIST OF MAPS

Map 1	Corsica 1790	30
Map 2	North Holland 1799	90
Map 3	Egypt 1801	114
Map 4	Portugal and Spain 1808	197
Map 5	Corunna 1809	227

INTRODUCTION

Soldiering, in the eighteenth century, was a heart-breaking profession for any British officer who wished to take it seriously. It was a century filled with wars, which took British soldiers all over the world: the War of the Spanish Succession, the War of the Austrian Succession, the Seven Years War, the War of American Independence and the French Revolutionary War. It is an astonishing and depressing fact that every single one of these occasions found the Army utterly unprepared. Every time, even the most elementary aspects of the business of making war had to be re-learned at vast expense of blood and pain and money. A staff officer in the Duke of York's campaign in Flanders and Holland (1793–5) wrote: '. . . we do not know how to post a picquet or instruct a sentinel in his duty; and as to moving, God forbid that we should attempt it within three miles of an enemy.'

That the Army was able to survive such constant ineptitude, rise from such depths, and face the disciplined, victorious legions of Napoleon, was due almost entirely to the devotion, eagerness and unquenchable professionalism of a handful of able officers, of whom Sir John Moore was one of the most important.

Moore's experience of war was derived from campaigns in both hemispheres, lessons well digested and passed on. He was a leader of high quality, revealed not least in his effort to create a new relationship between the officers and the men they led – a relationship founded on care, trust and mutual respect, not on the lash. He was repaid by the affection that his troops displayed for him, and by their response to his teaching in other matters.

Moore was, above all, a teacher, and his claim to enduring fame lies more in the method of war that he taught than in command achievements – although his last campaign called forth great qualities of penetration, decision and nerve. Moore did not originate the Light Infantry training system, calling for much individual initiative at all levels, which he expounded at his famous camp at Shorncliffe in 1803; but he was able, by his warm personality, to impart to the officers and men under him his own deep interest and enthusiasm. In turn, their skill and example was to impress the whole Army, and went far towards making it the instrument which, under Wellington in the Peninsula, defeated Napoleon's forces time and again, and played a great part in the final defeat of the Emperor himself at Waterloo. It could indeed be said of Moore, as of some other great teachers of war, that his finest victories were won after death.

John Terraine

Chapter One

*

DAMNED REBELS

His uniform still felt strange and restrictive in the Marseilles bustle. Back in Glasgow, John Moore's family waited impatiently for the first letter from the fifteen-year-old ensign, and his brothers and sisters bought the latest map of Europe so as to be better acquainted with his travels. The year 1777 would see dramatic military events far across the Atlantic; the War of American Revolution was twenty-three months old. Now, at stinking Marseilles in the March sunshine, the future opponent of the American rebels, and eventual victor against the French at Corunna, chaffed at his scarlet collar with its sea-green facings and tried to keep his tight white breeches clean. His powdered hair lay sticky beneath his gold-laced triangular 'Cumberland Cock'. His sword tended to become entangled between his legs. John Moore, the latest officer to enter the British army, awaited transport to join the 51st Regiment stationed at Port Mahon, Minorca.

He missed his secure Glasgow home, but that would soon pass. John had been taught to be independent by his wise father, Dr John Moore. The death of three boys in early life made Johnny – or 'Jack' or 'Jock' – born 13 November 1761 the eldest son. His sister Jane had arrived in 1758 and four more brothers followed: James in 1762, the future Admiral Sir Graham Moore in 1764, Francis in 1767 and Charles in 1770. Another, Hamilton, failed to survive the year of his birth in 1772; so did another sister, Marion, born in 1768.

The large family was boisterous and compact. James, a year younger than John, described his brother as a schoolboy at Glasgow high school: 'In his boyish days he was fiery and untractable, faults which were gradually suppressed by paternal

1

Moore's birthplace in
the Trongate, in
the centre of old
Glasgow.

Dr John Moore, wise and helpful father to 'Jack' throughout his early military career.

reproofs, and by his own masculine understanding; so that he acquired a complete command of temper, and a mild disposition. His figure was tall, and graceful, his features were regular, his eyes hazel, hair brown, and the expression of his countenance cheerful and benign.' The fair good looks would stay with him always; so too would the mild disposition, but beneath would still run an 'untractable' nature.

3

Independence had been further fostered by the unique opportunity offered to John in his eighth year. Dr Moore had been befriended by the Duchess of Hamilton, born Elizabeth Gunning, after his unsuccessful attempt to restore the health of her first son. Then, in February 1772, after her husband had succeeded to the duchy of Argyll, the Duchess invited Dr Moore to accompany her other son, fifteen-year-old Douglas, eighth Duke of Hamilton, while he travelled abroad for up to three years. Terms offered were £500 per annum for expenses and an annuity of £100; Dr Moore was to be tutor, guide and physician. The Duchess planned that her son should settle at Geneva for perhaps a year, after which he should visit the principal courts of Germany and Italy. Dr Moore, with some apprehensions about his headstrong charge, began the Grand Tour on Monday 13 April 1772, leaving his pregnant wife Jeanie in Glasgow. John travelled with the party.

The young duke and the doctor's eldest son became firm friends, and their relationship was strengthened by an incident in Paris. The Duke, fooling around with a small dress sword, nicked John in the side and appeared much mortified by the resulting stream of blood. John soon recovered; he had himself already almost inflicted a greater wound upon an innocent French *femme de chambre*: idly playing with a pair of travelling pistols, he had unleashed a shot which had splintered the fine panelling in the Duke's sitting room. His side was still unhealed when he became involved in a vigorous brawl with young French dandies in the Tuileries gardens, after they had dared to snigger at his plain English clothing.

Dr Moore rescued his son from further adventures, and the Duke from designing French females, and brought them safe to Geneva. There, until autumn 1774, John spent an arduous and lonely period in a stuffy little room, obliged to stick to his studies while his father fulfilled his duties with the Duke. 'I apply pretty much,' wrote John to his mother in October 1773, 'but find the Latin more difficult than the French. I am at the writing and arithmetic school, but Papa has learned me geography so nicely, I know every part of the world . . . I am trying all I can to make myself good for something. I will do whatsoever I am fit for, and Papa and you please.'

During these years John decided the 'something' must be the

Portraits of
Douglas, eighth
Duke of Hamilton,
centre, with Dr
John Moore and
young John,
painted at Geneva
in 1774. 'The
figures are like,'
commented Dr
Moore.

army. These were troubled times, and a military career
promised excitement: futile efforts were being made to restore
relations between Britain and her American colonies, and
George III told Parliament in November 1773 that these
attempts seemed doomed to failure. 'The New England govern-
ments are in a state of rebellion,' declared the King. 'Blows must
decide.' The idea of John being a soldier pleased his father, and
the diligent parent approached his patroness, the Duchess of
Argyll. She could only reply with a letter from the Secretary
for War, declaring His Majesty had decreed that no commission

should be given to anyone under sixteen. Dr Moore confided to his wife: 'I intend to make Johnny sixteen the moment he is past fifteen.'

By now the party had moved to Germany. 'I shall do all I can to profit by the good occasion which I now have of being abroad with my father,' John wrote to his mother in Christmas week 1774, 'and trie if I can to make a good soldier. I am very sure Papa does all he can to make me clever, and if I don't turn out good for something it will not be his fault.' He found German difficult, but would try harder, 'as it will be of great use to me when I am an officer, especially if I am sent into Germany, which is by far the best country to learn the art Military.' The group watched a review at Potsdam, and Dr Moore wrote to his wife: 'If Jack hesitated about being a soldier, this glorious scene would have confirmed him.'

He entreated the Duchess of Argyll for continued help. 'Your Grace may now declare Jack to be 16,' he wrote from Vienna on 29 August 1775, 'as he is actually turned of fifteen and in his sixteenth year.' The doctor's dates were certainly hazy: his eldest son was due to celebrate his fourteenth birthday the coming November. Before then the small band had moved to Vienna, where Emperor Joseph II offered to take the aspirant soldier into his service, but Dr Moore declined the invitation. John had heard that another member of his family also intended to enter service, although in the navy. 'I am pleased, my dear boy,' he wrote to his brother Graham, 'that you wish to be a sailor, for I am sure you will be a brave one. I hope that, in some years after this, you and I will thresh the Monsieurs, both by sea and land; but I hope we won't make war with the Spaniards; for the Spanish Ambassador is the best and kindest man I ever saw.'

In the winter of 1775 they travelled to Italy and Rome, and the welcome news arrived that the Duke of Argyll had obtained an ensigncy for John Moore in the 51st Regiment. The party celebrated in Rome, and travelled on to Naples, where Ensign Moore crept too close to the crater of Vesuvius and had to flee before a minor eruption. He fell upon burning cinders and was forced to spend some days on his stomach in bed. The Duke and his entourage moved north again, through the Alps to Mont Blanc and Geneva, where they spent the summer before heading for Paris. On 14 September 1776 they returned at last to London. John visited a West End military tailor, and travelled home to Glasgow resplendent in his uniform. Barely had Christmas and the New Year come and gone before Ensign Moore left home again for the journey south through Europe to his regiment and a new career.

*   *   *

His uniform had become familiar after a month's enforced delay at Marseilles, waiting for a packet to Port Mahon. The stay proved irksome, but by 3 April 1777 John could report his safe and happy arrival in Minorca. 'I have been hitherto, I must confess, exceedingly lucky, I have got into one of the best regiments in the service; as to officers, I never knew such a number of fine gentlemanly lads.' Another letter declared: 'I am very intimate with two or three of the officers, and I am upon a bad footing with none of them...never was I happier in my life, save those seven weeks I passed with you, dear Mother! in Glasgow.'

Ensign Moore was comfortably settled in George Town barracks, less than two miles from Mahon. He had a spacious sitting room, as large as his mother's drawing room, plus two closets–one for his servant–and he had bought sheets, blankets, towels and chairs. The company of his fellow officers continued to be excellent: 'There is no such thing as either drinking or gambling going on.' The commanding officer, Colonel Pringle, had been with the 51st almost since the regiment was formed in York in late 1755, and had played his part in the fine performance put up by the 51st during the Seven Years War, especially at Minden. John's boast was correct: the 51st was indeed 'one of the best regiments in the service'. The sentiment had even been echoed by the crusty General James Murray, overall commander in Minorca and leader of the left wing of Wolfe's army on the Plains of Abraham in 1759. Moore had been warned that Murray could be a veritable terror, but as John told his mother, the General was 'one of the best officers in the service, and a very agreeable fine old soldier'.

John Moore's career could have had no better beginning: congenial company and climate, excellent regiment and

Minorca, John Moore's first military posting, where he joined the excellent 51st regiment in 1777.

commanders, and duties which may have appeared dull to some but which were found interesting and educational by the zealous young ensign. Summer sped by with drill exercises and preparations ordered by Murray against sudden invasion by the Spanish and French. Many dismissed Murray's warnings: life seemed peaceful in Minorca – and in stark contrast to events across the Atlantic.

The year's campaign against those 'damned rebels' in the American colonies had begun with high hopes and grandiose plans: an army under General Burgoyne would slash south from Canada into New York State while Sir William Howe moved north from New York itself to join Burgoyne at Albany; a third column under Colonel Barry St Leger would strike up the St Lawrence to Lake Ontario, and sweep down the Mohawk valley to unite with the others. But the close co-ordination so essential for success, and especially difficult to achieve in the trackless North American forests, was rendered even

more elusive by confused orders from Whitehall. On 4 October Howe defeated Washington at Germantown, although the Americans only suffered 700 casualties out of their 13,000 strength. But within days came the turning point of the whole revolution: Burgoyne surrendered to the Americans at Saratoga. The remaining British forces in North America could barely cling to finger-holds at New York City, Rhode Island and Philadelphia. France recognized the independence of the United States, the prelude to her active participation in the war.

News of the Saratoga disaster had still to reach distant Minorca when the young ensign in the 51st decided he must seek more active duties – in America. Advancement in his military career would only come through actual fighting. Already, John Moore had begun to show a discontent with mere garrison duties which would remain with him throughout his life. Once again he enlisted his father's help, and the doctor, now resident with his family in London and embarked upon literary activities, applied his usual energy. The defeat in America aided Dr Moore: in a wave of patriotism, Manchester, Liverpool, Glasgow and Edinburgh volunteered to raise battalions at their own expense, and a number of Scottish lords promised the same – including the Duke of Hamilton. His would be the 82nd Foot, a Lowland regiment totalling 900 men. On 10 January 1778 John Moore was gazetted captain-lieutenant of the 82nd; his additional duties included those of paymaster. In the summer of 1778 he travelled to find his new regiment in Arran.

Twelve years later John Moore would return to the 51st, as commanding officer, and by then the regiment would have suffered stern trials: four years after Moore's departure, Murray's warnings proved correct, and 8,000 Spanish and French descended upon Minorca. The defenders endured a six-month siege amidst the battered fortifications at St Philip, finally capitulating in February 1782, with honour intact but their ranks decimated by scurvy.

It was not until late spring that Moore sailed for North America with six companies of the 82nd, under the command of General Francis McLean. The Duke of Hamilton had forsaken the attractions of military life for those of his new bride. Part of his regiment therefore went without him to the wild wooded coast of Nova Scotia, bringing with them news of Spain's declaration of war against England. McLean's men had the task of establishing a base at Penobscot Bay, close to Halifax, from which rebel trade with Boston could be severed. Within a month Lieutenant Moore had tasted combat for the first time. 'By my last you would be informed of our arrival here,' he wrote to his father on 24 August. 'Since then, our operations have been rather more interesting.'

The troops had landed on the rocky beach, and started to build a fort with timber from the conifers standing close to the shore; three sloops of war were moored across the harbour to establish a barrier against enemy shipping. But on 23 July 1779 the Americans moved against this British nuisance with vastly superior numbers, while the small British fort was still less than breast-high. About forty enemy ships appeared over the horizon, eighteen of them armed and the rest carrying troops and stores. The armed vessels immediately opened fire on the British

sloops, which returned the bombardment. A battery manned
by men of the 82nd at the half-built fort opened up on the
American ships, and the bay echoed with booming guns. First
American attempts to land were beaten off but early on the
morning of 28 July, three of the men-of-war moved close inshore
and turned broadside to the coast, heaving in the swell. Seconds
later the woods around Moore and the 82nd were rent by the
bombardment. Trees fell and branches crashed down on all
sides, to the consternation of the many men in the 82nd who
had never been under fire before. Moore controlled his fear and
tried to help the soldiers around him to do the same.

The cannonade ceased, and the British troops emerged from
cover to see crowded American longboats pulling towards the
beaches – heading especially towards an area defended by a
company of the Hamilton regiment, on the left of which stood
seventeen-year-old John Moore commanding twenty men, all
as inexperienced as himself. His superior officer, a captain of
the 74th, panicked – or, in Moore's words, became 'a little
startled' – and ordered his terrified men to retreat after firing
one ineffectual volley. Moore, however, stayed. 'Will the
Hamilton men leave me?' he shouted. 'Come back, and behave
like soldiers.'

Moore's twenty-man force stood firm, despite the growing
number of enemy on the beach. The firing intensified, musket
balls hummed in the branches above Moore's head, showering
splinters onto his shoulders. He saw a rebel officer flourishing
his sword and urging his men forward, and Moore raised his
fusil to shoot him down. His brother James later wrote: 'He
believed that he would have killed him; but he replaced his fire-
lock on his shoulder without discharging it.' The green lieutenant had still to overcome scruples about taking another man's
life. But men began to fall on either side of him; within minutes
his frail detachment had been reduced to almost half. To the
rear the retreating captain from the 74th reported to General
McLean: no hope remained of stemming the American advance. 'But where is Moore?' demanded the General. 'He is,
I fear, cut off.' 'What then is the firing I still hear?' McLean
turned to Captain Dunlop, from Moore's regiment, and
ordered him into the woods. Moments later Dunlop emerged
behind Moore, briefly congratulated him on his solitary stand,

but ordered immediate retreat. By now the enemy were feeling their way through the woods on both flanks. Less than half a dozen of the original twenty men of the 82nd emerged from the trees unwounded, among them Lieutenant Moore. 'I got some little credit, by chance, for my behaviour,' wrote John to his father. 'To tell you the truth, not for anything that deserved it, but because I was the only officer who did not leave his post *too soon*.' He added: 'I confess that at the first fire they gave us, which was within thirty yards, I was a good deal startled, or, in other words, as I'm writing to my Father, *devilishly frightened*, but I think this went gradually off afterwards.'

The enemy now prepared to rush the semi-completed fort. Further fortifications were hurriedly erected, and Moore, with fifty men posted in reserve, received fresh instructions: 'Should the enemy rush forward, as soon as they get into the ditch of the fort, you should sally out and attack them on the flank with charge bayonets.' But the Americans contented themselves with landing artillery and stores and building roads from the shore, along which they dragged cannon for two batteries, which

12

opened fire at a range of less than 800 yards. The inexperienced troops flinched at every shot, and McLean was determined to give them an example to remember. 'Throw wide the gates,' he snapped, and he walked forward into the open, brisk and correct, before stopping to examine the battery with his spy-glass. 'You see,' he shouted, 'there is no danger from the fire of these wretched artillerymen.' And then he stepped calmly back again.

The Americans mistakenly believed the British were short of supplies and settled down to a siege. The decision proved disastrous. Early in August the Royal Navy appeared in strength, and the American troops barely managed to scramble back on board in time. They attempted to sail upriver, but two vessels were taken by the British, and the remainder ran aground where they were burned by their crews or abandoned. Survivors fled through the woods back to Boston. 'This is undoubtedly the greatest coup for us, that has been done this year,' wrote a gleeful Moore to his father. John had learned to control his feelings under fire, but now he would experience a common military condition: boredom through lack of campaign activity.

Moore and his comrades stayed in camp near Halifax, enduring a dull daily routine, while for the next year British forces elsewhere seemed to be gaining the advantage over the rebels. The siege of Savannah, from 3 September to 28 October, culminated in a British victory, and on the evening of 18 June two fast frigates from New York brought news that Sir George Clinton had forced the Charleston garrison to surrender. Guns boomed in the camp in celebration as John Moore, now an acting captain, scrawled a letter to his father. The camp expected soon to be attacked by the French, and Moore eagerly awaited such excitement. 'The hope of being attacked is the only thing that renders this garrison supportable, we are all heartily tired of it, and would give the world to be sent to New York... If the French come here, you may expect an interesting letter.' The French refused to oblige. To Moore's boredom was added distress at the death of McLean, by now a close friend of the young captain. 'I am half thinking,' wrote John to his father, 'it very hard that a man who always exposed himself wherever there was the least danger, should die in his bed. To be killed

13

Fort George, New York, the headquarters of the British Army in America, where John Moore waited impatiently in 1781 while British forces surrendered at the disastrous siege of Yorktown.

is certainly in some degree more honourable, and certainly much more pleasing to a soldier.'

In this sombre mood, Moore left the camp and moved to New York to find employment on Clinton's headquarters staff. The tide was turning in favour of the rebels: in August 1781, when Moore reached New York, the Yorktown campaign began. The city of New York was heavy with rumours and depression. John Moore's spirits were only uplifted by the sudden arrival of his brother James, aged seventeen, now a military surgeon's mate. James and John quartered together first in New York, then at a Dutch farmer's house on Long Island, while the war dragged through its final months. By 28 September American troops under Washington had invested Yorktown; Cornwallis withdrew to inner fortifications two days later. Help failed to arrive in time from Clinton in New York and on 19 October, at nine o'clock in the morning, terms were signed for

the British surrender. At two o'clock that afternoon came the
final humiliation, when 6,630 British troops – including the
light company of Moore's 82nd – filed between the French and
American forces to lay down their weapons. This virtually
ended the war.

Now the scramble to find transports home to England began;
the two Moore brothers were obliged to wait their turn. John
spent the time reading and taking solitary walks along the banks
of the East River, while James offered his medical services at
the General Hospital in New York. They finally sailed early
in the New Year, 1782, and narrowly avoided destruction in
a hurricane close to the American coast. Many ships were lost,
but in James's words: 'Our transport was a stout vessel, with
a good crew which stood the tempest well.' A further hazard
awaited at the mouth of the English Channel, when a privateer
appeared early in the morning and decks were stripped for
action. John Moore and his comrades – most of them military
wounded – lined the rails as the privateer 'came dashing on
under a cloud of canvas and got into our wake'. James continued: 'The crew were all kept concealed, the captain only
appearing. I watched him from the poop, expecting every instant a broadside to be fired off. Instead of which, seeing our
soldiers and preparations, he hailed us with his trumpet, put
a few frivolous questions, and then dropping astern, sheered
off.' Twenty-four hours later the transport tacked into Falmouth, and James and John hurried ashore. Pooling their
slender resources, they took a post-chaise to London for the
reunion with Dr and Mrs Moore at their home in Clarges Street
off Piccadilly. Another brother, Midshipman Graham, was still
at sea, serving in Lord Byron's fleet in the Western Ocean. But
two of the Moore boys had at least come home safely, bronzed,
broadened, and infinitely wiser concerning the terrors and
tedium of war.

Chapter Two

*

CHAOS IN CORSICA

How was Moore to use the experience gained in North America? He now found himself on half-pay; the regiment to which he officially belonged, the 82nd, had only been raised for the emergency of the Revolution, and after England had proclaimed the cessation of hostilities on 4 February 1783 it was disbanded. Prospects for personal advancement were slight, and hopes for active employment even less. Moore could only wait.

Meanwhile, peace brought him an opportunity of an entirely different kind. The unpopular peace settlement led to considerable political changes, from which the 24-year-old William Pitt emerged as Prime Minister on 19 December 1783.

In the spring of 1784, a long-postponed general election was held to see whether Pitt could survive, and among the names of prospective politicians appeared Captain John Moore, attempting to win Peebles, Lanark, Linlithgow and Selkirk. The Duke of Hamilton had managed to persuade the young officer to leave his studies of field fortification and tactics and to plunge into the political battlefield – but only after promising that Moore would be allowed to remain uncommitted to either the Whigs or the Tories. With such a powerful benefactor, and perhaps aided by limited suffrage, Moore emerged successful on 26 April and took his seat when George III opened the new Parliament on 18 May. Pitt had come to power triumphant, with the Tories under Fox losing over a hundred seats. But the party conflict would intensify, and Moore become embroiled despite his refusal to be labelled as a party-man. After his death he would be branded as a 'Whig General' who owed his success entirely to his powerful Whig friends.

Yet Moore seemed unenthusiastic as a politician, although always diligent. He took little active part in the fierce debate over Pitt's India Bill during the summer of 1784, and endured rather than enjoyed the routine which became familiar during the years 1785–8: six months of the year at Westminster, the remainder in Scotland or studying military subjects at his parents' home in London. His father, now established as a well-known literary figure, introduced him into society, and he seemed presentable and attractive, though quiet. While welcoming and responding to female attention, he showed no inclination to marry and preferred his military manuals. He constantly sought a return to full soldiering, but the army remained small despite renewed hostilities in India.

In January 1788 Moore managed to regain a foothold on the military ladder. The addition of two battalions to the 60th had been ordered the previous October, to be trained ready for service in the West Indies, and Moore secured the appointment of major to one of them. In his brother's words: 'Then escaping from London and all its allurements, he flew to Chatham where the recruits were assembling. His spirits, which from lack of employment had become languid, were now stirred up by the drum and fife; and the drill became his morning business.' Major Moore was found to be skilful at training recruits. As James commented: 'The complete command he possessed over his own temper qualified him peculiarly for disciplining troops.' His battalion received commendation when a review took place later in the year.

Meanwhile, he still sought employment in the field, and especially with his original regiment, the 51st, which seemed likely to be sent overseas. Fresh trouble had arisen with Spain over the comparatively minor problem of trading rights with Spanish territory on the west coast of Vancouver Island, and Pitt had decided upon a firm stand. Early in 1790 it seemed possible that England and Spain might soon go to war – and France remained Spain's ally. Major John Moore therefore attempted a return to the regiment which he had forsaken to cross the Atlantic in 1778, and his bid proved successful.

Moore declined to stand for re-election to Parliament in the autumn of 1790, and instead suffered acute seasickness in crossing to Ireland to join the 51st at Cork on the afternoon

17

18

House of Commons debate, similar to those John Moore attended before serving in Ireland. Moore, on half-pay and anxious to return to soldiering, soon abandoned his Parliamentary seat.

of Saturday 23 October. The last time he had journeyed to the 51st he had been a raw ensign; now he intended to purchase the position of commanding officer, believing the present commander, Colonel John Jaques, to be 'stark staring mad' at the prospect of being separated from his wife and sent overseas. 'I shall feel his pulse,' wrote Moore to his medical father. He hurried to Charles Fort, Kinsale, twenty-four miles south of Cork, to find Jaques absent on a fishing trip.

Moore anxiously awaited information from home concerning affairs with Spain. By 7 November he had still to hear definite intelligence, and when his brother Frank forwarded a batch of bills with the scrappy note 'Dr. Jack. There's no News. Yrs. FM.' he displayed rare pique. 'This is rather too great a joke,' he wrote, 'at a time when not a day passes without something happening to increase or diminish the probability of war – and upon these events depend my going abroad, and perhaps my attaining the Lt. Colonelcy of this Regt... The weather is extremely bad, but when it permits we march about, fire etc. to prepare for this war, which no man here but myself has any doubt of. (I shall always have doubt till I hear a bullet pass my ear.) Our good Lt. Col. has retired to the Lake of Killarney. I hope we shall see no more of him.' Within hours delayed news arrived that the Vancouver business had been settled without war a mere three days after Moore had reached Cork, and simultaneous with this unwelcome information came Colonel Jaques, happy that the threat of overseas service had been removed, and anxious to withdraw previous suggestions that he might sell his command.

Moore decided to confront Jaques. The colonel's earlier hints that he would sell had amounted to promises, he claimed, and could not be retracted. If any attempt were made to do so, then he would see the matter became public. Under this pressure Jaques gave in; Moore scribbled a line to his father asking him to lodge £1,000 at Drummond's Bank in London and hurried to Dublin to obtain the necessary approval from the lord lieutenant. By 8 December all had been settled, not without sacrifice to the long-suffering Dr Moore in London. His son wrote: 'I drew upon Drummond's for one thousand and ten pounds. The odd ten is what is lost by the exchange. I am sorry to trouble you with that, but the expense of my equipment, Bed, Saddles,

Horses &c. and living in this place, with the bills I left unpaid in London, altogether amount to such a sum that for some years I shall have nothing like my pay to spend.' Five days later Lieutenant-Colonel Moore began the task of training the 51st to his own high standards. 'He has left me enough to do, but I have the winter before me, during which it is impossible to have any communication with the rest of the world, from the badness of the weather. I shall have nothing to divert my attention from my business. Of all the climates I ever was in, this is undoubtedly the worst.'

Recruits were instructed; unfit officers and men were weeded out. Throughout most of January and February the new commanding officer rarely left his cluttered desk and the oil lamps flickered late into the night as the wind howled and the rain drummed upon the misted panes. Moore's health began to suffer, and he wrote to his doctor brother James seeking cures for insomnia and rheumatism. James and his father hastened to send prescriptions, while his practical Scottish mother warned against damp sheets. Moore's health improved with the aid of a new bed, better sheets, a new saddle and a more sensible diet. He used the family prescriptions on his men, with excellent results.

By April the weather picked up and he was encouraging the troops to join him in a 6 a.m. daily swim in the sea, again for health purposes. His satisfaction with the state of his regiment increased: bad officers had been discarded not without some difficulty, and the newcomers seemed excellent, especially one of his new lieutenants, who became a life-long friend – Paul Anderson. His troops were becoming hardened, and Moore boasted that he would be 'proud to lead them against any enemy whatever'. The time had come to seek active service. He directed his pleas to Major-General David Dundas, Adjutant-General, and in return came a hint that regiments first on the list for overseas service would be kept as close to the coast as possible – and that the 51st would be moved into Cork. The transfer took place in May.

Events were moving fast on the Continent during the spring and early summer of 1791. The French Revolution was in its third year; now, in June, Louis XVI made his bid for freedom. The King and Queen slipped from the Tuileries palace on the

21

Paul Anderson, 1767–1851, devoted friend to John Moore. Anderson would nurse him through terrible sickness and battle injuries and Moore was to die in his arms.

20th, with Marie-Antoinette disguised as a governess. The attempt failed; the royal couple returned to Paris, and the King was obliged to sign the constitution on 3 September.

Moore felt considerable sympathy for the Revolution, and also for Marie-Antoinette – though not for her husband. He wrote to London: 'I thought the escape of the King and Queen, had it succeeded, would have created a civil war by numbers flocking to the royal standard . . . And as we thrive best in turbulent times, I wished their Majesties safe at Metz. I am, however, convinced now that no such event could have taken place, and that the idea of a counter-revolution is nonsense. The people of France are unanimous in the best of causes; they have begun by overturning the old constitution completely, and have every chance, from the good sense and moderation they display, of establishing a new one, probably better.' He also declared: 'As a man, I wish the French success, and as a soldier also. We shall have no war till they have established a good government – and begin to think that we have usurped a greater share of trade than they will think us entitled to.' Moore's attitude towards the revolutionary leaders soon underwent an abrupt change.

Moore's marching orders came at last, but they were disappointing: the 51st was selected for garrison duties in Gibraltar. On 17 February he informed his father that the transports had arrived, and on the 8th of the following month he reported from the *Brunswick*, in the Cove of Cork, that all men were aboard: 'I have been hurried to death with the embarkation . . . But I have been much pleased with the behaviour of the regiment . . . Upon the parade, the evening before we marched, I told them they might enjoy themselves, and be jolly with their friends till nine, when I expected every man to be in his quarters; and that at seven next morning they should come sober to the parade ready to march. They were glorious that night.' Only one man had deserted, and he had been recaptured.

Moore and his regiment landed at Gibraltar on 25 March. 'I have been up at daylight ever since we anchored,' wrote Moore to his parents, 'and seldom off my legs till bedtime. The weather is that of a hot July in England. Oranges, green peas &c. are in perfection . . .' The climate continued to please, and the Rock proved fascinating – as did a tour of Spain during Christmas 1792.

But the European situation was deteriorating rapidly. In February 1792 the Emperor of Austria and the King of Prussia entered into an alliance against France. In August the Paris mob invaded the Tuileries palace, and the royal family was imprisoned. The Austro-Prussian army invaded France, only to meet defeat at the Battle of Valmy. In September the French Republic was proclaimed. Very soon the Austrian Netherlands were overrun by the republican armies. Pitt, who had looked forward to fifteen years of peace, now gave promises of aid to

Holland against French invasion, and Britain began fresh preparations for war. Those, like Moore, who had at first wished
the Revolution well, were disgusted by the notorious 'September Massacres'; the final straw came on 21 January 1793,
when Louis XVI climbed the scaffold to his execution.

The news reached Gibraltar on 7 February. Next day John
Moore wrote to his mother: 'These monsters have disgraced
a good cause, and I can hardly now bring myself to wish that
they may at last succeed in settling for themselves a good
government.' Unknown to Moore, the French had already declared war upon England.

But many months passed before British troops could partici-
pate in strength in land operations on the Continent, and
Moore still despaired over the lack of opportunity for his 51st.
He told his parents: 'My sensations are very different at present
from what they were upon the armament against Spain. I was
then certain of being employed. The probability now is that
I shall not.'

The greater part of 1793 proved frustrating. In June
Moore examined plans for an army operation to seize Toulon,
but his hopes collapsed with the arrival of the elderly Admiral
Sir Samuel Hood in command of a strong fleet. 'As I had the
forming of the expedition myself,' wrote Moore to his mother
on 22 June, 'you may believe I gave myself a tolerable command in it; but now my castle is destroyed, and I am at times
as melancholy as a cat, at the thought of remaining here un-
employed in the whole war. But who would have imagined such
a fleet would have been sent to the Mediterranean, merely to
convoy the trade up and down.' An army expedition against
Toulon in any event seemed unnecessary: French royalists from
Marseilles and Toulon invited Hood to sail into the latter, and
he did so peaceably on 26 August with twenty-one ships of the
line. His force seized the great arsenal, together with some
seventy vessels, leaving Moore and his men still incarcerated
in Gibraltar.

Opposition to the royalists and the British at Toulon suddenly started to stiffen. The republican general, Jacques
Dugommier, adopted a plan prepared by the young Colonel
Napoleon Bonaparte, who commanded an artillery brigade,
and the ring around the Mediterranean port tightened. Hood

Lord Hood accepts the keys of Toulon from French royalists in August 1793.

sent urgent requests for troops: as Moore had feared, the two regiments longest in the garrison were selected, despite his pleas for the 51st to the governor of Gibraltar, Sir Robert Boyd. 'The old gentleman was timid,' complained Moore to his father on 30 September. A week later another letter declared: 'The two regiments from this [place] are embarked, but have not sailed; the wind is strong against them. A frigate arrived two days ago, with another requisition from Lord Hood for some guns, mortars, shells, &c....' The Toulon situation was clearly deteriorating – and once again Moore's hopes were raised: further troops might be needed. 'I shall write to you the moment I receive any orders,' he told his mother on 31 October. 'I expect them daily. The regiment is ready.' Another six impatient weeks passed before the 51st at last took leave of

25

Gibraltar. On Thursday 19 December, Moore made the first entry in the war journal which he would continue to write until three weeks before his death. 'Sunday, the 15th December. The 50th and 51st Regiments embarked on board four line-of-battle ships for Toulon.'

On the day Moore wrote these words, Toulon fell. Unaware of the disaster, but unsettled by disturbing rumours, the reinforcement fleet sailed on through worsening weather. Moore wrote in his journal: 'I have been so long accustomed to false reports at Gibraltar that I am not without hopes of finding upon our arrival at Toulon that this last is at least in a great measure so.' On 21 December a passing Spanish man-of-war gave confirmation to the rumours, but the force continued eastwards. The seas ran increasingly high and rain lashed the decks. Bad weather obliged Moore to stay in his cabin, and he could only pace up and down and curse the inactivity. 'In the ward-room I believe frequent recourse is had to cards and backgammon. To such as are not fond of these amusements and have no duty to attend to, a rainy day is particularly tiresome.' The fleet made land on the evening of the 28th and stood off for the night. One frigate, separated from the rest in the storms, sailed into Toulon where the French had deceived them by hoisting the British flag. Carried into captivity with the frigate was the entire baggage of the 51st, carefully collected and packed under Moore's supervision.

And now, during the morning of the 29th, came final confirmation that Toulon had fallen: a Spanish vessel approached the fleet with news that Lord Hood had evacuated the port and had sailed to Hyères Bay, taking three of the largest French ships with him. The naval commander, Captain Dickson, was determined to join Hood at Hyères – a policy which Moore strongly supported. But Dickson then delayed for forty-eight hours, to Moore's impatience. 'Both the ships and the troops may be wanted,' he jotted in his journal.

The fleet did not arrive until late on the last day of 1793. Hood's majestic flagship, the *Victory*, loomed on the horizon. Almost immediately Moore rowed across to the 110-gun warship to meet the irascible, seventy-year-old Hood – and to be criticized for the late arrival which Moore himself had so resented. So began a relationship between Moore and Hood which would go from bad to worse. 'He received the State of the Regiment, which I presented to him . . . expressed some surprise at the smallness of our numbers, said we were rather late, and then turned to one of the navy officers with whom he had been transacting business.' Moore retired, snubbed. He pushed his way through the crowd of refugees on the *Victory* to find his boat. 'I heard a fiddle and dancing in the ward-room, and was not a little surprised when I was told it was the French dancing out the old year; few of them have anything but the clothes on their backs, and the prospects before them are but gloomy, yet they contrive to make themselves happy.'

Moore returned to the *Victory* next morning, 1 January 1794, and discovered some of the reasons for the ill feeling between the admiral and the army. Army officers at Toulon had advised Hood that the port had become untenable, and should be evacuated. 'It was evident to them that they should be forced to do it soon,' wrote Moore, 'perhaps with the loss of the greater part of the troops, and possibly even part of the fleet. This was represented in the strongest manner to Lord Hood, who chose to follow his own opinion.' As a consequence of Hood's delay the British had eventually been obliged to evacuate in a disorderly, wasteful and humiliating fashion. And now a decision had to be taken over the next step.

Many naval officers seemed to welcome the setback at Toulon, believing they might now be allowed to return to England. Hood had other plans, and he summoned Moore eight days later to explain them. 'The intention was to send me with Major Koehler, Deputy Quartermaster-General, to Corsica, to report from observations upon the spot how far an attack upon that island with our small military force was practicable.' Moore and Major George Koehler prepared for their hazardous mission to French-occupied Corsica, and sailed in a fast frigate on the night of 11 January, after a 48-hour delay caused by contrary winds. Two days later they slipped ashore in the northwest corner of Napoleon's homeland. For a moment they feared captivity or worse: a cluster of heavily armed men waited for them on the beach – and all were dressed in French uniforms. But the colour of the cloth signified nothing, and a relieved Moore wrote: 'The people seemed happy to see us, and gave us three cheers.'

Yet Moore and his party, which included Sir Gilbert Elliot, lately commissioner at Toulon, had every reason for apprehension: the nearest French post, at Calvi, lay only about nine miles distant, and the island abounded with spies and armed agents.

Corsica had been in turmoil for the past three years. The inhabitants were sharply divided between those who welcomed the constitution of 1791, and those who opposed it.

In 1794 the dominating figure in the island was Pasquale Paoli, the famous patriot who had driven out the Genoese in

The precipitate retreat of British forces from Toulon, December 1793, leading to squabbles between the Royal Navy and the British Military over the handling of this unhappy affair.

1768 and was now trying to secure independence of the French. John Moore's mission was to meet Pasquale Paoli, to offer him weapons, equipment and perhaps the promise of military intervention. He received a warm welcome from Leonati, Paoli's nephew, and learned that Paoli was thirty miles away at Murato and the journey would take over a day, using a devious route. Leonati informed him that the French only occupied the coastal areas at Calvi, San Fiorenzo and Bastia and totalled 2,600 men including 'disaffected' Corsicans. 'All that is wanted, he says, is a few cannon to drive them from there.'

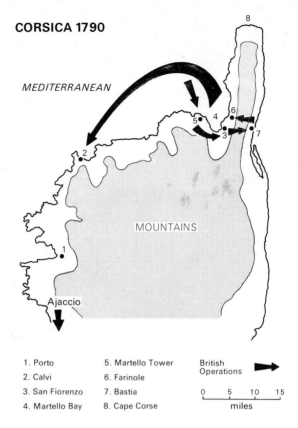

CORSICA 1790

MEDITERRANEAN

MOUNTAINS

Ajaccio

1. Porto	5. Martello Tower	British Operations
2. Calvi	6. Farinole	
3. San Fiorenzo	7. Bastia	0 5 10 15
4. Martello Bay	8. Cape Corse	miles

On the 15th Moore set out to see for himself. The roads were so bad that the mules could only carry them fifteen miles before dusk, and the party stopped for the night at a small village. 'The whole village poured in, and the people remained in the room till we had supped and retired to bed.' Moore's fears grew over the lack of secrecy surrounding the mission. After an uncomfortable night spent sharing a bed with Sir Gilbert, who snored, he rose early on the 16th to reach Paoli shortly after noon at a closely guarded convent.

The British mission found a tall, heavy man, with thick reddish-brown hair and piercing blue eyes, who surrounded himself with growling mastiffs. He delighted in quoting Livy and Plutarch, and declared: 'I defy Rome, Sparta or Thebes to show me 30 years of such patriotism as Corsica can boast.' He would agree to British protection, but he would not coun-

30

tenance any agreement which might result in Corsica being tied to the restored French crown following the defeat of the French republicans. 'I can say no more. Why, therefore, does his Lordship [Hood] tease me with more negotiation? *That man* has already injured me sufficiently with promises of succour which he has always withheld.' He threatened to abandon the fight and accused the British of failing to trust him. Sir Gilbert pleaded with Paoli not to misunderstand Hood's intention. The object of his mission was to know if there was any way of getting public assent to what Paoli claimed to be Corsica's wish. 'How can this be done at present?' growled Paoli. 'The enemy must first be expelled.'

While this diplomatic discussion took place Moore and Koehler started their military reconnaissance. Accompanied by about fifty Corsicans, they rode to the area around San Fiorenzo, and continued their reconnaissance on the 17th. They led their horses to the summits of ridges, from which they could see the French behind their fortifications; Koehler made sketches while Moore scribbled copious notes. In their eagerness to obtain details, they moved so close that they attracted the attention of a French patrol. Amidst the flurry Moore calmly noted the skill displayed by the Corsicans in taking up defensive positions and driving off the enemy. Only one man was wounded.

Moore had already conceived a possible plan for the attack on San Fiorenzo, by the capture of the defensive tower guarding the bay. This tower, named Mortella by the Corsicans, was always referred to as 'Martello' by Moore, and this spelling stuck when the word became a name in its own right. Further discussions with General Paoli after breakfast on the 18th formed the basis of the report which Moore prepared after his return to the coast on 20 January. The frigate *Juno* collected him on the night of the 25th, and next morning he boarded the *Victory* off Cape Corse to hand his report to Hood and General David Dundas, now the senior army commander.

The document revealed Moore's military mind at its best: detailed yet clear, with bold proposals backed by sound reasoning. 'The first object appears to be the possession of Martello Bay for the security of the fleet, and to enable it to effectively co-operate with the army when landed. The works which defend

MORTELLA TOWER. *Corsica.*

A *Middle Story*
B *Second Story*
C *Entering door*
D *Powder room*
E *Kitchen*
F *Embrasures for 2 Guns*
G *Cistern*
H *Space for contingency, see Cistern*

Mortella tower, Corsica, spelled 'Martello' by Moore: an excellent defensive structure later copied by the British for fortifications along the south-east to guard against French cross-channel attempts.

the bay are a stone tower with two or three light guns (4-pdr) at Martello point, another of the same kind at Farinole. The fort of Farinole consists of a strong battery immediately under the tower, and a redoubt open in the rear . . . The road leading to the heights has generally been thought impracticable for cannon. It is, however, by no means so for light guns or howitzers.'

Occupation of these heights would give an artillery position commanding the French defences. Moore put forward a detailed plan, concerted with Paoli, for the Martello attack: 500 men with light field pieces would land at the northern point of the bay and march to the heights by a path he had reconnoitred, under cover of the surrounding hills. The report then gave details of subsequent attacks and landings, and provided assessments of enemy strength at various points on the island. An invasion would stand every chance of success, but would have to be undertaken immediately or Corsican morale would slump. 'If delayed it is impossible to say what effect despair and the dread of being exposed to French violence and cruelty may have even upon those who at present are the best disposed.' Paoli had been so concerned not to endanger morale that he had asked Major Koehler to stay with him, as proof that the British would return.

Moore's report was well received, even by Hood, and the fleet made for Porto Ferrajo, Elba, to prepare for the invasion. Vicious storms continued to sweep the Mediterranean; another struck the fleet *en route*, and even the huge *Victory* seemed threatened as winds gusted the warship towards the rocks. At 1 a.m. Captain Englefield burst into Admiral Hood's outer cabin, which was being used by Dundas and Moore, and told the startled officers to dress immediately. 'He was afraid the ship would be ashore,' wrote Moore. 'He passed on and we could hear him make the same report to Lord Hood...My cot was immediately opposite to the Admiral's door, which Captain Englefield had left open. I turned round to observe his countenance. It was not the least discomposed. I could see him dress himself with the greatest deliberation.' The sight of Hood calmly pulling on one pair of thick worsted hose over another, to protect his thin legs from the cold, reassured Moore, and he turned to his cot again and fell sound asleep. By dawn the storm had passed and the fleet entered Ferrajo.

John Moore now faced his greatest opportunity so far: leading the first troops in the invading force. The Royal and his own 51st Regiment would be under his command, totalling about 600 troops with 120 seamen and 30 artillerymen with a 6-pounder and a $5\frac{1}{2}$-inch howitzer. The preparations on Elba included sorting out the confusion resulting from the precipitate

Toulon evacuation – guns were in one ship, carriages and ammunition in another – and Moore had somehow to find equipment for the 51st to replace that lost to the French. By 4 February all had been completed, and the force sailed in the evening.

On the morning of the 7th the invasion force anchored in a small bay behind Martello Point, and by noon the men were scrambling over the rocks. By nightfall Moore had led his troops a short distance inland, and they lay by their arms during darkness. The plan envisaged dragging the light guns up to the heights to bombard the Martello fortifications, as Moore had claimed in his report would be possible, after which an infantry assault was launched. His force accordingly marched at daybreak on 8 February.

Within an hour the road had deteriorated into a steep stony track, and the guns began to lag behind the infantry. Thirty soldiers were detailed to help the seamen drag the guns, but Moore now began to doubt whether they could be got forward. He nevertheless hurried on with the infantry to reconnoitre the ground, reaching the heights at noon. His panting men were allowed to pile arms and feed while he clambered to the summit with two officers. They crawled forward to a point less than 1,400 yards from the enemy. Moore hardly needed his spy-glass to see that all fears over lack of security in Corsica had been justified: the French had anticipated his attack. Frantic efforts had clearly been made to strengthen the defences and to build new fortifications; the advance redoubt at Martello had been enlarged, and new gun batteries had been installed. 'The attack on them was no longer an affair of two days, 500 men and two light guns,' wrote Moore. Even the arrival of his guns during the evening failed to raise his spirits. Major Koehler, now reunited with the British after his prolonged stay with Paoli, agreed that an attack by such a puny force would be useless. Moore accordingly wrote to Dundas, asking him to come forward and see for himself.

Meanwhile Hood attempted a naval solution to the problem. Moore and his men watched from the sunlit heights as the 74-gun *Fortitude* and the 32-gun frigate *Juno* tacked gracefully inshore to open fire upon Martello tower. Moore knew the attack would be useless: the fortifications had been designed specifically to withstand such an attempt. The boom of the cannon echoed up the hills to Moore's helpless force, answered by the sharper cracks from the French in the tower. The enemy defenders had only two field pieces, but they had the advantage of eighteen-foot-thick walls to cover them. The troops watching from the heights murmured in amazement as balls from the warships bounced off the tough masonry. In return, the French fire swept the decks of the British vessels with red-hot shot, and after $2\frac{1}{2}$ hours the *Fortitude* burst into flames. The warships sheered off under belching smoke, with the loss of sixty men killed and wounded. Next day 6-pounders were landed on the beach, but still the tower proved too strong. Finally an 18-pounder from the *Victory* was brought ashore, and began battering the tower walls while infantrymen kept up a steady fire into the embrasures to keep French heads down. The guns in Martello, positioned for defence against sea attack, were unable to reply, but the end only came after red-hot shot from the *Victory* ignited the lining inside the walls, and the young French commanding officer had to surrender. The garrison which had kept the British at bay only amounted to thirty-six men. The tower had proved so strong that the design became the model for many erected by the British for subsequent coastal defence against the French.

But the capture of Martello was only the first step in the seizure of San Fiorenzo. Still standing defiant were the massive and newly strengthened redoubt called the Convention and the neighbouring tower and redoubt of Fornoli. Dundas visited Moore at his positions in the hills, and agreed that an attack from this quarter was useless because of French activity since Moore had written his report. 'From the different conversations I had with him,' wrote Moore, 'he seemed undetermined what to do...He was firmly of opinion that light guns would not do from any situation, and the difficulty of getting guns of a large calibre over such rugged rocks frightened him.' While searching for a solution, Dundas ordered Moore to take his men down from the slopes, because they had no tents, and to quarter them in more pleasant conditions along the shore.

Koehler had meanwhile crept towards the enemy positions to reconnoitre, and came hurrying back with the news that there was an excellent site for a battery less than 700 yards from

A youthful-looking
John Moore,
sketched by
Lawrence.

the Convention; Moore inspected it and agreed. If two 18-pounders could be brought up, he told Dundas, no one could survive in the redoubt. Dundas gave him leave to make the attempt – while remaining sceptical about the possibility of the massive guns being dragged over such difficult terrain. But the British seamen accomplished the feat, described by Sir Gilbert Elliot in a letter to his wife: 'The ground was very steep and rough, considerably steeper than the green face of the Minto Crags at home . . . They fastened great straps round the rocks, and then fastened to the straps the largest and most powerful purchases or pullies and tackle that are used on board a man-of-war. The cannon were placed on a sledge at one end of the tackle, the men walked downhill with the other end . . . The surprise of our friends the Corsicans and our enemies the French was equal to the situation.' Two 18-pounders and one 8-inch howitzer, together with a 10-inch mortar and other smaller guns, were placed in position, and the bombardment began.

On the morning of the 17th, when the bombardment had been under way for forty-eight hours, Moore took his men into the prickly brown scrub near the camp to practise them in advancing in good order over broken ground. The men were still manœuvring when he received a message from Dundas: the attack would start that evening at nine o'clock. Moore was to move his men forward, ready for the storming, at 4 p.m. At a lunch-time briefing, while his men were cleaning their weapons, he heard that he would lead the frontal assault on the Convention while the 50th and 25th attacked a neighbouring battery and the Corsicans masked the other flank. Moore walked back to his regiment to give final instructions: the men would not fire during the assault but would trust to their bayonets.

The afternoon crept on. The troops were moved into advanced positions at four o'clock, and waited. Twilight fell. At 8.30 the advance began under the light of a full moon. The men walked steadily forward towards the enemy – the rough ground prevented anything but file formation. No sound could be heard except the occasional stone rattling underfoot and shouts and laughter from back at the camp. After advancing about 500 yards through tangled thickets, Moore came to a rough clearing suitable for forming up. Whilst this took place he walked a few paces further to view the ground. Almost immediately three or four shots cracked about his ears from an enemy advance picquet. The French were well prepared; the advantage of surprise had been lost.

Moore ran back to the column and ordered the advance. He moved the troops at a jog-trot down the slope of a hill until they reached a small area of protected ground, immediately beneath the redoubt. Here Moore called a halt to allow his men to regain breath and reform. Then came his sharp command to charge, and his men climbed from cover and up the hill to throw themselves upon the white-uniformed French. Moore stayed at their head. 'I called to the man next to me to follow me. Trusting to those who came after us to put to death such as defended that part of the work, I ran on to a traverse, where I knew there was a gun, with a view to prevent it being fired. We carried the traverse instantly. We found the gun elevated to fire on our battery. We instantly made for a second traverse, where there was another gun. This traverse was very high, with two embrasures and a narrow passage upon the right of it. I jumped upon the embrasure. One of the Frenchmen had a match in his hand lighted, but from some unaccountable accident he did not then fire the gun.'

Amidst the frenzied snapping of short-range French musket fire, with his men using their bayonets, as instructed, Moore made for a passageway on his left through which he could reach the centre of the redoubt. 'The enemy fired upon us and charged with their bayonets. Here, for the first time, our men began to fire; but the enemy showed so much firmness that we were fairly checked.' The British and French bayonets clashed and crossed; Moore's men began to fall back and his shouts of encouragement were lost in the screams, swearing and musketry. Then Moore heard fresh shouts from his rear: some men from the 51st had found another passageway into the inner fortifications, and the soldiers streamed through with Moore pushing into the lead again. Desperate hand-to-hand fighting continued in the shadowy, moonlit alleys. Moore thrust his sword into a Frenchman standing in his way, and the weapon bent as it jarred against bone; his second stroke struck clean through the man's body. Many of the French stood and fought till they were bayoneted and clubbed down, but others began to throw down their arms and beg for quarter.

The Royals and 51st reached the flagstaff in the centre of the redoubt; troops from the 50th and 25th, delayed by broken ground, joined them there, together with Corsicans from the other flank. There was great confusion and Moore feared a counter-attack while the British were in such disarray; raking grape-shot from nearby Fornoli could have caused severe casualties amongst the crowd of triumphant troops. Moore frantically tried to organize covering positions. 'The noise and crowd were such that it was difficult to know where to begin.' The Fornoli guns did open fire, but the bombardment proved beneficial: the men immediately sobered and Koehler and Moore found it easier to set them digging trenches. Then, just after midnight, Moore heard that the French had pulled back from Fornoli. His mission had been accomplished, at a loss of between thirty and forty men killed and wounded; the enemy had suffered 100 killed and captured.

Dundas came forward at dawn with profuse congratulations. The 51st consolidated their positions during the day, 18 February, and next day the French abandoned the remains of

San Fiorenzo and retired to Bastia. Hood added his congratulations, declaring in his usual fog-horn voice to Major Koehler: 'We should never have had any footing in Corsica but for the perseverance of yourself and Colonel Moore.'

Chapter Three

*

HOME IN DISGRACE

The next task was to drive the French out of Bastia, nine miles distant across a mountain range. Moore accompanied Dundas on a reconnaissance on 22 February. As the two officers stood amidst the scrub and scanned the enemy positions, they realized that this presented considerable difficulties. The actual fortifications – four detached redoubts and a citadel – did not seem formidable, as they were badly constructed. The shifting of supplies, weapons and ammunition forward for the attack was a greater problem. The open coastline offered no protection for reinforcement from the fleet, and the deplorable mountain road had been cut by the fleeing French. Paoli's men had failed in their promise to cut enemy communications between San Fiorenzo and Bastia, where the enemy garrison had now been reinforced by a further 600 troops. The British would be met by about 1,300 crack troops, plus the crews of two frigates, and probably more than 1,000 Corsicans. The French gained a further advantage on 24 February when they drove Paoli's Corsicans from high ground badly needed by the British for battery positions.

The next few days were extremely depressing. 'The cold upon the top of the mountain was very great,' wrote Moore, 'and the fog so thick, as in every sense to make our situation uncomfortable.' Moore slept on loose straw strewn with hay, and for a month after taking San Fiorenzo never took off his battle-stinking clothes. Each night he made an arduous two-mile tour of his positions. Sir Gilbert Elliot commented: 'He is in love with his profession, and as all the services one renders to a mistress are pleasant, he enjoys discomforts.'

As always in his career, however, Moore found the difficulties

Bastia: an eye-witness impression by Captain Percy Fraser, RN, in 1794.

of dealing with superiors infinitely greater than the harshness of campaigning life. A rift developed between Dundas and Hood over the feasibility of attacking Bastia, in which Moore struggled not to become involved. Dundas told Moore that the attack would be impracticable with the force at his disposal; but Moore believed the attempt should nevertheless be made. 'I did not pretend to say that it would be successful – far from it; but perhaps the situation of affairs required the attempt; if it failed, the island had better be abandoned. San Fiorenzo was unhealthy, and not a post by itself to be kept; to fortify it was nonsense.' Moore had given his opinion to Dundas when asked, but accepted the decision of his superior officer. Then, at the end of the first week of March, Moore received surprising visitors. High-ranking naval officers picked their way through Moore's army camp on the clammy mountain ridge, led by the Adjutant-General of the Fleet, Captain Englefield. They brought an astonishing message. Hood desired Moore's opinion upon the practicability of attacking Bastia. 'General Dundas had said to his Lordship it was impracticable and chimerical,' reported Englefield, 'but Lord Hood thought differently, and was willing, if it was attempted, to take the whole responsibility upon himself, and wished to know what the different officers at the head of corps thought upon the subject.' Englefield said he would withdraw from the tent for a moment, to allow Moore to discuss the matter in private with Colonel William Villettes of the 69th. Moore told him not to bother. He could give an answer now. 'I did not conceive that I could with any propriety give Lord Hood an opinion upon such a subject.' Dundas, as his superior officer, would have to make the decision: Moore would obey orders. The naval officers hastily departed.

Moore reported the conversation to Dundas the following morning. The General expressed surprise, though he added that 'it was a piece with his [Lord Hood's] whole conduct'. He took Moore into his confidence and read out correspondence between himself and the Admiral. Moore commented in his journal: 'The General's letters were full of good sense and moderation. His Lordship's were not remarkable for those qualities. The General said Lord Hood was a man who never reasoned himself, nor would he listen to reason from others.' At the end of the meeting Dundas, with whom he had always had excellent relations, told Moore that he intended to quit Corsica and return home.

Further trouble loomed next day: Dundas showed Moore a letter from Hood claiming overall authority. 'His Lordship said that upon the evacuation of Toulon he conceived the General's command to have ceased; and from that moment he, Lord Hood, had the supreme command of the fleet and the army, and it was from courtesy only that he had admitted the General to interfere.' Dundas called a meeting of his commanding officers and told them he intended to depart as soon as possible; ill-health would be the public reason. 'We all agreed,' wrote Moore, 'as to the absurdity of Lord Hood's pretension to command the land forces, and agreed to resist any such attempt.'

Dundas gave up his command on 10 March to Colonel Abraham D'Aubant of the Engineers, the senior officer present. The old general left within twenty-four hours, with kind words for Moore: he had hoped that Moore would be his successor, and asked if he could perform any favour. 'Emolument was not my immediate object,' replied Moore. 'All I desired of him was that if an opportunity offered, wherein by mentioning me or the regiment, he could get me employed, he would use it.'

Moore had clearly fallen far from Hood's grace. On 13 March his journal entry declared: 'Within this hour I have re-

General Sir David Dundas, 'Old Pivot', friend of John
Moore whose departure from Corsica precipitated the
quarrels in the British Command.

ceived a letter from Lord Hood, expressing concern and disappointment that I should decline giving my opinion respecting
an attempt for the reduction of Bastia. Having been led to come
to Corsica by my report, he had therefore an undoubted right
to expect my opinion.' Moore disagreed: the question of loyalty
had to be considered, and French reinforcements and preparations had in any case made his original report out of date.

Bad weather prevented him venturing from his camp on the
14th, despite a summons from the new force commander, so
the first official interview with D'Aubant took place next day.
From the start, relations were poor. 'He seems much averse to
the attack on Bastia. He had not the boldness to say so. It is
difficult to speak more nonsense than he does with more gravity
and decorum of manner.' Moore felt no confidence in D'Aubant: even if he attempted the attack he would be 'unequal to
it and would bungle it. I therefore could not help wishing it
might not be attempted.' Instead, reliance should be placed
on a naval blockade to force the enemy into submission.

Moore's opinions were strengthened by a council of war held
at the army HQ at 10.30 next morning, 16 March. 'I cannot
recollect all the nonsense that was spoken by D'Aubant. Major
Koehler and I were the only two who spoke our sentiments
openly.' Moore and the Major maintained that the lost position
at the village of Carda must be retaken, as a bombardment
could be brought down upon the port from there. 'This in time
might force a capitulation, especially as the place would be
simultaneously closely invested by the fleet.' The meeting
agreed that Moore and Koehler should reconnoitre the position, and this they did on the 17th, taking advantage of fog
to creep close to the enemy lines. The reconnaissance left them
even more convinced that an assault under D'Aubant would
be too hazardous. A further council of war on the 20th resulted
in a decision against the attack, after D'Aubant had tried to
avoid giving his own opinion. Moore's scathing entry in his
journal declared: 'He deserves, in my opinion, to be broke for
deciding without having attentively reviewed the situation
himself. I have no conception of a commanding officer deciding
an affair of such importance from the report of others ... but
it was evident from the beginning that whatever report was
made he was determined to do nothing.'

Hood remained determined to do something and intended to push the navy in where the army apparently feared to tread. Koehler resigned in disgust. 'I shall feel his loss much,' wrote Moore, still convinced that Hood's effort would be ineffectual; he considered the Admiral ill-advised, ill-humoured and bigoted.

Another young officer serving in the combined British force held an entirely opposite opinion. 'The Lord [Hood] is very good friends with me,' wrote Captain Horatio Nelson. 'He is certainly the best officer I ever saw ... His zeal, his activity for the honour and benefit of his country are not abated. Upwards of 70, he possesses the mind of 40 years of age. He has not a thought separated from honour and glory.' The main fleet had been suffering at sea while the army delayed attacking Bastia and Nelson had informed Hood: 'We are really without firing, wine, beef, pork, flour, and almost without water: not a rope, canvas, twine or nail in the ship ... We are certainly in a bad plight at present, not a man has slept dry for many months.' Now this inactivity would be ended: Hood had given Nelson command of the invasion attempt north of the port.

Nelson's attack went in on 2 April, and his brave seamen made a successful lodgement. Guns were hauled across the beach and a battery began the bombardment of the port. But Moore commented on 5 April: 'Lord Hood is persuaded that the townspeople will revolt the moment the fire commences and will force the garrison to surrender. Of this I am no judge. The heights seem as well guarded as ever.' The bombardment from the fleet and shore batteries continued throughout April. 'We have not gained an inch,' wrote Moore on the 23rd. 'People are now persuaded of the absurdity of the attack. The report of the surrender the moment our batteries should open is proved to have had no foundation.'

Admiral Hood urged D'Aubant to assault from the heights in support of Nelson, but D'Aubant refused. Moore heard this decision with relief; his confidence in D'Aubant had continued to ebb, and he repeated his opinion to Sir Gilbert at a meeting on the *Victory* on the 25th: 'If they must be attacked it had better be delayed for a few days, when in all probability a general officer would arrive from England: under D'Aubant nothing could be undertaken.'

Nelson suffers the wound which was to leave him partially blind in one eye.

Day after day the cannon fire continued, and by 2 May further complications had arisen. A meeting of commanding officers heard the content of letters from the British ministers at Florence and Turin: it seemed that the French intended to move on Leghorn or Genoa, or both, and the ministers each requested that Lord Hood should send squadrons to cruise off the harbours. Hood again requested an army attack on Bastia, or at least a display of force, warning: 'The speedy surrender of that place became more important from the situation of affairs in the Mediterranean, and it was probable we might soon be obliged to withdraw the naval force from Corsica.' To do

46

this without taking Bastia would leave the troops 'in a very unpleasant situation'. D'Aubant once more asked his commanding officers for their views. Moore gave an irritable reply. 'It
was impossible for me to come every 8 or 10 days and give an
opinion upon what ought or ought not to be undertaken.' He
still believed the force available to be insufficient; the attack
undertaken by Nelson had not weakened the defences; the only
chance of taking the port lay in continued blockade of the
harbour, which might be done equally well whether the heights
were taken or not. Moore, who had heard that a replacement
for D'Aubant had been chosen, added in his journal: 'I am
anxious that *he* should do nothing. General Stuart may be
expected hourly.'

The siege dragged on. Moore's hopes of a successful con-
clusion were not even raised by the news that reinforcements
were being sent from Gibraltar. 'I dread the arrival of a reinforcement before [Stuart] comes to command it.' His fears
seemed justified. About 600 extra men reached the area on 13
May and the following morning D'Aubant informed his officers
that he now intended to move forward and co-operate in the
attack on Bastia. Moore was appalled at the ill-conceived plan
of operation which his superior now presented, and criticized
the fact that all communication between D'Aubant and Hood
was now by letter, rather than verbal contact. He obtained
D'Aubant's agreement that he should report the proposed
attack to Hood in person, and he set foot on the *Victory* at 2
p.m. the same day. The interview with the Admiral proved
frosty, as expected. 'If the General had advanced ten days ago,'
boomed Hood, 'when I applied to him to show himself upon
the heights, I had positive information that the place would
have surrendered. Now indeed I believe he need not give himself that trouble, as Bastia must, from every account, give up
in the course of six or seven days at furthest.' Hood added: 'All
communication between the General and me has hitherto been
in writing. I wish it to continue so. Words are often misinter-
preted. The whole must come to a hearing hereafter, and what
has passed between us has been sent home. I therefore must
decline giving any answer to your message.' Hood at least invited Moore to dine on board; Moore described his manner
during the uncomfortable meal as 'very polite'.

Moore now acknowledged that the French might capitulate through bombardment alone, but believed it could have been brought about far more economically. 'Bastia is distressed from want of provisions only. The ammunition we have expended has been literally thrown away. Had the fleet blocked the port without landing a man or firing a shot the place would at this instant have been equally near surrender.'

On the morning of the 17th D'Aubant told Moore that he intended to leave the island: he wanted to be away before Stuart arrived and hence avoid 'the mortification of serving as second after having been first'. He had asked Hood for a frigate to take him away, and would leave Moore as his successor until Stuart arrived. Hood, however, was determined not to let D'Aubant shuffle out of his responsibilities. D'Aubant told Moore on the 18th that he had been informed by the Admiral that no frigate could be spared. 'He did not seem inclined to enter into conversation,' wrote Moore in his journal, 'and I left him. I returned to dine with him. There was something extremely odd in his behaviour . . . I conjectured that the refusal of the frigate was not couched in the civilest terms.' D'Aubant continued to make half-hearted plans for an attack; fortunately for Moore's peace of mind, and the safety of the troops, these were never put into effect. On 19 May the defenders of Bastia, short of provisions and probably fearing fresh British reinforcements, at last surrendered.

'When I reflect what we have achieved,' wrote Nelson, 'I am all astonishment. The most glorious sight that an Englishman can experience, and which, I believe, none but an Englishman could bring about, was exhibited – 4,500 men laying down their arms to less than 1,000 British soldiers – who were serving as marines.' D'Aubant ordered Moore to march his men forward over the mountains for the triumphant entry into Bastia. The Brigadier-General, previously so hesitant, now seemed full of bustle and boast. 'He never seems to have had such a desire for action,' wrote Moore drily. His men had to clamber up the hills and stumble with full packs over the terrible roads. 'Numbers of men fell down from the excessive heat, badness of the road &c. As we reached our ground there came on a thick fog, followed by hard rain, to which we were exposed for more than three hours before our baggage and camp equipage came up. I never recollect suffering more from cold. The men were shivering. The sudden change from heat to cold, wet clothes &c. must have sent many to hospital. When the provisions arrived I ordered a glass of raw spirits to each man.' Moore was incensed by this unnecessary hardship inflicted on his soldiers.

His anger increased still further on 22 May when he received news that Lord Hood had demanded that certain units be embarked with the fleet for an expedition to Leghorn. The soldiers left on Corsica would be insufficient for the attack on the next and last objective, Calvi, and in Moore's words: 'The part of the army employed, being a mere appendage, would be sunk in the general name of the fleet and marines, and the capitulation would be made to Lord Hood alone. General D'Aubant had the weakness to consent to this slur being thrown upon himself and the troops under his command.' Moore immediately hurried to see D'Aubant. He reminded him that he, Moore, would be in command if D'Aubant left, and he therefore had the right to a say in affairs. D'Aubant's reply revealed his fear of Hood, and the damage which he believed the Admiral might do to his reputation at home. Moore told him that if he would stop the senseless forward march of the troops, he himself would confront Lord Hood; D'Aubant agreed.

Early next morning Moore boarded a boat which would take him to the *Victory* for the unpleasant meeting with the Admiral. 'The ill-will of Lord Hood is probably all I shall get by it,' he had written in his journal late the previous night. 'There are situations, however, which decide a man's character. This I think is one of them, and no consideration shall induce me to yield to what I conceive to be disgraceful.' His apprehension increased as his boat cut through the swell and the *Victory* towered ominously ahead; he climbed the high side of the warship and stepped on deck, hat under his arm. Lord Hood was at breakfast; Colonel Moore was asked to join him in his cabin. He entered, and found to his intense relief that Hood had two guests: Sir Gilbert Elliot and D'Aubant's successor, General Sir Charles Stuart. Happily, Moore told Hood that he need no longer trouble him, and soon he had entered into a long and animated conversation with Stuart, which continued when they returned to shore later in the day. At last the troops would be commanded by a man in whom Moore had complete faith. He immediately struck up a firm friendship with his new superior officer. Moore believed his troubles were over. 'The General said I had acted very properly,' he wrote. 'For these two or three months past I have lived in hot water.'

A visit to the surrendered French positions reinforced Moore's belief that his opinion had been correct throughout. 'Upon the whole I am convinced that Bastia with our force could only have been taken by famine. The land attack made by Lord Hood, though he will gain credit for it at home, was absurd to a degree. Three times his numbers could not have penetrated from that quarter. He never advanced one inch. If he had he must have been cut up. The distance of his post, together with the unaccountable want of enterprise in the enemy, saved his troops from destruction.' The ambitious and self-confident Captain Nelson, with whom Moore would soon be closer acquainted, would hardly have agreed.

Stuart soon showed himself to be an able and conscientious commander; 800 reinforcements arrived from England to garrison Bastia, and Stuart reorganized the remaining forces at his disposal. All the flank companies were formed into one battalion, named the reserve, under Moore's command. In mid-June the army moved by sea to Calvi; by the 18th the troops had landed and had marched inland to the heights immediately above the French positions.

The coming fight promised to be tough. Stuart confided to Moore after a reconnaissance that the advanced French fortifications at Mozzello were 'a regular casemated work. We must lose men.' Sudden downpours delayed preparations for the assault, and for the next few days Moore rarely enjoyed dry clothing. He spent long hours supervising unloading down on the beach, or risked his life closely reconnoitring the French positions.

Relations with the navy worsened again. The French fleet had slipped past the Toulon blockade, and Hood immediately put to sea. Once again Moore suspected his motives. 'We are much in want of sailors,' he wrote on 19 June. 'The listlessness of the navy is remarkable. Lord Hood, on the report of eight sail of the line having got out of Toulon, thinks proper to assemble and cruise with 17. I have long been of opinion that his Lordship's zeal was not for his country, but to gratify his own vanity.'

Captain Nelson now had a delicate and potentially unpleasant task: Hood ordered him to stay behind with the *Agamemnon* to co-operate with the army. Relations between Moore and Nelson soon revealed a complete lack of mutual sympathy. On a higher level, relations between Stuart and Hood, with the latter still chasing the French, proved equally deplorable. On 29 June a message arrived from the Admiral enclosing a summons for surrender which the Admiral believed should be presented to the Calvi garrison. Stuart refused to accept Hood's advice: 'As he had received so very little assistance from Lord Hood, he begged to be allowed to carry on the operations as he chose.' Hood immediately confided in his protégé, Nelson: 'I say this to you alone. If things do not go altogether right, no blame shall lay at my door.' Nelson, in fact, had a high opinion of Stuart, but suspected the influence which Moore might have upon him: he thought Moore had displayed over-caution over the degree of bombardment required before the infantry could advance. 'I hope to God the general, who seems a good officer and an amiable man, is not led away,' wrote Nelson to Hood, 'but Colonel Moore is his great friend.' Moore, for his part, blamed lack of naval support for the delay in bringing up sufficient guns, though in fact bad weather and determined sallies by the French were also responsible. He continued to insist that the fortifications of Monteciesco and Mozzello should not be attempted before the walls had been sufficiently breached.

The batteries opened up on Monteciesco at 4 a.m., 4 July. Considerable damage was inflicted almost immediately, and by 6 July two of the French guns had been silenced, and the third only fired at infrequent intervals. A successful attempt was made to establish a forward British battery, although with considerable casualties when the French retaliated during the early hours of the 7th. Moore escaped unhurt, but only just. He wrote: 'Captain Serigold of the navy was killed in the battery, and a man's thigh shot off, both close to the General, when I was speaking to him.'

At 8 a.m. on the 7th the new British battery opened fire but the French counter-fire continued to blast the trenches throughout the day. By now Corsica's summer sun had become fierce; hot winds seared the faces of the reserves in the trenches; flies swarmed everywhere. The reserves were not relieved until evening: they had been exposed to shot and sun for two days and two nights, but at least had the satisfaction of knowing that Monteciesco had finally been abandoned.

Attention now turned to Mozzello. Heavy French fire pounded the British positions on the 8th: 'Our battery was hit almost every time,' wrote Moore. 'A shell fell in the middle of us, blew up some cartridges and set fire to some live shells, and yet nobody was seriously hurt. The General got a knock with a splinter on the back.'

By 11 July the guns in the Mozzello fort had been destroyed, but the breach remained impracticable. The French continued firing from the town, and Moore commented: 'I was in the trenches with the Grenadiers all yesterday and the night before. We were fortunate enough to have but three or four men touched... My batman was knocked down by my side by rubbish and a good deal bruised; the ball struck a heap of stones close to us.' And Moore also wrote: 'Captain Nelson was wounded by stones in the face. It is feared he will lose one of his eyes.' Nelson was more optimistic. 'Amongst the wounded, in a slight manner, is myself,' he wrote to England, 'my head being a good deal wounded and my right eye cut down, but the surgeons flatter me I shall not entirely lose the sight.' He refused to stay away from his duties for more than a day. Meanwhile Moore was urging greater activity, and at 10.30 p.m. on 18 July he noted with satisfaction in his journal: 'The breach in the Mozzello is practicable. I am to storm it at the head of the Grenadiers; the whole arrangements are so good that the business must succeed.' He ended this journal entry by noting that he would move forward in thirty minutes' time.

The Grenadiers shifted into position soon after midnight, with the 50th and 51st waiting in the rear to give support. Anxiously, the troops watched for the first faint streaks of dawn. Dim light appeared on the horizon at about 4 a.m.; a solitary gun suddenly cracked from the new British battery to signal the advance. Moore rose and called his men forward, leading them at such a pace that they reached the French palisade before the pioneers who were supposed to cut it down, and Moore

Napoleon Bonaparte, confident and rising rapidly to fame while British troops continue the battle for his native Corsica.

jumped through a smoking hole torn by British shot. The Grenadiers followed him into the bottom of the breach. 'We were annoyed both by shot, hand-grenades, and live shells, which the enemy had placed on the rampart and rolled over upon us.' The tall Grenadiers pressed forward, bayonets rigid and deadly in front of them, and the French fell back.

Moore swung to the left to attack the nearby breach, with Captain McDonald, commander of the Grenadiers, hard on his heels. Sword unsheathed Moore stepped into the entrance, and then collapsed, blood gushing from his scalp. Striking an inch or so further down, the shell splinter would have decapitated him. Captain McDonald and his men pushed on, while Moore clambered to his feet, brushed the blood from his eyes and hurried after them up the debris-littered slope. Within a yard of the top Captain McDonald sagged to his knees, badly wounded in the face; four or five other men also fell. By now Moore had regained the lead, and within moments the fort was filled by swarming, shouting Grenadiers. So well had Moore kept up the momentum of the attack, and so swift had been its success, that the light infantry had been unable to move to the rear in time to block the enemy escape. Moore directed his men to defensive positions, ready for a possible counter-attack. General Stuart ran up, throwing his arms around him in jubilation, then ordered him to the rear when he saw that he was wounded. Moore wrote in his journal: 'The wound in my head became troublesome.'

The British had gained possession of the fort at the cost of about thirty men killed or injured. Now the French hold on Calvi became precarious. Firing ceased from the town, and Moore believed the enemy would soon capitulate. But the French requested that they should be given a breathing space: if help had not reached them within a specified period, they would surrender. To save British lives, Stuart agreed to give them until 10 August. Meanwhile the British strengthened their positions, and suffered increasingly from the heat and from sickness, and disease spread by the filth of trench existence. Moore wrote on 4 August: 'Considerably more than two-thirds of our number are in hospital; men and officers tumble down daily in the most melancholy manner.' Moore escaped the fever, but looked ill and wretched with his head shaved and thick bandages wound around his scalp; he believed the harsh sun and wind had made him look ten years older.

On 10 August the French in Calvi laid down their arms, and Moore entered the town. 'It is inconceivable the destruction our fire has occasioned; there is literally not a house which has not been damaged by shot or shell. The whole is a heap of ruins.' Moore expressed his feelings in a reminiscent sentence: 'Never was so much work done by so few men in the same space of time.' He wrote to his mother on the 11th: 'Upon the whole I am as happy as man can be ... You have heard how the thickness of my skull saved my life. The last plaster fell off to-day; and as soon as the hair, which was shaved, grows, there will not remain any trace of the hurt.' But he added: 'I have, however, my distresses. My servant William, and another I had, are both in the hospital with the fever, which almost everybody but myself has had: he was my valet, cook, groom; and without him I am helpless.' William Hillows, who had been with Moore for four years, died soon afterwards. The next few days were spent dismantling the French defences and trying to reorganize the 51st, after the ravages of fever. On 31 August Moore left for a tour of Corsica with Stuart, returning to Bastia on 25 September to find the sick list unaltered. 'The number of deaths was considerable.'

Officially, Moore's duties were restricted to command of the 51st; unofficially, he would soon be adjutant-general, though this depended upon the departure of the present incumbent, Sir James Erskine – who showed little inclination to leave. Confusion in the command became much more serious on 3 October, when a courier arrived from England bringing Sir Gilbert Elliot's appointment as viceroy. The grand title immediately presented difficulties, inferring as it did a far superior position to that of governor – and yet the island would have to be governed by martial law for some considerable time.

Friction between Viceroy and Commander-in-Chief became apparent almost immediately. Sir Gilbert told Stuart that he would like to visit the army hospitals, to which the army commander replied: 'If as Sir Gilbert Elliot you have a curiosity to see the hospitals and to have information respecting them, I shall be extremely happy to give it [permission] to you. But if you mean that as Viceroy you have any authority over them or any part of the army, and that this is to be the first act of your reign, I shall not consent to it. You have no authority whatever over the army.' 'I am totally of a different opinion,' snapped Sir Gilbert. Moore's sympathy clearly lay with Stuart: Sir Gilbert, he believed, had been 'infinitely dazzled' by the splendours of aides-de-camp and liveried servants. 'I fear he will involve his country in difficulties. It is particularly fortunate that a person of General Stuart's manly, liberal understanding happens to be at the head of the army . . . I dread his departure.'

Relations between Sir Gilbert and Stuart deteriorated during October. The General showed Moore the correspondence between the two men, in which the Viceroy asserted his rights to the command of the army, though he said he would not insist upon those rights for the moment. Moore described Sir Gilbert's letters as 'tediously long, mean, from too much forced flattery, but artful ... Corsica was to be considered in exactly the same light as Great Britain or Ireland – a wonderful assumption in the case of a country which cannot defend itself, nor even pay its civil establishment.' The General, on the other hand, had replied in terms which were 'polite, manly, and concise'. By the end of the month the quarrel centred upon Stuart's proposals for a Corsican regiment: Sir Gilbert insisted upon naming the officers and altering the battalion and company structure.

On 5 January 1795 a courier reached the island from London, bearing letters from Downing Street. These made clear that the powers of the Viceroy would be similar to those of the lord-lieutenant of Ireland. Stuart, who had delayed his departure in an attempt to improve the situation, realized he could do nothing against such august authority, and made ready to leave with the adjutant-general, from whom Moore would take over. On 7 February Moore bid his friend farewell, declaring: 'It will be long, probably, before I serve under an officer for whom I have so much esteem and attachment.'

Moore now had a lonely and frustrating task, and his longing to be away and in action grew daily. He had to endure glittering functions at the Viceroy's residence, in rooms heavy with the scent of myrtle, orange blossoms and arbutus, where regimental bands played non-martial music on the terrace. 'Lemonade is handed about and there are cards,' wrote Moore disdainfully. 'It is a mixture between a drawing-room and a *conversazione*.'

Sir Gilbert appointed Sir Thomas Trigge commander-in-chief, with the rank of lieutenant-general. 'The power to make such appointments has hitherto been supposed to belong to the King alone,' wrote Moore. He established a reasonable relationship with Stuart's successor, but soon realized Trigge's deficiencies. 'He is a worthy, easy-tempered man, but seems never, in the course of between thirty or forty years' service, to have thought upon his profession beyond the mere details of his regiment. The scene he is now engaged on is perfectly new to him. He has no confidence in himself, and is so unused to action, that he cannot even execute the ideas suggested to him by others.'

Pasquale Paoli, fiery Corsican nationalist. Indiscreet discussions with Paoli would lead to Moore's rapid departure from the island.

And now politics, the bane of Moore's reputation, threatened his career. Leading Corsican patriots shared Moore's opinion that too much power had been entrusted to Sir Gilbert Elliot. Moore remembered Paoli's passionate outburst when he had met him during his first reconnaissance of the island. To Paoli

57

acceptance of a British viceroy's authority smacked of subservience to London. Tension increased; by mid-February Moore wrote in his journal: 'Several have told me that Sir Gilbert's government is the completest despotism ever exercised in Corsica. I expect daily a revolt in some part of the country.' Added to these fears of internal struggle were the dangers of French invasion, against which no effectual measures were being taken. 'No country requires them more,' wrote Moore.

Moore's disgust at Sir Gilbert's policies grew, and he took the dangerous and highly indiscreet step of discussing the situation with Paoli, whom he admired. His journal entry for 16 May commented: 'General Paoli left ... yesterday; he had been here some days; he was closeted twice with the Viceroy. They differed entirely, and Paoli now speaks openly against him. Paoli told me that he had written home.' At the end of July he spent two days 'very pleasantly' with Paoli, accompanied by other officers, during which the Corsican patriarch spoke 'without affectation of the impropriety of the Viceroy'.

Moore's apprehensions about the possibility of civil war and outright insurrection against the British increased, and his criticism of Sir Gilbert's handling of Paoli – shared by many other officers – became stronger. 'Paoli's party,' he wrote on 4 August, 'the one Sir Gilbert has quarrelled with, wish to be united with us as a nation, and dread the misconduct of Sir Gilbert as most likely to bring about a rupture.'

Nevertheless, Moore could still send home reasonably cheerful letters, which revealed a close acquaintance with other Corsicans besides fiery politicians. 'Apply to my mother to buy some white cotton thread,' he wrote to his brother James on 10 August, 'such as is used for embroidery, and send it to me by a messenger. Send a good quantity of it, it is for a fair Corsican.' The letter also showed Moore to be seeking ways out of Corsican service. 'I have written to the Duke of Hamilton, and I make no doubt but, in case of a dissolution, he will bring me into Parliament, *if he can*!' Escape from his present service seemed attractive even in exchange for enforced idleness in the House of Commons.

Moore's departure, however, was clouded with disgrace. The blow fell on 1 October. Early in the morning General Trigge summoned him for an urgent meeting. Embarrassed, the commander hardly looked up from his papers as he revealed that the Viceroy wished to be rid of the troublesome colonel, and had already written to London. According to Elliot, 'my connection with the people of the island who opposed his measures, the countenance and support I gave them, helped them to thwart his views, and made it impossible for him to carry on the government if I remained.' Sir Gilbert had assured Downing Street that Moore seemed 'an exceedingly good officer' but would be better promoted or employed elsewhere. London had replied with instructions for Moore to return home immediately. Sir Gilbert would insist upon these orders being obeyed unless Moore promised to sever his connections with Corsicans who opposed the Viceroy's rule. Moore replied with solid Scottish indignation: Sir Gilbert had 'taken upon him to represent to the Minister and the King what was utterly false and had thereby done what he could to injure me. His recommending me for promotion and employment elsewhere by stating my misconduct was absurd.' The unfortunate Trigge tried to calm his young subordinate by asking him to think the matter over. Moore agreed, but returned later in the day with his attitude unaltered. 'Being conscious of no crime or impropriety of conduct, I could promise no change; but I expected before he [Sir Gilbert] took any final determination that he would point out more distinctly what he meant or alluded to.' Moore demanded a meeting with the Viceroy, to be attended by General Trigge.

The unpleasant interview took place at nine o'clock the following morning, 2 October. Moore demanded to be given more details of his alleged misdemeanours. Sir Gilbert replied by saying that Moore had taken 'a decided part' in opposition to his measures and had had a significant influence upon the Corsicans. For thirty minutes Moore attempted to gain further information, without success. The contrast between the two men, one a soldier and the other a diplomat, was striking. Moore, so calm on the battlefield, grew so indignant that tears came to his eyes and sometimes he could barely splutter out his words, while the urbane Sir Gilbert remained cool and refused to go further than he wished, interspacing his quiet criticism with smooth compliments on Moore's military abilities. 'As long as I execute my military duty,' stormed Moore, 'I conceive I am

William Pitt, 1759–1806, sketched by Gillray: Moore had now to confront this young, brilliant British Minister to explain his Corsican conduct.

at liberty to give my opinion of different measures, either of your or any government...you might send me home, and others might follow, but, till you send away every officer of the army, you will not carry your point. Officers will continue to avow their opinions of your measures; as long as these do not affect their actions, they will consider you have no business to check them. Your conduct to me is, to a high degree, arbitrary and oppressive. The army will think so.' Sir Gilbert thought not; nor did he care. Moore continued to storm. To attempt to deprive officers of their opinions was 'a degree of tyranny till now unexampled'. Sir Gilbert refused to alter his own opinion: Moore had meddled in the politics of the country, and must either change his attitude or go. 'You can't give a single example,' exclaimed Moore, and stalked from the room.

A few hours later he received curt instructions to leave the island within forty-eight hours; Moore obliged within a week. So Moore, who had fallen from favour with Admiral Hood for refusing to give him his military opinion, now found himself ejected for giving his political views too freely. He headed for London and a confrontation with no less a person than the prime minister, William Pitt.

Chapter Four

*

YELLOW JACK
AND
BLACK BOGS

A crackling fire in the hearth of the study at 10 Downing Street did nothing to melt the atmosphere. Pitt's manner seemed stiff and cold. Outside, the early December day remained foggy and the mud squelched thick between the Whitehall puddles; the sun of Corsica seemed far away. Pitt explained the reason for Moore's recall: Sir Gilbert Elliot's reports had been so strongly worded that the Government had no choice. 'Nobody had acquiesced without regret, and he should be happy to hear that Moore was able to justify himself – no officer's character had stood higher,' Pitt added politely. Moore, whose righteous wrath had continued unabated throughout his journey to England, complained of the injustice of being brought back and deprived of his situation in Corsica without trial. 'Corsica was the place for me to have justified myself... now I have nothing to offer against Sir Gilbert's representations but a complete denial.' Moore declared: 'If I had associated with those only who approve of Sir Gilbert's measures I must have lived alone, for I knew no persons, whether British or Corsicans, who did approve of them, except those in his immediate pay.' Pitt declined to enter into argument: Moore had better see the Duke of Portland, Secretary for the Home Office and Colonies. So Moore took his leave.

Portland proved 'kind and obliging' but powerless. Moore described the meeting in his journal. 'He said that what had occasioned the order by no means affected my military character, which stood as high as ever.' Moore repeated his argument, without apparent success. 'His Grace was either silent or repeated what he had at first said. Upon the whole he was

62

embarrassed, and I retired perceiving that nothing was to be got out of him.'

Yet Moore's spirits were beginning to revive: the attitude of the Government indicated that it was not opposed to another appointment for the promising colonel, and he learned that the Duke of York, commander-in-chief of the army, had intervened on his behalf; Trigge had written a complimentary report; Stuart, his firm friend, had added his weight. Moore believed Sir Gilbert might soon regret his action: 'Upon the whole, he will find he could have done nothing less politic than to send me home.' And within a few days Moore discovered that the Viceroy, who had driven him from Corsica, had also inadvertently helped him with his military career. Mr Henry Dundas, Secretary for War, informed his fellow Scot that he had made a good impression on Pitt after all, and he would now be promoted to the rank of brigadier-general for service in the West Indies. Moore, after a short leave, joined his brigade in the Isle of Wight. He had scarcely been given time to unpack his baggage.

*   *   *

Corsican service had wrought considerable changes in John Moore. He had experienced prolonged action, extensive campaigning discomforts, and the problems involved in fighting alongside an unreliable ally against a determined and skilled opponent. Militarily, Moore had amply proved his ability. Politically he had displayed an almost naïve indiscretion. All these aspects of his character would continue to be revealed, especially the contrast between his aptitude for fighting and his lack of diplomatic dexterity. Now, as 1796 opened, the 35-year-old brigadier-general prepared to journey overseas again, hardened by his experience on the harsh Mediterranean island. He would need all his endurance to withstand the ordeals of service in the West Indies.

Soldiering in this far-flung corner was unpopular, and with reason: the climate was terrible, and the troops felt neglected and forgotten. While war flared again in Europe, British and French troops struggled amidst the malaria-infested swamps and jungles of St Lucia, an outpost of empire considered so vital for maritime power.

St Lucia, whose
malaria-infested
jungle and swamp
nearly cost John
Moore his life.

Moore's departure from England was inauspicious. He awaited orders all through February, hearing of more unpleasant reports from Sir Gilbert Elliot, then suddenly received instructions to leave within a matter of hours. The fleet was to sail on the morning of the following day, 27 February; he had arranged no passage, no baggage had arrived and he had no money. He swiftly purchased bedding, ready-made shirts and stockings with the help of a £40 loan, and at dawn he leaped into a small boat to take him out to the vessel on which he hoped to travel. He spent almost five hours being sculled up and down the foggy, choppy Solent attempting to find his ship, and when he did so he discovered the main fleet had already left. The wind blew fresh and Moore managed to catch up with the other vessels after the Needles, but other complications arose. The captain opened his sealed orders, expecting them to give a destination for the fleet, but found only instructions in case he should be separated from it. Moore, despite his exhaustion, saw the humorous side. 'It is therefore only upon supposition that we are proceeding to Barbados, but should be justified in returning to Portsmouth or steering for any other part of the globe.' Confusion over Moore's appointment continued after the arrival at Barbados on 13 April, and for a while it seemed he might even be given the command of cavalry units. Moore hastened to rectify the mistake, and by 25 April he was at sea again and making towards the island now showing as a distant smudge on the Caribbean horizon – St Lucia, occupied by the French.

Moore was attached to General Alexander Campbell's division, which was intended to spearhead the invasion. A landing was to be attempted at Ance le Cap, after which an advance would be made with two light guns and a howitzer to Longueville House; two columns would then strike left and right along the coast to unite at Grenado for the attack on the main French batteries commanding the vital anchorage in Choc Bay. With the aid of attack from the rear, General Sir Ralph Abercrombie, the commander-in-chief, intended to land the main body of troops in Choc Bay, and General William Morshead would then make another landing in the south to gain the island's high ground at Morne Petit.

The longboats rode over the rolling swell at 8 a.m. on 26 April carrying Moore's detachment to the jungle-fringed beaches. Moments later the men splashed hurriedly ashore, relieved at the absence of enemy. Moore rushed them into the woods and along the quarter-mile track to Longueville House, whose strong walls and narrow windows offered good defensive positions. Intermittent firing took place during the morning; one British soldier was killed and six or seven wounded, as the enemy recovered from the surprise attack. General Campbell had now landed with more troops – and with disturbing news. General Abercrombie reported that the navy was not yet ready to bring the main force into Choc Bay, and the landing must be deferred. But the bulk of Campbell's troops were already ashore, and Moore protested strongly that to re-embark would be impossible; moreover, it would be extremely dangerous to defer the next stage of the advance. He urged Campbell to post picquets at sunset, as if the British intended to spend the night at Longueville, but instead he proposed that they should advance by moonlight. Campbell agreed to seek Abercrombie's permission, which came late that night. Campbell, suffering

Sir Ralph Abercrombie, Commander-in-Chief in the West Indies, whom Moore would meet again in Ireland, Holland and Egypt. 'A truly upright, honourable, judicious man,' commented Moore.

from fever, asked Moore to give the necessary orders, and the march began at three o'clock on the morning of the 27th. The column had barely moved a mile before the leading Grenadier company clashed with a small French party, but the enemy soon fled and the force reached the heights of Choc unmolested. All seemed to be going well: the French batteries covering Choc Bay were found abandoned, and the British fleet moved into the anchorage. Abercrombie landed immediately, and by the evening of the 27th a good proportion of the troops had been brought ashore.

Moore now received orders for the next step: an assault upon the heights of Morne Chabot, from which an attack could be launched on the dominating position, Morne Fortuné. Moore would march at midnight with a detachment of about 650 men, and a second detachment under Brigadier John Hope would leave thirty minutes later. Hope's attack would open after Moore had engaged the enemy. The prime responsibility for success or failure therefore rested on Moore, who was by now extremely exhausted: he had been forty-eight hours without sleep, constantly on the move in the hot, sticky climate. He conferred with the commander-in-chief, discussed the route for the march with guides, gave his orders to his subordinate officers, then dropped for an hour's heavy sleep.

Just before midnight the march began. Moore had promised Hope to strike at dawn; there was therefore no time to spare. The path proved to be so narrow that the men could only proceed in single file, and frequent halts had to be made to avoid breaking the line as the men wound their way over the broken ground through the thick woods. Just before 4 a.m. musket flashes in the darkness announced that Moore's advance guard had been seen by the French advanced posts. This early discovery ruined the timing of the attack, for Moore could not wait in vulnerable single-file while the minutes dragged by to dawn. 'I had therefore no alternative but instantly to push on an attack. I accordingly gave, without hesitating, orders to advance and attack.' Luckily, the path ahead widened to permit six to eight men to form line, and this narrow British front advanced against the forty or fifty men in the French picquet. The latter drew back, out of the woods. There was still no time to lose: the enemy in the main defensive positions would now be falling to arms.

Moore's guides fled at the first musket shot, but were dragged back and requested to explain the ground. Moore learned that the land in front was 'tolerably smooth', sloping gently to the left while a thick hedge bordered the advance on the right. Moore feared this hedge might be lined with enemy infantry, but had to take the chance. He immediately ordered the Grenadiers to advance into the dark again. Along the hedge went the British line, for 200 tense yards, with Moore expecting a French fusillade from this cover at every step. None came, but then the British found the way barred by a heavy fence, too heavy to pull down. Musket balls were now whistling about the troops, and the men hesitated to present themselves as easy targets by climbing over the obstacle. Moore jumped over himself, calling them to come with him, and the rest followed to form line for the advance up the hill to the French position.

The French fire increased in intensity and accuracy, and as the line began to climb more and more gaps began to appear. Moore ordered his men not to fire, but the inexperienced British troops became nervous and discharged their muskets. Others in the second line also began to fire and the confusion increased. 'I was hoarse and exhausted with calling to them,' wrote Moore. By sheer will-power, he kept the men together. The line, though ragged, continued to advance. The ground levelled; the British had reached the summit. Moore gave another order, and in drove the British with stabbing bayonets, and within minutes the fight had finished. Most of the French fled, leaving about eighteen dead and the same number badly wounded.

The victory had been costly: the British casualties totalled about eighty, and Moore admitted: 'I do not think I ever made greater efforts or ever ran more personal danger. A Grenadier was shot in my arms, as if Providence had thrust him there at the moment to receive the ball levelled at me.' The men, though brave enough, were inexperienced and confused by night operations. 'I don't know that I ever felt more satisfaction than upon gaining the height. I had almost despaired of it. The consequences of a failure were strongly imprinted on my mind; besides, it was my *coup d'essai* in an army where I was unknown, and by its success my character would be judged.'

Brigadier Hope arrived at the base of the hill with the second division, but when the firing ceased he had hesitated to advance, not knowing who had won; then his men heard a solitary staccato drum beating the Grenadiers' march, and Moore's men at the top heard an answering cheer from the darkness below. Hope joined Moore as dawn broke over the hills to the east. They scanned the slopes and valleys to their front and could see no sign of the enemy, and, despite his personal exhaustion and the weariness of his men, Moore decided he must push further forward to take advantage of the enemy's disadvantage. Ahead lay another hill, Morne de Chasseur, which commanded an excellent position: possession of this would enable him to open communication with General Morshead who had landed in the south to take Morne Petit. Moore urged his men on. They had only three miles to go to reach the objective, but the roads were so bad and the men so stiff that it took as many hours to reach the summit. The British encountered no opposition, and by noon were safely entrenched with Moore's forward position thrown out to within 700 yards of the French.

Yet his exertions were still far from over; his attack the previous night had shown the troops to be raw and the officers inexperienced, and he found no time to rest. 'I found the picquets asleep, and Brigadier-General Hope and I were obliged to patrol the whole night. Being so close to the enemy as we are, our safety depends on our alertness.' Early next morning, 29 April, he received warm congratulations in a note from Sir Ralph Abercrombie, now at Chabot: 'My best thanks are due to you for the judicious decision you made on falling in with the advanced post of the enemy; any hesitation would probably have defeated your purpose. Your determination has given us success...'

Hopes for a rapid ending to the campaign faded during the following days. Moore strengthened his positions as best he could, but they remained vulnerable to surprise attack and 'the officers and men are, unfortunately, so bad, that little dependence is to be put on them'. Moore added: 'I am therefore obliged to be the whole night on my legs.' To the discomforts of humidity, mosquitoes and poor provisions, was added French artillery fire. Yet for almost a month the British and French lines remained virtually static. Morne Fortuné had still to be taken, and attempts to gain possession of the enemy's positions at Cul de Sac failed. Tempers grew strained under the stress, and Sir Ralph Abercrombie complained of poor progress in establishing a road between Moore's position and his neighbour's. Moore's journal entry revealed exhaustion: 'He is blind, and, never having been in the plain or crossed the country, he has no conception of the impenetrable stuff which covers it.' Casualties steadily mounted, from fever and from sallies to capture French gun positions which had become 'nuisances'.

More British guns were gradually hauled to the front and a massive bombardment opened on Morne Fortuné at dawn on 24 May. Shortly after 6 a.m. Abercrombie considered opposition had been sufficiently weakened, and Moore stepped from his trench to lead the light infantry and the Grenadiers into the attack. Skirmishing and savage bayoneting drove the enemy from the advanced position, despite the discovery of more survivors from the bombardment than had been expected. Moore went on to secure the surrounding ridge, then hurried back to report to Abercrombie and to urge forward working parties to clear a road for cannon.

While he was speaking to Sir Ralph, Moore noticed groups of French infantry coming from the fort on Morne Fortuné towards the post he had just taken. He sprinted back over the rough ground and threw himself panting into the defences just as the enemy emerged from the rough terrain which had helped cover their approach. 'Fire from the enemy was brisk and well-directed. They had the means of covering themselves, and they were clever in availing themselves of it; our men were falling fast.' Moore ordered the Grenadiers and light infantry to move out and charge the advancing line; the men formed and advanced with Colonel James Drummond at their head. Moore saw Drummond hack down a French officer with his sword and heard him shouting at his men to press back the enemy with their bayonets. The first French assault fell back, but barely had Drummond and his sweating men reached the trenches again when a second attack began, more determined than the first. The French pushed to within a few yards of the British position, firing one close-range volley after another. In a moment would come the final charge. Never before had Moore been in such a dangerous situation. 'The front I could present was small. Many officers and men had already been knocked down; more were falling every moment. The regiment showed great spirit, but the enemy's force was superior to ours. The ground was so confined that the whole of our men could not be brought into action or to support each other, and if the men continued to fall so fast, it was to be dreaded they might give way.'

Moore knew General Abercrombie would be able to see the struggle; he glanced constantly through the smoke to see if reinforcements were on their way, but none were visible. Hope rushed back to beg for help, and Moore organized yet another charge. Two companies of the 27th rose from their trench; many men were cut down almost immediately as they tried to form under fire, including their commander, Major Dunlop. His successor, Major Wilson, was struck down just as he ordered the charge. But the men advanced, with Moore standing on the parapet, shouting himself hoarse as he urged them on. They advanced towards the French, bayonets flashing; the two locked lines swayed, and at last the French began to turn. A tremendous cheer burst from the trenches. The survivors of the magnificent 27th returned to their position – leaving 120 killed and wounded behind, including two majors, two captains and four subalterns. The firing died down. Guns came up to reinforce the British line, and Moore reorganized his decimated ranks.

But the enemy had made their last bid: next day negotiations for surrender began, and so the conquest of St Lucia was completed. On 26 May Moore had the honour of heading the march to possess the fort of Morne Fortuné. Further honours were soon forthcoming, although Moore received these with less enthusiasm. Sir Ralph Abercrombie had been so impressed with his performance that he now wished to leave him as commander of the island, with 3,000 troops. Moore's reaction was summed up in one sentence in his journal: 'Of all things, I dislike a garrison.' Yet he knew refusal would be useless. He would have the exalted title of His Excellency the Governor, even though his appointment would only bring him 30s 6d a day.

Even before Sir Ralph departed, Moore's troubles had begun. 'I am involved in a most disagreeable scene,' he wrote. 'A considerable number of the negroes are in the woods in arms. The work in the Morne, called Fort Charlotte, is quite open, with no cover for officers or men. Everything military or civil is in the greatest confusion, and the rainy season has commenced; whilst it lasts it is almost impracticable to do anything.' Moore had only one consolation: his close friend Anderson, now a major, who had fought alongside him throughout the campaign, was to be his assistant. Sir Ralph Abercrombie and the bulk of the army sailed on 3 June; this precipitate departure increased Moore's burden. It would have been better if Sir Ralph had waited a while longer and used the time to send detachments throughout the island to quell the armed negroes. These 'brigands' came from three sources: runaway slaves from the plantations; trained black soldiers who had

71

slipped into the jungles after the French defeat; and new arrivals from Guadeloupe, trained and equipped by the French. Together, they would provide Moore with the second biggest problem of his governorship: the greatest of all would be the terrible climate and consequent ill-health amongst his men. Immediately the fighting ceased, the sick lists lengthened to horrific proportions; Moore realized that activity would provide the best antidote to the fever, and, always a firm believer that he should practise what he preached, he himself began to work with greater intensity than ever before, so much so that it seemed that overwork would kill him even if the fever did not.

The next eleven months proved damnable. Moore had a position of authority which many would have considered enviable. 'My powers are great,' he wrote to London. 'I am head of the law; my decisions are final.' Yet the responsibility which accompanied the power would have crushed a lesser man, so tremendous were the problems facing him. And for all its beauty St Lucia was full of poison, from the snakes, scorpions, centipedes and tarantulas in the jungles, to the 'Yellow Jack' fever which struck down the men as surely as French bullets. In one month alone – October 1796 – the garrison of St Lucia buried 663 men, and Moore became almost frantic in his vain attempts to cut fatalities. He refused to acknowledge that this enemy could not be beaten. 'It is not the climate alone that kills the troops in this country,' he wrote to Sir Ralph, 'it is bad management... I differ from most people I meet with, on this subject, but *I am sure I am right*.' He insisted that personal cleanliness, regular meals with sensible food, the minimum of liquor and vigorous sea-bathing were the weapons with which to fight this enemy. Above all he urged the need for activity: limbs must be driven when they felt utterly weary.

Moore's existence was spartan, though the word he used himself was 'Roman'. He spent days and weeks chasing the brigands through the jungles, harrying them wherever possible. He pleaded with Sir Ralph, now at Martinique, for more troops and supplies; he drilled and trained his own black troops; he attempted to restore the plantation economy; he tried to organize coastal defences against possible French invasion. He had no relief – nor would he have wished for the trappings of a governor's life which Sir Gilbert had so relished in Corsica. Moore never much enjoyed society, and preferred his 'family' of young staff officers, all of them as keen as himself, and all with a love for their quiet, conscientious commander which bordered on worship.

'My government continues as turbulent as ever,' he wrote to his anxious mother on 16 December 1796. 'The enemy within would be soon subdued, was it not for the supplies and encouragement he is constantly receiving from without. My means for preventing this communication are much diminished by the sickness and mortality which have prevailed among the troops. If I succeed in keeping this island, under all the disadvantages I have to contend with, I shall think myself very fortunate: nothing short of such success can compensate for the vexation of body and mind I have, and must continue to suffer.' Fever had touched him, but only slightly, and he hastened to reassure his mother. 'I am perfectly recovered, and *am so prudent*, that there is no fear of me ...'

Early in the new year Sir Ralph summoned Moore to Martinique and offered him a means of escape. The governorship of Grenada had become vacant, and he was convinced Moore could have this lucrative and prestigious post. But he added that the appointment would continue after the war with France had finished. Moore declined; he gave his reasons in a letter to his father on 18 January. 'I do not know if you are one of those who will blame me for refusing such advantageous offers. My dislike of this country is the chief cause – nothing would induce me to remain in it at present, but a sense of duty ... I feel it would be unbecoming to leave it during the war, as long as my health will permit me to serve.' He finished this sad letter to his parents: 'The Blacks, to a man, are our enemies; the few Whites who are not so afraid to be, our friends. I am convinced that nothing but my exertions, and the attention I have paid, would have kept the island in our possession – but it is every moment in danger: be prepared, therefore, to hear that it is wrested from us. I wish sincerely I was quit of it.'

Deaths from fever mounted when the hot rainy season arrived. This time 'Yellow Jack' refused to spare John Moore. Early in April the first symptoms began to appear; within hours Moore was covering his sweat-soaked bed linen with black vomit before sinking back exhausted on the limp pillow. His eyes glazed and closed, and the doctors departed, having given up hope of his recovery. But his staff officers refused to give up. Paul Anderson dragged the inert body upright, prised open the patient's mouth, and poured down strong wine. Careful nursing brought a faint flicker of life. Moore opened his eyes again; the whites were so bloodshot that they appeared scarlet, but they showed recognition. The doctors rushed back; reports which had been prepared announcing the news of the Governor's death were cancelled. Each day Moore fought for more strength, and each day he succeeded, despite excruciating pain from a huge abscess at the base of his right hip. He began to work again, from his bed, and vowed he would stay on the island until his duty had been done. But his young officers pleaded and better sense prevailed. In the second week of July, a short and vastly welcome note reached Clifford Street, London. 'My dear Mother. It will surprise you, I hope agreeably, to hear I am arrived at Falmouth, from the West Indies ... I was told by everybody that if I remained during the hurricane months, I should probably die. The campaign in the West Indies was completely over ... I am this day landed from the packet, not an invalid, but in perfect health.' Moore left for London on 10 July, and with him travelled the loyal Major Anderson; Moore asked his mother to arrange lodgings for this excellent friend in the neighbourhood of Clifford Street – 'the nearer the better'.

*   *   *

The summer passed pleasantly for Moore, now a colonel again – his rank of brigadier-general had only been for the duration of his West Indian service. For five months he rested, apart from occasional meetings in Whitehall and the writing of a typically businesslike report on the St Lucia campaign. Moore spent most of October touring Essex, Suffolk and Norfolk, with his friend Major Lewis Hay of the Engineers, who had been instructed to study coastal defences, and Moore's journal revealed his own close attention to detail.

The international scene remained gloomy and there were fears of French invasion: on 10 March Bonaparte had invaded Austria and in little more than a month dictated peace terms,

eventually formalized in the Treaty of Campo Formio. Bonaparte's victory resulted in Belgium becoming part of France,
so giving him a larger springboard for an assault across the
Channel. Already, in February, a half-hearted attempt had
been made upon the coast of Pembrokeshire. The resulting
panic had stimulated recruiting for home defence – and had
almost caused a disastrous run on the Bank of England. Now,
in autumn 1797, it still seemed that before long the British army
would be fighting on British beaches.

In November, however, Moore left for overseas service
again – though not far away. Sir Ralph Abercrombie had been
appointed commander-in-chief in Ireland. His admiration for
John Moore did not flag, and he now sought Moore's services
as a brigadier. Moore left London on 24 November, sailed from
Holyhead on 1 December, and landed in Dublin the following
day after 'a most boisterous, disagreeable passage'. With him,
as always, went Anderson.

'Had there been any prospect of service in Portugal,' wrote
Brigadier Moore in his journal, 'I should have preferred going
there, but as I suppose our troops will immediately be recalled
from there, and the West Indies presents no service, there was
no alternative but Ireland or idleness at home, of which I was
already tired.' Sir Ralph informed Moore that he would command the forts of Cork harbour, Kinsale and Middleton, under
Lieutenant-General Sir James Steuart, commander of Ireland's
southern district, who had still to arrive from England. The
commander-in-chief also told Moore of the appalling state of
military preparations in Ireland, and of the poor relationship
between Abercrombie's office and that of the lord-lieutenant,
technically his superior.

Moore disliked intensely the current methods of keeping the
country quiet. 'The mode which has been followed,' he wrote,
'has been to proclaim the districts in which the people appeared
to be most violent, and to let loose the military, who were
encouraged in acts of great violence against all who were supposed to be disaffected. Individuals have been taken up upon
suspicion, and without any trial sent out of the country. By these
means the disturbances have been quelled, an apparent calm
produced, but the disaffection has undoubtedly increased. The
gentlemen in general, however, still call out aloud for violent

measures as the most proper to be adopted, and a complete line seems to be drawn between the upper and lower orders.' Such unjust repression contrasted sharply with the policy he had employed in St Lucia, where he had fought against known dissidents with every means at his disposal, but had offered mercy to all who surrendered and had tried to win over the peaceful population by good treatment and economic progress.

Moore left for Cork on 6 January 1798, disturbed by what he had learned. He soon found further reasons for disquiet. The troops in Ireland consisted mainly of militia, whom Moore considered extremely unreliable. Many of them felt considerable sympathy for the French, especially the recruits who formed the bulk of the force, and this attitude was only natural after the harsh treatment of the Irish dealt by the British. Even more serious, Moore considered, was the lack of respect shown by the rank and file to their officers: the men were usually Protestant while their seniors were Catholic. Nor could Moore find much that was worthwhile amongst the officers; he condemned them as 'profligate and idle, serving for the emolument, but neither from a sense of duty nor of military distinction'. Corrup-

76

tion proved rife in the militia and in the country generally. 'In the management of this country there appears to have been a great want of probity and talent. If there ever was a time when such an officer as a dictator was required, it is the present. If a man of sufficient character and talent was to be found to fill it, he might still save Ireland.' But Moore insisted that such a leader would have to be a benevolent dictator, serving the interests of his country, not his own. Meanwhile, Moore lost no time in attempting to reform his own particular command. The attempted French landing in Ireland in 1796 had failed miserably, but another expedition might meet with more success – especially in view of the deplorable state of coastal defences.

Sir James Steuart, commander of the south, reached Cork in early March, and Moore found his superior officer, whom he had known in America, in a very sorry state of health. 'I found [him] completely unfitted for business.' Then, in April, Sir Ralph Abercrombie told Moore he had asked to be recalled, following criticism of his liberal policies, and especially opposition from some officers to his attempts to root out corruption. His successor as commander-in-chief arrived at the end of May:

Lieutenant-General Gerard Lake, whose appointment Moore considered of doubtful value in view of his apparent unwillingness to check military scandals.

In this tense, unhappy situation, Moore's skill in building excellent relations with his men, and persuading them to give their best, proved invaluable. He believed the militia contained good material, if it could be properly moulded. The method he used was trust: if he showed his men that he trusted them, he believed they would back him up. His commonsense approach to Irish problems was displayed in a speech to his troops on 16 March. 'Ireland is composed of Roman Catholics and Protestants. The Government has entrusted both equally with her defence . . . For a man to boast or be proud of his religion is absurd. It is a circumstance in which he has no merit; he was the one or the other because his parents were so before him, and it was determined for him before he had a choice. Any man might fairly pride himself upon being just and honest, but not on his religion. If you follow the doctrines of the one or the other, you will be good and honest.' Moore was speaking to his men in a manner they had never experienced before, and in a way which few commanders could bring themselves to do. 'I am as much at my ease amongst you as I ever have been amongst any soldiers whatever . . . It is melancholy to be obliged to act against one's countrymen. I hope sincerely it will never be our case; but, as soldiers, we engaged not only to fight the foreigner, but also to support the Government and laws, which have long been in use, and framed by wiser men than we are.'

Gradually Moore forged the link between himself and his men, and to strengthen it he stamped firmly on inefficient officers. He demanded high standards of leadership and personal behaviour. A captain in his corps was found to be drunk on picquet duty, and Moore immediately threw him under arrest. 'I hope sincerely he may be broken . . . Soldiers are flogged for it. I do not see how I could look them in the face if I was not to punish it equally in officers.'

Civil war erupted on the evening of 23 May; confusing rumours flitted along the muddy, rutted roads. Communications with Dublin had been cut, except by sea, and while the rebels in the capital were easily put down the insurrection

Irish troops caricatured by Gillray, yet Moore believed –
and proved – that they could be excellent military material.

remained dangerous in the rural areas. Wexford fell to the insurgents. For two weeks Moore waited impatiently for action,
and on 9 June he leaped to obey an order to march his light
battalion and two 6-pounders to Cork, where he arrived the
same day. After further delays and confused orders he marched
again at dawn on 14 June, with instructions to reinforce troops
in the Wexford district ready for an attack on the rebels at
nearby New Ross. By 18 June he reached the vicinity of New
Ross where he joined other English forces.

The advance began at 6 a.m. on the 19th, after a four-hour
postponement because of heavy rain; Moore led the right
column of three. The rebels were deployed on a hill about a
mile and a half from Ross; they waited for the English to come
just within cannon range, then turned tail with the English in
close pursuit. About seventy Irish stragglers were killed. A
further advance was to be made next day, and Moore was
ordered to move on Taghmon, seven miles from Wexford. He
waited until 3 p.m. for other troops to join him, but as there
was no sign of them he decided to start for the Taghmon objective with the 1,000 men already under his command. Within
a few minutes Moore was involved in a sharp fight which
revealed the fruits of his training methods, his control over men,
his superb tactical appreciation, and his ability to act quickly
and decisively in moments of extreme stress.

'We had not marched above a mile when a cloud of dust
was seen moving towards us. This we immediately perceived
to be a large party of rebels.' Moore, with his usual foresight,
had reconnoitred the ground earlier in the day; he immediately
ordered a part of his troops to advance and skirmish, covering
the movement of his light infantry to the right and left of the
road. Guns were run forward to a commanding position at a
crossing of two tracks. The rebels plunged forward, outnumber-
ing Moore's force six to one. Moore's light infantry companies
fought with courage, but were forced to give ground. Moore
then threw himself from his horse, ran to their front, and
jumped a ditch to advance on the enemy regardless of the muskets aimed at him. His men followed his example, and soon
the enemy were driven back downhill. Next Moore sent three
companies to block a large force of rebels attempting to creep
round the left flank.

Almost immediately the commander of these companies sent word back that the rebels, making use of thick cover in a nearby wood, were too strong for him. Moore's troops were in danger of being outflanked, surrounded, and slaughtered. The conflict had reached its most crucial point. Moore sent reinforcements to his left flank, but the calls for further help became increasingly urgent. He sent his faithful brigade-major, Anderson, to assess the situation, and Anderson quietly returned to tell Moore he must go there himself, or all would be lost. Only Moore's presence could stiffen the outnumbered troops. He called to Anderson to take charge of the front sector, and spurred his mount towards the threatened flank. He galloped over the muddy fields, clods of turf flying from his horse's hooves, and met his men retreating in disorder with the enemy close behind. Grabbing the panic-stricken men by their collars, he pushed them into ditches on either side of the road and shouted to them to make a stand; then he rounded up more men, urging them into a semblance of order. 'Face the enemy,' he shouted. Other men rallied when they saw the figure of Moore amongst them. 'When I saw them ready for it, I took off my hat, put my horse into a trot, gave a huzza, and got them to make a push. The tide immediately turned. We drove the rebels before us, and killed a great many.' The insurgents tried two or three times to make another stand, but could not, even though they numbered about 6,000. The pursuit continued until darkness fell at about 8 p.m., and night passed uneasily with the men by their arms. Moore pushed forward towards Taghmon early next morning.

Grey clouds clung to the hills; rain splattered into the faces of the British troops. Two horsemen came galloping along the boggy road towards Moore's advancing column, one rider waving a white handkerchief. They carried a letter from Lord Kingsbury, taken prisoner by the rebels, which said that the insurgents in Wexford offered to lay down their arms if their lives and property were spared, and this was confirmed by Matthew Keogh, the rebel governor. Moore made no answer, having no authority to start negotiations. Clearly the lives of captives in Wexford were in great danger, and he decided to press on for the town instead of stopping at Taghmon as instructed.

Defeat of the rebels
at Vinegar Hill,
June 1798. At one point along the route Moore narrowly escaped death.
He had climbed a dyke to view the way ahead, but behind
lurked half a dozen rebels. A staff officer unsheathed his sword
and jumped in amongst them, only to stagger back with a
pike thrust in his arm. But the rebels ran off and the march
continued.

Later, Moore and his men were threatened by an ambush
on a far larger scale. The road ahead lay along a wild hillside.
Moore swept the summit ridge with his glasses and discovered
parties of armed men amongst the peat bogs. He immediately
halted the column while an advance guard climbed cautiously
up the hill, then Moore took the main body forward within
supporting distance. With their ambush discovered, the rebels
disappeared, and the column approached the town of Wexford.

Black smoke curled upwards. Moore had intended to wait
on the outskirts until reinforcements arrived, but fearing the
rebels might raze the town and slaughter the prisoners he
ordered a party of 200 men to rush forward into the streets.

Once again the rebels fled before his unexpected onset, and Moore rode into Wexford to a tumultuous welcome: released prisoners flocked round him, sobbing hysterically and flinging their arms round weeping wives and children. 'Forty prisoners had been shot and piked the day before,' wrote Moore, 'and it was intended to have shot the rest that evening if I had not come on ... I, therefore, had the good fortune to perform one of the most pleasing services that could fall to the lot of an officer.'

Soon after this reinforcements arrived led by Generals Lake and Henry Johnson; Moore dined with his commander-in-chief, still battle-stained, and had a brief but joyful meeting with his brother Graham, whose ship lay off the shore. General Lake paid credit to Moore's exploits in a despatch published in a London Gazette Extraordinary on 26 June: 'General Moore, with his usual enterprise and activity, pushed on to this town, and entered it so opportunely as to prevent it from being laid in ashes and the massacre of the remaining prisoners.'

One by one the main rebel pockets in Ireland were eliminated and captured leaders brought to trial and execution. Among the latter was the ex-priest 'General' Philip Roche, who had commanded the troops opposing Moore – 'a great, fat, vulgar-looking beast' who proved so heavy that the rope broke when the first attempt was made to hang him. With him died Keogh – even though he had made such a convincing speech, claiming he had been forced at pike-point to command rebel troops, that Moore had appealed to Lake for his reprieve.

But a new policy was now inaugurated at Dublin with the arrival of the sixty-year-old veteran of the American revolution, Lord Charles Cornwallis, appointed both lord-lieutenant and commander-in-chief. Cornwallis preached calmness and conciliation – methods which Moore strongly supported, and the two men became friends. Moore received a further encouragement during the first week of July; he wrote to his father from Taghmon camp on the 7th: 'My promotion [to the rank of major-general] is in orders.' And in the same letter Moore described 'highly flattering' instructions which he had just been given: he would command the force intended to hunt out the remaining rebels from the murky mountains and bogs of Wicklow. His corps would be completely separate and independent, giving him full scope to use his own initiative.

For the next three weeks Moore revealed his remarkable energy to the full as he chased his elusive enemy through pouring rain and over terrible terrain. 'The rebels waited for us nowhere,' he wrote to London. 'We found the country deserted; villages and houses burned; nothing could be more melancholy. Though we have had no fighting, the fatigue and inconvenience of the troops has been very great.' The countryside had proved so rough, and the need for speed and flexibility so great, that the baggage had been left behind, and the troops slept on the ground without tents or covering for seven nights of sluicing storms and bitter cold. Moore 'chose to share the fate of his men'. At occasional stops at local inns, inhabitants were amazed to see this English general actually pay for his meal. The expedition and subsequent forays into the wild wastes proved successful, but not without cost: Anderson's health collapsed and he had to return to England to recover, and in early August Moore had to take to his bed with aching limbs and bouts of shivering and sweating. Exaggerated tales of his illness reached Clifford Street in London, and Moore's doctor brother James climbed on the Holyhead coach to rush north and over to Ireland. Unknown to James, John had already recovered. Still weak, and with his clothes hanging from scrawny limbs, he had felt fit enough to answer an urgent summons from Lord Cornwallis, and had reached Dublin on 24 August. 'I found Lord Cornwallis looking over the great map of Ireland. He immediately told me that the French had landed.'

The scanty intelligence reports indicated an invasion in the region of Killala Bay, on the north-west coast near Sligo. The French were apparently few in number, but had been enthusiastically received by the locals. General Lake was to organize a force to the south of the area, in Galway; General Nugent was to move towards Sligo from the north, while Taylor, who commanded at Sligo, probed the enemy strength without becoming entangled in battle. Moore received orders to take his men north to the centre of Ireland at Athlone or Longford where the principal army would be assembled, led by Cornwallis in person. General Moore now became so busy that his journal, abandoned on 26 July during his hectic rebel-chasing, would not be re-opened until 17 September.

By 27 August Moore had joined the main army at Athlone. During the night an express messenger brought news of a French victory at Castlebar, and news of further enemy successes against Lake reached Cornwallis next day, as he advanced north. By 29 August contact had been made with Lake and his retiring force, and on the last day of the month the English were drawn up within half a mile of the advanced enemy posts at Mount Bellew.

The first of September dawned fine, and brought a happy surprise for Moore. Two horsemen rode to his position as trumpets, bugles and drums were sounding reveille and the order to strike camp. Moore was squatting by a table-cloth laid on the grass, upon which breakfast had been spread, with his 'family' of officers around him. His brother James trotted up, escorted by a dragoon, tired but triumphant after his rushed journey from London. 'Well, James!' exclaimed General Moore. 'Have you come to see a battle?' 'I came to bring you health to fight one,' replied his brother, 'but your looks show that you've got it already.' James joined the march – an extra doctor might always be useful.

Initially the army presented a glorious spectacle. 'The view of the column was very striking,' wrote James, 'now ascending the heathy hills, then descending the valleys in long array, with glittering arms, and with all that martial pomp and ceremony, which is so captivating to the ambitious.' But soon there appeared the usual hardships of campaigning which his brother knew so well – weariness and sheer frustration.

Spies brought information that the main French force was still at Castlebar, where Irish dissidents were being enlisted and armed, but they disagreed over the size of the enemy force: some said 20,000 men; others subsequently proved more correct, claimed just over 1,000. Lord Cornwallis advanced cautiously. Although the march may have been relatively slow, James Moore found the going increasingly exhausting; as soon as the army halted for the night on 1 September, two miles beyond Tuam, he slumped with weariness. 'Not so my brother, whose labours seemed then only to commence. He galloped all round the country, examined every wood and eminence, questioned the country people respecting every road and path, and compared their different accounts with a good map.' After posting picquets and patrols General Moore snatched a brief meal, then rode off to confer with Cornwallis, returning late in the night to fling off his boots, bid his brother goodnight, and stretch out on a truss of straw.

For the next six days the English and the French manœuvred for position, with Cornwallis gradually drawing his regiments around the enemy, and with the French apparently heading towards Sligo. Moore's men were especially exhausted with this constant movement: on 6 September he received orders to march across country to reinforce Lake, shadowing the enemy's rear; late on the 7th, he received fresh orders to counter-march back to Cornwallis. Lake meanwhile continued harassing the outnumbered French, pushing forward wherever possible, while Cornwallis loomed closer. The French were unable to stand the pressure, and surrendered on the 8th, knowing their position to be hopeless. James Moore returned to London without witnessing a battle.

John Moore was about to march into the Killala and Castlebar area to quell the French-armed rebels, when disturbing reports arrived from England: a French line-of-battle warship and eight frigates had put out to sea from Brest, believed destined for Ireland. Cornwallis immediately informed Moore that he must have his men ready to move to likely landing areas at short notice. But on 14 October Moore wrote in his journal: 'It is not yet known what has become of the squadron from Brest, but all apprehension of their coming to Ireland is over . . . It is to be hoped that Nelson's glorious victory off the Nile will stop the relish of the French for naval expeditions, and enable us to be quiet during the winter.'

Moore spoke too soon. Within twenty-four hours news reached his camp that two French men-of-war had anchored in Donegal Bay and were attempting to land troops; more ships lay in the offing. He immediately gave orders to stop troops already marching to their winter quarters. But next day came more news: the ships in Donegal Bay had put to sea, and reports indicated an action at sea between the French fleet and the Royal Navy. For almost a week Moore waited in acute suspense. Then came more news, and this time the reports gave him special joy. The British fleet under Sir John Warren had played havoc with the French force, and the name of Moore had been predominant in the action: his brother Graham had thrown his frigate *Melampus* against two enemy vessels, and after twenty-five minutes had caused one to flee under full sail and had taken the other. Six more French ships had been seen off Killala but had since disappeared.

Wet weather ended the campaigning season. The French had been scared away, the rebels were defeated or scattered, the English army was firmly in control. Moore wanted to be gone. A chance of release came at the beginning of December, when he heard that his old commander in Corsica, General Charles Stuart, had sailed with troops from Lisbon and Gibraltar to capture Minorca, and had asked that Moore should command the reinforcements being despatched to him. Moore hurriedly informed London that he would be pleased to accept such a command, and waited three weeks in growing impatience for official confirmation. The wait ended in disappointment. Moore had to pay the price for his own efficiency: the matter had been discussed with the Duke of York, and it had been agreed that Lord Cornwallis had laid so much stress on the esteem he held for Moore that to remove this favourite from Ireland would give umbrage. So Moore had to endure the Irish winter, and so inactive did he become that a huge gap appeared in his journal. Instead, he occupied himself with another kind of writing.

Sitting in his damp Athlone garrison rooms, he turned his thoughts to a subject which had always been of immense interest to him: the training and organization of infantry, based on his experiences in America, Corsica, and the West Indies and especially the methods used by him in training the light infantry of the Irish militia. He began with the declaration that light infantry should start with sound training in the drill and movement used by ordinary foot battalions. He then examined the drill required for all the multiple manœuvres and tasks which these specialists might be called upon to perform, giving each section a separate heading: file movements, extending and closing, firing at close order, firing at extended order, firing advancing in extended order, firing retreating, file firing in battalion order with files touching ... All these complicated movements were described in Moore's clear style – though the descriptions were written in his usual illegible sloping scrawl, which always gave the impression that his thoughts were running too fast for his hand to keep pace. Moore's work during this sodden winter of 1798–9 would provide a solid foundation for training methods he would later see put into practice. First however would come more action, and more desperate battles.

In early June 1799, Moore applied to Cornwallis for two months' leave, and began to pack. He never had a chance to enjoy the break. A message reached him from Dublin Castle: General John Moore must go at once to the south of England. He re-opened his journal: 'It was the intention of His Majesty's Ministers to employ me upon a secret expedition...'

Chapter Five

*

WOUNDS OF WAR

Ahead lay a misty coastline so flat that Moore had difficulty
in distinguishing where sea ended and land began. All around
swayed Royal Navy warships and cumbersome transports;
spray showered the greasy decks; troops huddled together, their
faces grey with cold. General John Moore had written in his
newly opened journal: 'We are now upon a voyage of
adventure.' For the first time in four weary years, British troops
were about to land on mainland Europe. Holland had been
selected as the immediate objective, and Moore commanded
the fourth brigade. His old friend Sir Ralph Abercrombie was
the commander-in-chief, and the total army numbered 17,000
men. A Russian force of similar strength was to fight alongside
the British, and if the enterprise prospered the Duke of York
himself would sail over to command the conquest of Holland.

The fleet had sailed from Ramsgate on 13 August, aiming
initially for a landing on Walcheren. Then the plans were
altered, first to an attempted landing at Goeree and Voorne,
then to an attack on Texel. Such changes augured ill, and as
Moore wrote during the voyage: 'The expedition has undoubtedly been hurried beyond reason, but the country having
been put to the expense of assembling it, it is necessary that
we should be sent to attempt something.' Besides, the international situation seemed hopeful: Marshal Alexander
Suvorov's Russo-Austrian army had defeated MacDonald's
French force at Trebbia in June, and might now drive the
enemy from Italy, while the Austrians were pressing hard in
Switzerland. Archduke Charles of Austria might march north
through western Germany to join the Russo-British force in ex-
pelling the French from the Netherlands, and Suvorov would

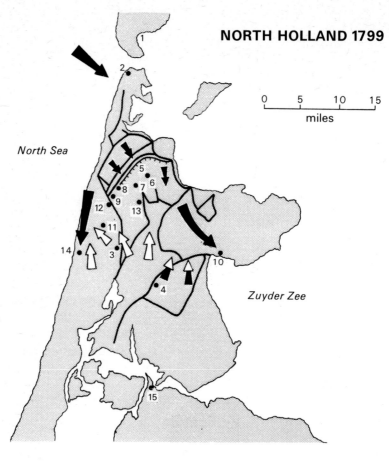

NORTH HOLLAND 1799

North Sea

Zuyder Zee

1. Texel
2. Helder
3. Alkmaar
4. Schermeershoorn
5. Zype Sluys canal
6. Groenevelt
7. Harings–Karspel
8. Ennigerburg
9. Krabbendam
10. Hoorn
11. Bergen
12. Schorldam
13. Wannenhuizen
14. Egmont–Op–Zee
15. Amsterdam

British   French   Dutch   Dyke   Canal

British troops
bivouac amongst
the sand-dunes of
the Helder, 1799.

make use of this northern offensive by striking from the south, pressing Masséna back into France. But first the British army had to land on the Dutch coast – if the weather permitted. But the weather was on the side of the French. So plans had been changed again: now a landing was to be made on the northernmost tip of mainland Holland, around the Helder, and the fleet gathered offshore on 21 August. Then the clouds fell, wind whipped the waves, and the warships and transports had to put out to sea once more. Storms prevented a return until the 26th; early next morning the disembarkation began.

Fortunately for the British, enemy opposition proved negligible. 'We landed with great confusion and irregularity,' commented Moore. He had been put ashore with a mere 300 of his own men, and these a mixture of every regiment in his brigade, but within an hour more troops had arrived and Moore rushed them into positions fronting the Helder. The British forces to his right ran into a stiffer defence, and in driving the enemy back they encountered a large body of enemy cavalry and infantry in the sand-dunes. 'A very hot action commenced,' reported Moore, so hot that the British lost 452 killed and wounded. Enemy infantry now also began to wind round the

British left, and Moore feared the position on both flanks had
become 'extremely bad'.

The British bridgehead was still far from secure; the soldiers
so far landed might soon find themselves trapped. Abercrombie hurried over to Moore's position in the centre and
explained the situation. He had just visited the right flank, and
in his view only one chance remained to avoid failure: Moore
must strike boldly with his brigade to seize the town of Helder.
The attack was to be launched during the night, and, as Moore
wrote: 'It was evident that if we failed, immediate measures

Surrender of the Dutch fleet to the British, August 1799. 'The greatest stroke that has perhaps been struck in this war has been accomplished in a few hours, and with a trifling loss,' declared an over-optimistic Moore.

must be taken for re-embarking.' Even the arrival of a cutter with news of a 6,000-man reinforcement sailing from England could not alter this assessment. And the attack would be extremely hazardous – Dutch deserters informed Moore that the enemy had 2,000 men in the fortified town.

Early in the evening Moore made his way forward to view the ground; he observed enemy troops in movement and believed them to be taking up positions for the night. Then, just before dark, he was astonished to see these troops marching off by the coast towards the Alkmaar road. The enemy were evacuating Helder. Moore immediately pushed forward patrols and followed with the Royals; outside the town he was met by a man with a white flag; the enemy had spiked all their cannon and departed. Moore rushed in his men; by dawn he was in possession of the town and the enemy batteries, and more good fortune came with the news from Abercrombie that the enemy fleet had surrendered on 30 August without firing a shot. 'Thus the greatest stroke that has perhaps been struck in this war has been accomplished in a few hours, and with a trifling loss ... The chances of war are infinite. The number which were against the success of this expedition were incalculable.'

Moore's relief was short-lived. Reinforcements reached the enemy army, which by the end of the first week in September numbered 5,000 French and 8,000 Dutch. The French were centred on Alkmaar with posts stretching to the sea, while the Dutch lay to their right based on Schermeershoorn. The British troops, still suffering without tents in the wet weather, were precariously situated, especially at the right of the line, and during the evening of the 5th Moore received orders to reinforce this sector. These positions must be held until Russian forces arrived for the advance into Holland. By early morning, 6 September, Moore had deployed his regiments along a line of defence provided by a dyke to the front of Zype Sluys canal, and with outposts as far forward as the villages of Groenevelt, Harings-Karspel, Ennigerburg and Krabbendam; at some points his men were within easy hailing distance of the French, and here he awaited attack. Late on the 9th the rumble and squeak of gun carriages and the tap of drum beats were heard in the darkness ahead. Moore prepared his brigade to meet the coming assault.

Just before dawn he received a message that the enemy were moving on Krabbendam. Moore guessed the enemy intended more than an attack on this village. He knew the defence of Krabbendam was in capable hands, and had greater fears for the Harings-Karspel and Ennigerburg areas – a good road ran through these villages and along the dyke to the rear, and 'the impediments of the country made it extremely difficult for an enemy to advance except by roads'. This, Moore believed, would be the point where he would be needed most, and as usual he proved right. He galloped across the flooded fields and arrived just in time. Dawn had begun to break, and in the half-light he could see dim grey masses of men moving towards Harings-Karspel, and could hear French voices shouting commands. Guns began to thunder; cannon balls thudded into the soft soil. Moore's outposts fell back before the weight of numbers, but Anderson had the presence of mind to order the bridges over the canals to be raised as the men retired. The crackle of distant musket fire showed that the French were attacking at two other points in the British line, including Krabbendam. A message reached Moore from Abercrombie at the latter village asking for reinforcements, and also requesting Moore's presence. Moore sent the extra men, but declined to go himself. 'I thought that my presence was indispensable where I was.' He rode backwards and forwards behind the main dyke, reassuring his men and ordering them to stay under cover of the bank until the last moment.

And now the main attack began. Moore could see a large French column advancing, supported by artillery, and the shouts and drums and bugles grew louder as the enemy approached. A musket shot shattered Moore's finger, and only his spy-glass prevented the ball from tearing into his body. On came the French, their faces now easily visible, no longer shouting and calling to each other, but ready for the bayonet charge over the last few yards of ground. Moore waited, then shouted an abrupt command, echoed by other officers. The long line of British infantrymen climbed to their feet, scrambled up the dyke, formed line, and poured their fusillades into the French. Scores of the enemy fell and the rest hesitated, then halted, and the enemy column began to splinter; the French troops turned and ran in confusion and Moore allowed his men to cheer them on their way. The other attacks were repulsed at about the same time, and by early afternoon Moore could order his men forward to retake the villages to the front. Enemy casualties from the day's battle totalled over 2,000; the British lost only a handful, owing to the excellent protection of the dyke.

Later in the day the Duke of York stepped ashore to take command, his face sprouting a four-day beard which to the meticulous Moore 'gave him the look of a savage'. During the next forty-eight hours Russian and English troops were disembarked, bringing the army's strength to nearly 40,000. The

Gillray caricature
of the campaign in
Holland: a well-fed
Duke of York
served by starving
Grenadiers.

allied line began to move forward, and by 19 September the Dutch in the Hoorn area had capitulated.

No further advance could be made until the Russians had pushed forward on the allied right, and this they failed to do. On the 19th the Russian contingent received a serious setback after attacking Bergen. Two Russian generals were captured, and up to 3,000 men were killed and wounded. Moore's comments were scathing: the Russians, from the beginning, had failed to preserve order. 'Their retreat was precipitous and as unsoldierlike as their advance. The whole attack was hurried, before the Generals perfectly understood their parts, and before those who were to lead the different columns had communicated together. The first check caused confusion, and there was

The capture of the Russian commander, Hermann, at Bergen, 19 September 1799: Moore believed the Russian general had allowed himself to be taken.

nobody to remedy it.' He suspected that General Hermann, their commander, whose action 'fell short of his talk', had purposely allowed himself to be taken prisoner to cover his misconduct.

Now the allied line had to retire to stronger positions and seek the opportunity for another attack. The troops still suffered from the regular downpours, and Moore still had his arm in a sling – he had been obliged to ask Anderson to write his letter home on 18 September. He suffered further discomfort from a fever, for which he took tartar emetic. The second offensive, planned for the 29th, had to be postponed because of the terrible weather: rough seas sent surf high up the beaches, preventing his men from outflanking the enemy by this route.

By 2 October Moore's fever had diminished and his sling had been cast aside; he felt fit and ready for the battle that was to take place that day. The Russians, numbering 8,000 under General Essen, were to march in the direction of Bergen, with General Sir David Dundas following with the reserve; General Sir Harry Burrard was to lead the Guards towards Schoreldam and Wannenhuizen. The main attack was to be launched by

97

Skirmishing in the sharp and bloody Dutch campaign. Sir Ralph Abercrombie with 10,000 men: they were to move along the beach to Egmont-op-Zee, with the aim of turning the enemy's left. As Moore commented, 'The whole evidently depended upon the success of Sir Ralph's column' – and Moore was to lead the advance troops. But much also depended on the Russians: 'It was very necessary for the Russian columns to advance pretty boldly towards Bergen in order to enable Sir Ralph to advance with safety.' The past Russian record warranted no confidence that they would do this.

At 6 a.m. the tide had ebbed sufficiently for Moore's men to march past the Duke of York and make their way forward along the wet beach. Plans soon started to go wrong: Colonel MacDonald, commanding a force which should have stayed in the sand-dunes to the immediate left of the column as flank-guard, moved too far inland. About four difficult miles of dunes now separated him from the main advance, thus exposing its left flank, and increasing numbers of French could now be seen gathering there. A messenger cantered up from Sir Ralph: Moore must form his men to prevent the French from falling upon the flank of the column. Already Moore's leading units were skirmishing with enemy light infantry and hussars, and he had scarcely time to form the 25th and 79th Regiments before the French thrust forward.

This initial attack was repulsed, but the next five hours were very difficult for Moore and his hard-pressed regiments. The French fell back, but constantly turned at bay in good defensive positions; the British troops had to trudge on, exposed to incessant, harassing sniper fire. As they struggled over the dunes, with sand in their boots and mouths, the French kept always in front of them; the sound of battle swelled with continual skirmishing fire and occasional violent, shattering volleys. Moore suffered a glancing wound in the thigh early in the day, but he rode on; later his horse fell beneath him, shot through the chest, and he barely managed to fling himself clear. He limped across to another mount, one leg stiff and aching. The advance slowed, but Moore urged his men forward, constantly protecting the threatened left flank, until his troops reached within two miles of Egmont-op-Zee.

It was here, when the British were sufficiently wearied and weakened, that the French had decided to make their main stand. A body of fresh troops, so far unengaged, came rushing down on Moore's brigade: wave after wave of shouting, cheering men flooded over the sand ridges. Within moments the whole area had become a seething mass of blue uniforms with the redcoats pressed into small islands, and acrid musket smoke shrouded the whole conflict. Moore, as usual, was at the front and now fought with his leading regiment, the 25th. The French attacked the regiment's flank; three companies of the 92nd were cut down as they struggled through to reach them. The British troops were falling fast, and the survivors looked anxiously over their shoulders; more and more began to flee. 'I saw the impossibility of rallying or stopping my men under such hot fire,' wrote Moore. 'I had given up the point, and had just determined in my own mind to let them go a certain distance to the rear and then to rally and bring them back.' Moore, almost surrounded, turned to force his way through.

It was then that a shot, fired at close range, threw him hard onto the sand: the bullet had entered behind his ear and came ripping out of his cheek under his left eye. With blood pouring from his face, and only semi-conscious, Moore thought half his head had been blown away and gave himself up for dead. He lay sprawled on the sand while hand-to-hand fighting continued around him. Then he heard a shout, and felt hands hauling him up; he opened his eyes to see a British soldier dragging him to his feet and the French only a few yards away. Moore was half-carried, half-pulled, back through the ragged British lines and through the advancing 92nd Highlanders. A field dressing was rapidly tied round his wound and his groom came running with another horse; the general was helped into the saddle, and with blood seeping through the bandages and his groom holding the bridle he began the painful journey back to the rear – but not before he had heard that the arrival of the Highlanders had bolstered the falling front, and another gallant charge stopped the French. The groom led him back ten miles, with Moore reeling in the saddle and clutching the pommel with both hands. He collapsed in his bed, and knew nothing until dawn the following day.

He woke to find Anderson at his bedside, with the Duke of York's own surgeon there to dress his wound. The surgeon declared he had had a miraculous escape: neither the jaw nor any other bone had been broken, the eye seemed undamaged, and Moore would probably recover completely. Propped on his pillows, Moore heard more details of the previous day's fighting. The column had advanced no further after he had left the field, and the remainder of the day had passed in skirmishing. A vigorous enemy artillery and cavalry attack in the evening had been repulsed. Sir Ralph, who had had two horses shot under him, reported disappointing news of the Russian operation: General Essen had been unable to reach Bergen.

But Moore's efforts had not been totally in vain. The presence of Sir Ralph Abercrombie's column threatening the French left induced the enemy to retire: Abercrombie entered Egmont-op-Zee on the 4th, and Bergen and Alkmaar had fallen the previous evening. Stalemate now ensued. The Duke of York realized he had insufficient men to drive the French from Holland, especially in view of Russian unreliability and lack of support from the Dutch; moreover, the Dutch fleet having been taken, one of the main objects of the expedition had been accomplished. The French, on the other hand, realized that to drive the Russo-British army from Holland would be difficult and extremely costly. Negotiations for an armistice therefore began, and on 18 October the Convention of Alkmaar was signed by which the British kept the Dutch fleet but agreed to withdraw from Holland.

By now General Moore was at sea, having embarked from Helder on board the frigate *Amethyst*, bound for the Nore. But before departure Moore had again had a narrow escape from death. The surgeons had been bathing his inflamed wound with a strong solution of sugar-of-lead, and this poisonous liquid had been left on his bedside table. Moore, reaching for a draught of whey to slake his perpetual thirst, had taken the sugar-of-lead instead. He realized his dreadful mistake as he set down the cup; he called Anderson from the adjoining room and quietly asked him to pass a quill pen from the nearby writing stand, and to bring an oil cruet and water. Moore then thrust the feathers down his throat and retched out the poison.

On 24 October he arrived in England, naturally still weak. News of his wound had preceded him; he had dictated a letter to Anderson on 3 October, addressed to his father, and had managed to write the final sentence himself: 'With my own hand, and from my bed I subscribe myself your affectionate son ...' With this letter had come a message from Sir Robert Brownrigg, adjutant-general and secretary to the Duke of York: 'His conduct in the serious action of the 2nd, which perhaps may be ranked among the most obstinately contested battles that have been fought this war, has raised him, if possible, higher than he before stood in the estimation of this army. Everyone admires and loves him; and you may boast of having as your son the most amiable man, and the best General, in the British service: this is a universal opinion, and does not proceed from my partiality alone ...' Similar praise came from Sir Ralph, who had made the time to write a note to Dr Moore on 4 October. 'The General is a hero, with more sense than many others of that description. In that he is an ornament to his family, and to his profession.' Within thirty minutes of receiving his son's letter, Dr Moore had scribbled a paragraph to his wife, who was staying at Richmond: 'My dear Jane – our dear Jack is alive, and in a fair way of recovery ... How many merciful escapes has he had!'

The year and the century closed with General Moore – now a
recognized public figure and a highly respected general – making firm steps towards full recovery. Dr John Moore and his
doctor son James attended him, and noted with concern the
saliva still oozing from the two holes in his cheek, but after a
few sleepless nights and much complaining by 'Jack' that he
would rather have lost an arm, the wounds began to close, and
by November 1799 he was about again. James penetratingly
observed his brother's behaviour during these weeks of convalescence. 'Whilst tending him I often noticed that he was revolv-
ing the events of the war in his mind and that his whole thoughts
were bent on undertaking new enterprises; for his character was
of that stamp in which exertions amongst dangers and difficulties is preferred to idleness.'

By the close of 1799 practically all Bonaparte's gains of 1796–7
had been wiped out, but Masséna had swept the allied army
under Korsakov from the field of Zürich on 25 September, and
Suvorov had been forced back across the central Alpine spine
to the upper Rhine. So although the French had been driven
from Italy except for the Riviera coast, the allies had failed to
seize the opportunities which had been offered to them, and
Russia withdrew from the coalition in disgust. And on 9
November 1799 Napoleon Bonaparte became First Consul of
France.

For Moore 1800 brought false hopes and familiar frustration.

Before the New Year opened Moore had managed to escape the shackles of London society to go to Chelmsford, to train the troops assembled there. In February 1800 came an opportunity which sounded excellent: Sir Charles Stuart had been given permission to lead a force of 20,000 men in the Mediterranean, where they were to assist the Austrians in driving the last French from Italy; Stuart invited Moore to accept a command in this expedition, and Moore very gladly agreed. But the plans fell through. Sir Charles Stuart shortly afterwards resigned and Sir Ralph Abercrombie became commander-in-chief in the Mediterranean and Portugal instead, with Moore as one of his major-generals.

The army sailed from Portsmouth on 13 May, arriving at Minorca on 22 June in a belated attempt to help the Austrians. The French at Genoa had capitulated on 4 June, but the Austrians had nonetheless been obliged to allow terms favourable to the enemy because Bonaparte was sweeping over the Alps with a new army. Sir Ralph hurriedly despatched troops to reinforce the threatened Austrians, but calm seas and contrary winds prevented the arrival of the fleet at Genoa until 30 June, and by this time Bonaparte had inflicted terrible defeat on the Austrians at Marengo. The British force retired to Leghorn. Moore was thankful that they had escaped destruction alongside their allies: 'From the turn affairs have taken I cannot but consider it was a fortunate event that we were detained.'

Sir Ralph Abercrombie's army joined with the Mediterranean fleet, commanded by Admiral Lord Keith, and the question arose over what to do next. The Queen of Naples urged Abercrombie to help defend her kingdom, claiming that Lord Keith had already promised assistance. Abercrombie was unwilling to embark on such an unproductive expedition, and said he intended to send Moore with the troops back to Minorca and await instructions from London. Before leaving Moore had a chance to visit Leghorn, where he met the British ambassador and his wife, who had with them an illustrious companion, subject of a disgusted entry in Moore's journal of 15 July. 'Sir Wm. and Lady Hamilton were then attending the Queen of Naples. Lord Nelson was there attending upon Lady Hamilton. He is covered with stars, ribbons, and medals, more like the Prince of an Opera than the Conqueror of the Nile. It is really melancholy to see a brave and good man, who has deserved well of his country, cutting so pitiful a figure.'

The long-awaited instructions arrived in late August, and the army sailed for a secret destination, which soon turned out to be Gibraltar. The fleet arrived there on the 14th and Sir Ralph then received orders to land and destroy the arsenal at Cadiz, if he could be certain of bringing off the army again. Lord Keith assured him this could be accomplished, and the fleet sailed on 2 October to reach Cadiz forty-eight hours later. There Sir Ralph learned to his dismay that naval officers well acquainted with the coast doubted the possibility of a successful landing. A period of bickering and ill-feeling between the army and naval commanders now began with half-hearted attempts to land and confused orders resulting in complete fiasco. On top of this came a distressing letter from the governor of Cadiz to Lord Keith, pleading with him to desist from attacking a town which had already been stricken by plague. It was not until 24 October that fresh orders from England resolved the confusion: Sir Ralph Abercrombie was to sail on a fresh expedition, this time to the far end of the Mediterranean. Moore, heartily sick of the whole deplorable Cadiz affair, wrote: 'It appears by the letters from England that the [Austrian] Emperor and the French have made peace, but no hopes are entertained of England being included, and it is thought to be of importance to force the French from Egypt ...'

The Austrians sued for peace on 25 December, but Britain continued to wage war. Egypt was known to be Bonaparte's most prized conquest, even though the French occupation forces had been much reduced. Abercrombie's expedition might enjoy numerical superiority, especially if it received co-operation from the Turkish army at Jaffa with a tiny British detachment led by General George Koehler who, as a major, Moore had known well in his Corsican days. There were long discussions between Sir Ralph and Moore during the winter resulting in a plan of action: the British army would land at or near Damietta and march on Cairo; its supplies would be transported up the Nile. Moore received special instructions, dated 3 January 1801: 'Major-General Moore is to proceed to the Turkish Army near Jaffa, where he will endeavour to make himself master of the real state and condition of the Ottoman

Army. He will ascertain, as far as he has an opportunity, the means that army has of acting in the ensuing operations, and what resources the British Army may receive from their co-operation.'

Moore landed at Jaffa six days later, only to find that Koehler, on whom he had relied for detailed information, had died of putrid fever on 29 December. Sadly he proceeded to the Turkish Vizier's plague-ridden camp, where he was entertained with pipes, coffee and sherbet, sitting cross-legged on a sofa. He outlined Sir Ralph's plan: Damietta had been chosen as the British objective because it lay closer to the Turks and would enable the latter to co-operate. The Vizier, whose forces had been driven from Egypt by Napoleon in July 1799, seemed well satisfied. Moore then inspected the Turkish army and was appalled. 'From a view of his troops, and from everything I could learn or observe of their composition and discipline, I could not think they were otherwise than a wild ungovernable mob...while their chief, the Vizier, was a weak-minded old man, without talent, or any military knowledge.' He added: 'It was in vain to expect any co-operation.'

His visit was depressing not least because plague was still prevalent in the Turkish camp. 'The army has lost 6,000 persons by plague within these seven months.' Scores died during Moore's five-day visit; nine of the Vizier's staff were buried in one day. 'The Turks are so extremely careless that the clothes of the persons who die of the plague are sold publicly at auction.' Custom dictated that important guests should receive the present of a pelisse, which the Vizier threw about the recipient's shoulders; not surprisingly, Moore took precautions: 'It is not proper to refuse this present, but I requested it might be sent to me, not wishing to run the risk of catching the plague by wearing it before it was fumigated.'

He hastened to Abercrombie, now at Marmaris Bay, Asia Minor, to give his report. The commander-in-chief said he had expected a depressing assessment of the state of the Turkish army, and ruled out all hopes of co-operation. He also changed his plans. Instead of attacking Damietta, he decided to land in the vicinity of Alexandria: occupation of this harbour would sever enemy communications between Egypt and France. The actual landing would be made at Aboukir, about eighteen miles from Alexandria itself, and the scene of Bonaparte's last great triumph over the Turks and Egyptians.

Moore and his superior fully realized the difficulties: all supplies, even water, would have to be landed at Aboukir and carried up to the army as it advanced to besiege Alexandria; the British might well have to face 10,000 French troops, and the enemy would probably employ harassing tactics, making use of their cavalry superiority, rather than become involved in a pitched battle which might favour the British. Moore wrote in his journal on 24 January: 'I cannot but think the enterprise in which we are about to engage extremely hazardous and doubtful in its event. We cannot, however, hesitate; we must attempt it.'

The expedition had to wait for artillery and cavalry and shipping to transport them, giving the French further time to prepare. On 11 February Moore wrote more gloomy words: 'Fresh orders from France, the promise of further reinforcements, together with the account of the success against the Austrians, the truce and peace which must follow with that power, the war which is likely to take place between us and Russia; these circumstances, of which they have now heard, will all tend to raise the spirits of the French in Egypt, and to make their resistance more obstinate.'

Contrary winds and bad weather delayed departure until early in the morning of 22 February; on 1 March the Egyptian coast appeared on the southern horizon. The fleet sailed so close to Alexandria that ships in the harbour could be distinguished and even the colour of their signals: Moore could not understand why Admiral Lord Keith was so adventurous. The fleet then continued along the coast to Aboukir, and by dawn on the 2nd Moore could see the ship which had gone ahead to mark the anchorage. Soon after daylight came the signal to cook three days' provisions and prepare to land, and by 9 a.m. the warships and transports were swinging on their anchor chains. But the weather continued boisterous; and the troops had to stay on board, watching the enemy prepare positions directly opposite the landing area, for five more days.

Moore made good use of the time, taking a cutter close to the beach to reconnoitre the positions with his usual eye for detail. The final plan was to land along a one-mile front extending south from a dominating sand-hill, behind which the enemy could be expected to concentrate. The area in general consisted of a confusion of lesser sand-dunes, offering good defensive positions for the French, and on the northern horn of the bay stood a castle, from which the enemy could enfilade the landing with artillery and mortar fire. The British first division amounted to 5,500 men. On the left were the Guards and another brigade, commanded by Generals George Ludlow and Eyre Coote. Moore with the reserves was on the right of the British line, landing directly beneath the dominating sand-hill and in the position most exposed to the castle's enfilade fire.

The wind dropped late on the 7th, and the weather promised well. Orders were given for the troops to climb into the flat-bottomed boats and launches at 2 a.m. on 8 March, and the second wave transferred from the large ships to shallow draught vessels. Soon after daylight the majority of the landing craft moved to the rendezvous close inshore, but it took another two hours for the line to be dressed. Sir Ralph Abercrombie appeared concerned over Moore's chances against the large sand-dune and asked whether he 'continued of the same mind, to land exactly opposite to the hill, or if it would not be better to incline more to the right, as the hill appeared to be very steep in front'. Moore answered: 'The steepness is not such as can prevent our ascending, and is therefore rather favourable.' When Sir Ralph received this reply he declared: 'This is really taking the bull by the horns.' He sent a further message: 'If the fire from the enemy was so great that the men could not bear it, he would make the signal to retire; and therefore desired that Moore and Cochrane should look occasionally to the ship in which Sir Ralph was.'

At 8 a.m. a blue rocket spluttered up into the deeper blue sky and hundreds of oars rose and dipped. The uneven line began to pull for the shore. The troops sat tight-packed in their boats, their white uniforms – which the surgeons preferred them to wear as evidence of cleanliness – already stained with tar, grease and sometimes vomit. The French, spectators of the final British preparations for the last two hours, awaited them, fully prepared.

Chapter Six

*

EGYPT AND HONOURS

Moore was in the barge of Captain Alexander Cochrane, naval commander of the landing, positioned a few yards to the front of the first line. Fifteen artillery pieces opened fire from the dunes, and others joined in from the castle on the British right flank, first with round-shot to sink the boats, then with grape-shot to tear holes in the crammed ranks. In the centre, two craft carrying men from the Coldstream Guards suffered direct hits, and disintegrated in a mess of splintered wood and broken bodies. Next came the crackling infantry fire from the beaches; more men in the boats were hit at every yard. The British soldiers cheered to relieve their tension, but the thin 'huzzas' sounded shrill amidst the tumult of the guns; the soldiers were helpless until the bluejackets could put them ashore. Sir Ralph Abercrombie stood on the deck of the flagship, and in his hand he clutched the flag which could have signalled retreat. But by now the boat had reached shallow water and the crunch of sand grated beneath Cochrane's boat. Sailors vaulted the gunwales to prop planks across to dry land, over which ran Moore and his staff – Brigadier-General Oakes, Colonel George Murray, Brigade-Major George Groves, Major Paul Anderson . . .

The first line touched the beaches, almost as straight as when the move to shore began. Out swarmed the men. Some fell in the shallows; others were bayoneted by Frenchmen rushing from the dunes; but the rest splashed through to the sand and formed a firing line; the advance began. Moore formed up the flank companies of the 40th, 23rd and 28th, ordered them to load but not yet to fire, and led them towards the forbidding sand-hills. The musket fire increased; the soldiers stumbled and slithered for footholds in the sloping sand; but on they marched with Moore at their head. 'The flower of the British Army was in action,' wrote one midshipman watching from the waiting fleet. 'I saw General John Moore in front, waving his men onward with his hat.' Up the slope they went; no one disobeyed the order not to fire, despite the fire they had to endure from the French. As they neared the summit, the line seemed thin, and the way behind was studded with bodies; some soldiers had to scramble the last few feet on hands and knees. They reached the summit, straightened, formed into line and charged. They swept all before them, bayoneting all who stood in their way; the French ran, and cheers broke from the sweat-sodden soldiers. Four cannon were captured, and Moore's men plunged on, halting only to fire volleys into the backs of the fleeing enemy. Then Moore formed his survivors on favourable ground and hurried back to the summit to observe the situation elsewhere along the beach.

On Moore's left General Hildebrand Oakes had found the enemy ready to receive his troops with infantry and cavalry charges, but as Moore reached his vantage point he could see these attacks being repulsed and Oakes' men moving forward. Further along the smoking line the Guards brigade and some of Coote's were also pushing inland. All along the beach the French were being driven from their defensive positions: the British bridgehead was won. For the moment the French would have to be allowed to go: lacking cavalry and artillery the British could attempt nothing more ambitious than consolidation. French sharp-shooters were still active, but by 11 a.m. firing had dwindled into a silence broken only by the groans of the wounded, shouted commands, and creaking rowlocks as stores and reinforcements were sent ashore.

The remainder of the expedition was disembarked during the afternoon and the British moved two miles inland. Moore summed up the success in his journal: about 600 British troops had been killed or wounded, two-thirds of whom had been in his reserve, but the French had lost considerably more. 'The enemy had had eight days to assemble and prepare; the ground was extremely favourable for defence. Our attempt was daring, and executed by the troops with the greatest intrepidity and coolness...' More stores were brought ashore next day, 9

'The boats continued to row in steadily,' Moore wrote, 'and the sailors and soldiers occasionally huzzaed.' The landing of the British troops, Aboukir Bay, March 1801.

110

Troops establish a camp in the Egyptian sand-dunes, before advancing inland for the violent clash with the French at Alexandria.

March, but soon the winds increased and hindered communications with the fleet. Clearly, the army would have to advance as soon as possible or else be stranded on the beach; Alexandria lay eleven miles away along a narrow sandy strip bounded on the north by the sea and on the south by lakes, Madie and Mareotis, the latter being dry.

Moore spent the 9th and 10th studying the position: he wanted 'to feel what was in my front'. In the distance he could see the mosques and minarets of Alexandria; immediately in front lay uneven terrain thickly covered with palm and date trees which would give the advantage to the defence. The French were also preparing themselves for the coming battle: on 10 March Moore and his reconnaissance party clashed with a similar force sent forward by the enemy, but after some sharp skirmishing the French broke contact.

By late afternoon on the 12th the two armies were in battle positions. Moore's brigade was reinforced by two additional regiments, the 90th and 92nd, and the General positioned these in front. 'I ordered each body to throw forward one-third of their numbers, with the officers belonging to it, as sentries in front. This formed a strong chain, which was relieved every hour by one of the thirds in reserve.' His journal entry continued: 'The enemy was so close to us that it was evident that neither army could move without bringing on an action.' At

6 a.m. on the 13th the preliminary manœuvring began. Sir Ralph had deployed his army in three columns: the left, under General Hely Hutchinson, would attempt to turn the enemy right, with the centre column under General John Cradock moving in unison. Moore's reserve would hold the right flank.

Billowing dust showed that this time the French intended to strike first, and from the sand-storms erupted enemy cavalry to fall upon the leading British troops, especially men of the 90th and 92nd whom Moore had posted to the front. Moore could see the lines of French horse wheel towards the British picquets and charge, while the Highlanders hurried into defensive squares. The two sides clashed amid dust and smoke – and then Moore saw the French galloping back again in confusion; the British outposts had held.

Now it was the turn of the British to advance. But with the enemy making full use of his cavalry and artillery superiority, ground could only be gained yard by yard. Sir Ralph Abercrombie had a horse shot under him and owed his life to a man from the 90th who dragged him to safety. The air was full of cannon and musket balls. Repeated waves of French cavalry broke against the British bayonets and volleys. Moore displayed all his skill at keeping his men under close control amidst the appalling confusion of battle. 'I kept the reserve in column, covering the right flank of the two lines. We advanced rapidly, exposed to a most heavy cannonade from the front, and of musketry from hussars and light infantry on the flank. The men, though mowed down by the cannon, never lost their order, and there was no period during the action or pursuit that I could not have halted the reserve and instantly wheeled to a flank without interval.'

The advance continued throughout the day, the French constantly turning to fire back whenever they reached suitable defensive positions, supported always by their artillery. Clouds of dust and surging smoke hung over the battlefield, and beyond them sparkled the minarets of Alexandria to tantalize the British troops. Moore could see that the plan to turn the enemy right was failing. Instead, the British right – his own column – was in front of the rest of the army; if he moved on alone into the plain before Alexandria his column would receive the full

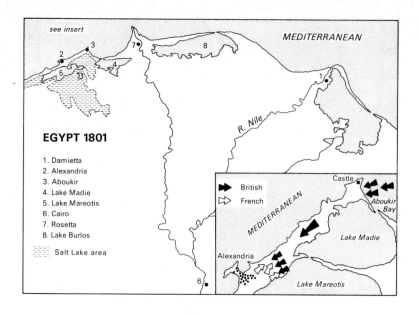

EGYPT 1801

1. Damietta
2. Alexandria
3. Aboukir
4. Lake Madie
5. Lake Mareotis
6. Cairo
7. Rosetta
8. Lake Burlos

Salt Lake area

British
French

force of the guns concentrated on the heights defending the city. He 'begged' Cradock, whose brigade lay next to his, to halt with him until the rest of the sprawling army came forward, but the advance continued when the remainder of the brigades came up, out into the waiting plain. Another halt came in the middle of this exposed terrain. Moore hurried over to Sir Ralph: the attack on the left had still to force the enemy's right and Sir Ralph decided to send extra regiments to Hutchinson. But this additional deployment took time, and although Hutchinson eventually advanced he soon slowed again, believing the ground before him was too strongly defended by artillery. He sought further orders; first General Hope and then Sir Ralph himself galloped over to see the ground; further frantic discussion took place – during which the enemy were given time to see the threat being mounted and took the opportunity to reinforce their positions.

During this wait the rest of the army, including Moore's battered reserve, had to endure the full weight of the enemy's cavalry and artillery assaults in the open plain. Each cannonade and cavalry charge littered the ground with more mutilated men; the troops drove off the enemy horsemen but stood helpless beneath the ruinous grape- and round-shot. Moore paced the sand, even more impatient than his men to be off and increasingly incensed by the delay. 'We were ... destroyed by his [the enemy's] artillery without the power of retaliation.' He watched the sun sink red through the dust in the west. And then came the most galling order of all. His men, who had punched their way forward with such sacrifice and so much courage, must now pull back over ground they had painfully won; hours lost in discussion meant that the day had grown too late and the enemy too strong for the attack on the left to be launched. The men who had fallen in the plain had been wasted.

And so the army retired to defensive positions, about five miles back from Alexandria, and the hours of darkness passed with the dreadful business of attending to the wounded. Surgeons worked throughout the night on makeshift tables; men lay in rows before them, waiting to have limbs amputated. Scores of wounded remained on the plain to the front, and had to be abandoned until the following day when parties came out from the opposing camps to bring them in and to heap the slaughtered onto bullock carts. British and French soldiers helped each other. The tacit truce received official confirmation after an exchange of messages between the two commanders: Sir Ralph wrote to General Friant 'expressing a wish not to aggravate the calamities of war by any acts which, without benefits to the general cause, tended only to distress individuals', and the French commander agreed.

But soon the advance would have to continue, and meanwhile the British line remained vulnerable to a determined French counter-attack. To the right the British positions extended to the sea, and on the left up to the Lake of Madie where the ground levelled into a plain without defensive features. Gunboats and supply vessels managed to sail up the lake to within half a mile of the British line, and the officers – though not the men – were allowed to bring ashore a change of clothing. Moore thankfully stripped off his tattered uniform. Water had been found by digging beneath the palm trees, but fuel for cooking remained in extremely short supply – the green palm branches merely smouldered. The heat intensified daily as the Egyptian summer wore on, and the flies buzzed in increasing hordes, but at night the men shivered in their holes in the sand, clutching blankets about them. Moore found time to dash off a note to his father. 'I am sitting on the ground and writing on my knee. I fag from morning to night, and am perfectly well. I have had the good luck to escape unhurt, but many of my friends have suffered. This is the black side to which we must endeavour not to look.'

But now the black side would loom predominant: for the third time within two weeks the British and French would clash in battle. Reports reached Sir Ralph that the French in Alexandria had been reinforced by 6,000 men under General Jacques Menou, and by 19 March an attack seemed imminent. Even before Menou's arrival, Moore had become pessimistic over British prospects. 'All we know', he wrote in his journal, 'is that the enemy fought us upon the 13th with six or seven thousand men; that the position they have taken opposite to us is extremely strong and studded with artillery; that if we carry it we have still the siege of Alexandria to carry on, defended not by a simple garrison but by an army, with another army on our flank and rear. The operation is beyond our force.'

On 20 March Moore had been appointed duty major-general of the day. After visiting the picquets he stayed on the left of the reserve until four in the morning of the 21st. The enemy had been quiet during the night; nothing had been observed but the occasional rocket. Moore mounted his horse and began to move down the line, ordering commanders to stand down their men at daylight if all still seemed peaceful. Sudden musket fire jarred from further to the left, but soon died down – during the previous evening Moore had noticed that the officer commanding the picquet in that area had seemed jumpy, and he believed the men had merely been firing at shadows. He turned his horse again and continued along the line. But then came more firing, insistent now, and from even further left – and this would be where men from the 28th Regiment were holding an important central redoubt. Moore reined round his horse, and as he dug in his heels exclaimed to his aide: 'This is the real attack!'

He galloped through the dark to the redoubt, to find it a

mêlée of struggling men. 'The day had not yet broken, and the darkness was made greater by the smoke of the guns and small arms.' Plans had previously been prepared whereby General Oakes would despatch the 42nd to assist the redoubt if the enemy assaulted; Moore prayed these men were on their way. He believed the entire position of the British army would be rendered untenable if the redoubt fell, and already the enemy were thrusting all about the positions, covered by the night. 'We could feel the effect of the enemy's fire, but it was impossible as yet to see what he was about.' Moore could hear the French drums beating the charge and excited voices encouraging one another to advance. Enemy musket fire increased in intensity; to the front and to one flank the black of the Egyptian night was slashed by malevolent yellow and red flashes. Bullets drummed into the wood of the redoubt and into the earthworks and thudded into bodies. Moore's horse suddenly gave a gigantic quiver and reared, throwing its head in the air with a high-pitched whinny as a stray shot found its face; Moore wrestled with the reins, but finding the animal unmanageable flung himself from the saddle. Colonel Paget, commander of the redoubt, who was standing next to Moore on the platform, fell shot in his neck; Moore knelt beside the Colonel as he moaned that he must be finished, and Moore believed him.

Then came fresh shouts from the dark, and added confusion. Moore ran to the edge of the redoubt, and through the murk could see men forming in the position where the 42nd should be. Paget had dragged himself to his feet and found a horse, and now clattered over to Moore, blood streaming down his chest. 'I assure you the French have turned us,' he shouted. Moore ran to the newly arrived 42nd, shouting as he reached them: they must face to the right about and strike at the enemy behind the position. 'I showed them the French completely in their power.' The troops charged, and terrible screams issued from the night as their bayonets punctured the exposed French line. 'Not a man of these French escaped being killed, wounded or taken.' The 42nd returned, and Moore immediately led them round the flank of the redoubt to scatter another column. But then a bullet seared into Moore's thigh; he collapsed, then hauled himself up again and hobbled over to Sir Ralph, just arrived at the fight.

The 42nd had continued to chase the enemy, and had gone too far: enemy cavalry were piercing in through the half-light and within moments were cutting through the disorganized defenders. Men ran together to form hasty defensive groups; back to back they stood, muskets raised; volley after volley spurted into the enemy cavalry, and the horsemen sheered off again. Two more cavalry charges broke upon the British. A sabre sliced across Sir Ralph's chest, ripping open his uniform yet only grazing his flesh, then a French dragoon seized the commander but fell immediately, shot by a soldier of the 42nd. Moore found himself surrounded; hacking and slicing with his sword, he managed to struggle to safety. The 42nd, their ranks shattered, continued to fight man for man; flank companies of the 40th were hurried up, and Moore ordered them to fire to their immediate front, even though these volleys might inflict casualties amongst British troops still in the line of fire. On came the French cavalry, straight into these terrible fusillades. 'The field was instantly covered with men and horses, horses galloping without riders – in short, the cavalry were destroyed. Every attack the French had made had been repulsed with slaughter.'

118

John Moore at the
Battle of
Alexandria: detail
of a painting by
James Northcote,
R.A.

More men from General John Stuart's brigade arrived to
drive back any further French attempts, and the shattering din
of battle subsided – except for the enemy artillery shells which
continued to crash around the redoubt. Moore's soldiers had
exhausted their ammunition, both cartridges and artillery shot,
and for sixty minutes remained helpless. 'Had their infantry

119

again advanced we must have repelled them with the bayonet.
Our fellows would have done it; I never saw men more determined to do their duty; but the French had suffered so severely
that they could not get their men to make another attempt.'
Ammunition for the British guns arrived at last and a counter-
barrage opened. Among the last French shots came one which
killed the horse Moore had borrowed after his own had been
wounded. Men at the redoubt had succeeded against an attack
launched by over 12,000 French veterans; in those four hellish
hours about 1,300 British troops had been killed and wounded,
and about 3,000 French. Harsh daylight revealed the carnage.
'I never saw a field so strewed with dead,' wrote Moore. At
least 500 horses lay heaped on the battle-ground.

By now Moore could barely walk. His wounded leg had
swelled; his stiffened uniform was stuck to his skin; pains shot
through his hip when he tried to move. General Oakes had also
been hit in the thigh, and both men were helped to their tents:
surgeons probed the holes and pronounced them clean – no
bones had been touched. A damaged bone might have meant
amputation and the end of Moore's career, or worse. While
being dressed, Moore heard that his friend and aide, Anderson,
had also been wounded: he had been taken by French hussars,

but captured and capturers had then come under fire and the enemy had made off, leaving Anderson with a badly gashed arm.

Also among the casualties was the commander-in-chief, Sir Ralph Abercrombie: he had been hit in the thigh, but had refused to leave the field until the battle had ended. At first, hopes were high for his recovery; Moore wrote in his journal on 24 March: 'Sir Ralph is, I hear, much better this day; the ball is not extracted, but he is tolerably free from fever.' But five days later he added: 'Sir Ralph was seldom free from fever, got no sleep but from opium, and had occasional delirium; for some days past the surgeons have had little hope of his recovery. I received a note this morning from his son, which informed me that he had expired last night at 11 o'clock without pain.' Moore believed that his friend could not have died at a better moment and in better circumstances. 'He has conducted the only part of the expedition which is likely to be brilliant.' He had beaten the French on three successive occasions – 'more than has been done by any General this war'.

But Moore believed these successes would be insufficient; the French still held Alexandria, and, as Moore had written before the last battle: 'The operation is beyond our force.' Sir Ralph would have been unable to go beyond the limited bridgehead carved by his gallant army, even though French prisoners claimed that the campaign in Italy under Bonaparte could not be compared with the ferocity of fighting they now had to endure. 'It is difficult to say as yet what the issue of all this will be,' wrote Moore to his father on 25 March. 'Government had undoubtedly been deceived with respect to the force and situation of the French in Egypt; the Delta is a most plentiful country, their army wants for nothing, and in the last action their numbers exceeded ours. Unless, therefore, Ministers, apprised of their error, send reinforcements or the Turks act with energy, what chance have we?'

Moore wrote these words from a cabin on HMS *Diadem*, anchored in Aboukir Bay, where he had been transferred to allow his wound to recover. He told his father: 'Having lost so many of my men, it was but decent to get a lick myself... My wound is in the left leg, in the outside of the bone, which is not touched. The wound is deepish, and has about three inches of passage. I shall be at my duty in a fortnight.' His assessment proved extremely optimistic; he had not left the *Diadem* five weeks later, and wrote in his journal on 1 May: 'My wound, which was at first thought slight, has proved extremely troublesome and painful; the ball, it seems, passed between the two bones of the leg, and though fortunately it hit neither, it did sufficient injury; my leg continued inflamed for a long time and matter collected between the wounds.' He now had every hope of being fully recovered within a month. 'My left [leg] and thigh are much wasted, and my body from long confinement is very weak; but I can now move with crutches.'

Hutchinson had meanwhile succeeded Sir Ralph Abercrombie as commander-in-chief, and his despatch to London on 7 April had praised both Moore and the men he commanded: 'It is impossible for me to do justice to the zeal of the officers, and to the gallantry of the soldiers of this army. The reserve, against whom the principal attack of the enemy was directed, conducted themselves with unexampled spirit.' But, Hutchinson continued: 'I regret however the temporary absence from the Army of this highly valuable and meritorious officer, whose command and co-operation would be so highly necessary to me at this moment.'

The three successes against the French led to better results than the pessimistic Moore had believed possible. Those prisoners to whom Moore had spoken were correct: they had never had to contend with such opposition before. The French in Alexandria were shaken and demoralized; they had thrown all they could at the British, and still the British stood firm. Moreover, the successes stimulated the Turks into action. Up to 5,000 Turkish troops were landed under Captain Pasha at Rosetta on the far side of Aboukir Bay, and the Grand Vizier sent forces across the desert; the French were further discouraged when regiments despatched from Cairo to meet this army suffered defeat.

Hutchinson now made Cairo his primary objective. On 29 June Moore rejoined the army, still limping but determined to be at the front. But the enemy refused to fight; on 10 July they evacuated Cairo and the marauding Turks swarmed in. French troops from the city fled to the sea and thence to France, and only Alexandria remained in enemy hands. By now all

Turkish troops
march across the
desert to threaten
the French flank in
Egypt: a decisive
moment in the
Egyptian
campaign.

Sir Henry Paget,
the brilliant cavalry
officer who served
with Moore in
Egypt, Sweden and
in the Peninsula.

123

manner of nationalities of troops had flocked to join the British –
Turks, Arabs, Syrians, Copts, Mamelukes – and further reinforcements had arrived from England. A French fleet from
Toulon failed to reach Egypt, and Menou, commander at Alexandria, knew he could expect no further help. On 30 August
he agreed to capitulate. With this anti-climax came the end
to French domination in Egypt, begun so gloriously by Napoleon Bonaparte three years before.

Fresh orders came from London on 15 September, to be
revealed by Hutchinson the following day: Moore had been
appointed commander at Alexandria, with about 6,000 men,
while the remainder were to leave for Malta, Gibraltar and
England. The prospect did not please Moore, and for reasons
which he had been obliged to use on previous occasions.
'It has never been my object to remain in garrison anywhere,'
he wrote. This time he had a special reason for wishing to decline: letters from home reported that his father was ill. Moreover, the Duke of York had very kindly written to him in June,
pressing him to return to England to allow him to recover from
his wound. Moore explained the situation to Hutchinson, and
the commander agreed to his departure. On 10 November 1801
his ship reached Portsmouth, just in time for him to get to London before his much loved father died.

On 27 March 1802 the Treaty of Amiens between France
and England brought general peace to Europe for the first time
in a decade.

*   *   *

For the moment Moore's eternal thirst for action had to remain
unquenched. His period of peace began with a touching
memento of war: in April 1802 he received a graceful sword,
together with a letter signed by Colonel the Hon. Henry
Paget, now recovered from the neck wound suffered in the
redoubt before Alexandria. The sword came as a gift from the
commanding officers of those corps 'who had originally the
good fortune to be placed under your command', and Paget
continued: 'It would be presumptuous, Sir, in me to attempt
to point out in you what are those rare talents which you possess,

the application of which has rendered you the object of so much veneration to the corps . . .' Paget and his colleagues had experienced one of Moore's most valuable attributes: his ability to train and lead his men in such a manner that he inspired worship.

Now, in peacetime, Moore could develop his training skills. After a short time at Brighton he moved to Chatham in October 1802, where he initially had to spend many hours on the unpleasant task of weeding out officers and men so as to reduce the army to non-active strength. Then he turned to happier employment. On 18 January 1803 an order issued by the War Office after representations by Moore declared that the 52nd would become light infantry; he would now make his contribution to the development of this important military arm.

Until Egypt the bulk of Moore's fighting career had been concerned with light infantry tactics: the skirmishing in the American forests; the hand-to-hand struggles in Corsica, with the irregular local troops playing a significant role; rebel-hunting in the bogs and misty peaks of Ireland. Moore's specialization in the use of light infantry troops was therefore to be expected; in addition to this he was always interested in training methods, and firmly believed that individual soldiers must be allowed to use their initiative as much as possible. Light infantrymen, operating separately from the rigid regular lines, had already become accepted. In 1800 the Experimental Rifle Corps had been created with detachments from fourteen regiments, and this had been brought into line in 1802 with Coote Manningham as colonel and William Stewart as lieutenant-colonel. This corps was to develop the practice, instituted as far back as the American revolution, of having a 'light' company in each foot regiment, usually detached from its regiment or battalion for covering the advance or for some other special mission. Instead of the smooth-bore musket known as 'Brown Bess', the green-jacketed riflemen were armed with the Baker – which was harder to load and needed frequent cleaning, but was easier to carry and above all had rifled barrels, which gave reasonable accuracy up to about 300 yards. The Baker opened new vistas for skirmishing and light infantry tactics.

In autumn 1802 Lieutenant-Colonel Stewart received orders from Moore, now at Chatham. The Rifle Corps would move to Shorncliffe, in Moore's command area, and the General hoped 'that you will find the station...adapted both to your target practice and field movements'. Thus Shorncliffe became the training camp for the light infantry Rifle Corps.

Moore then turned to the selection of personnel for this highly important new branch. First-class officers would be required, who could display a high degree of individual judgement, and the same applied to the rank and file; unlike normal line regiments, the ordinary soldier would have to be capable of acting independently. Thus Moore wrote: 'The service of light infantry does not so much require men of stature as it requires them to be intelligent, handy, and active, and they should in the first instance be young, or they will neither take to the service nor be easily instructed in it.' The words 'take to the service' reveal an attitude of mind which lay at the base of Moore's policy towards the troops under his command, and especially with regard to discipline. Men must obey orders and fight not through fear of the lash, but through more positive motives: both officers and rank and file must be wedded to their profession – like Moore himself.

This attitude received clear expression in a letter written by Moore to his friend Robert Brownrigg, military secretary at the Horse Guards, on 11 June 1804, declaring his opposition to suggestions that men should be enlisted for short service. At first glance it would seem that Moore would have supported such a liberal move to reduce the existing lifelong period spent by the troops in the army. But Moore saw further. Short service would merely increase dissatisfaction and unhappiness: men, knowing they would be leaving soon, would grumble at the length of time left to serve, and would be unwilling to risk their lives, even if by not doing so they endangered their comrades. Soldiers, like Moore, should want to stay in the army for good. A change to short service 'suggests much evil but no good is likely to arrive from it. The soldier is contented, I have heard no complaint originating with him against the terms of enlistment – I dread a change which might affect troops, who as they are, combine qualities very uncommon, and which make them perhaps the best soldiers in Europe...no troops are so obedient or so attached to their officers.' He continued: 'The discipline of the mind is as requisite as that of the body to make a good

126

soldier. The English are less prepared for this in their civil state than other nations and are more likely to acquire it when they enter the service for life than for a limited period. The impression on the mind at his entrance into the service that his profession is decided for life, tends as much to the happiness of the individual as it does to make him a good soldier. He considers the officers and soldiers of his regiment as the persons with whom he is to pass his life, he endeavours to gain their friendship, and good will, and to distinguish himself by the qualities which are likely to gain their approbation.' A soldier's regiment should be his family.

Moore tried to instill this attitude into his officers and men, and he succeeded. At Shorncliffe every man was urged to think and act for himself; the drills and exercises were explained, so that all might see the reasons for them rather than carrying them out without thinking; the men were treated as human beings, not mere cannon fodder, and were encouraged to develop self-respect. Floggings were never carried out at Shorncliffe: the men were encouraged by example and not subdued through barbaric discipline. The last thing Moore desired was a cowed soldier. Men should be clean-living and healthy: swimming and physical exercises should replace drinking and whoring. And yet Moore's policy at Shorncliffe merely formed part of his lifelong method.

Indeed his accomplishments with the Rifle Corps can be overrated. In a sense he merely carried out training orders which his commander-in-chief, the Duke of York – for some years a firm believer in light infantry – had issued; and the actual mechanics of training were based on a manual written by General Sir David Dundas, though Moore added to this with his own observations written while wintering in Ireland. Moore, despite his enthusiasm for light infantry, remained convinced of the predominant role still to be played by the rigid regular lines.

But Moore's real contribution was more important than any drill manual or support for one type of infantry as against another: it was his appreciation that the troops under him had feelings similar to his own – that they felt fear, had hopes, were capable of loyalty and love, and would follow him to the death if need be, because they trusted him and each other, and because they knew he would be just as willing to die for them. Moore, throughout his career, set a superb example.

*   *   *

Even by spring 1803, a bare six months since arriving at Chatham, Moore had other preoccupations besides the Rifle Corps. Rumbles of war against France had again become insistent. On 8 March the King sent a message to Parliament, announcing that it had become necessary to prepare for conflict. On 15 May a private letter from Brownrigg reached Moore's HQ at Chatham, warning the General of the need for immediate steps for the defence of the kingdom; within twenty-four hours Britain had ordered the naval blockade of the Continent. Napoleon began preparations for the invasion of England, and tension rose in the southern counties. By 2 June Moore had moved to Sandgate, where he was to command a brigade in the most likely target area for a French invasion attempted from Boulogne; Sir David Dundas had been given command of the whole southern district.

Moore's energy had to be directed to improving fortifications and communications, organizing the regular forces, and above all attempting to recruit local volunteers. He disagreed with existing plans to retreat before an invading force, in the hope that the enemy could be drawn onto disadvantageous ground, and told Dundas on 1 July that such a system would lead to 'confusion and despondency'. Instead, 'the language and the system should be to head, and to oppose, and not a foot of ground ceded that was not marked with the blood of the enemy'. Eventually the Defence Act ordered lords-lieutenant to furnish lists of all able-bodied men between the ages of fifteen and sixty in their counties who were willing to serve as volunteers, and Bonaparte's boast that he was going to dictate peace terms from conquered London no doubt helped swell the ranks of those coming forward for home defence. A grand total of 340,000 enrolled, though the importance of the force was diminished by the fact that only a third could be supplied with muskets.

But winter weather destroyed any hopes Bonaparte may have entertained for an invasion in 1803. Preparations to repel an

offensive continued during the spring and summer of 1804, but with dwindling expectations that the forces would have to be used. On 15 August gunfire from Boulogne could be heard at Shorncliffe, but the martial noise only signified official celebrations of Bonaparte's birthday, the day of St Napoleon. Eight days later the guns at Shorncliffe replied, to celebrate the arrival of the Duke of York, come to review General John Moore's troops. The visit passed well. 'We came off with flying colours,' wrote Moore to his mother. But he added: 'Notwithstanding all the honour, and all the flattering compliments, still the four days' attendance completely wore me out. I rejoiced most heartily when they were over.' On 30 September he wrote

Fears of French invasion, 1803; propaganda cartoon warning against seeking peace with the enemy.

129

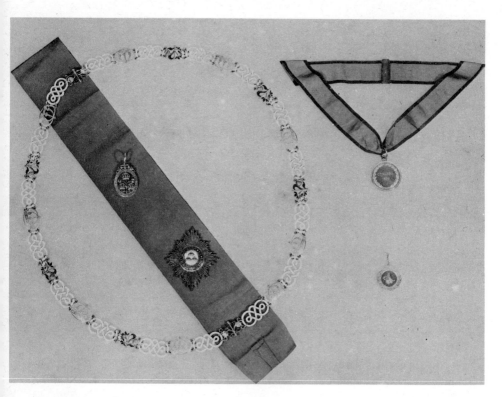

Sir John Moore's insignia of the Order of the Bath: the large Star (*opposite*) is a replica in diamonds presented to him in 1805 by the officers of the 52nd Light Infantry.

again to his mother: more flattering compliments and even greater honour had been bestowed. 'Sir John, and a ribbon, seem not in character with me – but so it is.' His investiture as Knight of the Bath took place at Windsor on 12 November. Sir John stripped off his fine new mantle of strawberry satin as soon as he decently could and returned to Shorncliffe, where he gave an unusually curt reply to an aide-de-camp who delighted in showering him with an abundance of 'Sir Johns'. 'Sir!' snapped Moore. 'I am your General. I am General Moore.'

By now his anti-invasion routine had become extremely dull, and increasingly Moore longed to be away. But he had found one consolation: the fair and fascinating Lady Hester Stanhope, niece to William Pitt for whom she acted as hostess. Pitt, who had resigned in 1801, resided for much of the time at nearby Walmer Castle, and there Moore and Lady Hester became acquainted. The friendship ripened after Pitt's return

to office in 1804 and would continue after her uncle's death in January 1806. Many men and more women disliked this vivacious, dark-eyed woman – unconventional, talkative, opinionated, and apparently uncaring of what others thought of her. All these characteristics found favour with Moore: quiet and reserved himself, he delighted in the company of this 23-year-old. Visits between Sir John and Lady Hester would become increasingly frequent, and, as far as Lady Hester was concerned, the meetings could not come too often. Her face,

131

Major-General of
the Infantry,
Knight
Commander of the
Bath.

which just failed to be beautiful, became radiant in his presence; her sensual nature became highly attracted to this extremely good-looking officer. In later years Lady Hester would
allow the rumour to circulate that she had been engaged to
Moore; certainly she desired more than mere friendship. At one
time she enthused to her brother, a young member of Moore's
staff, about Sir John's magnificent physique: he was a perfect
example of a man, she declared. 'But Hester,' replied Charles,
'you should see him in his bath. He's like a god!'

Within a month of his knighthood in November 1804, Moore
left his camp again for London, this time for a far more serious
purpose. Ministers had received secret intelligence at the end
of September: Spain seemed about to give way to Bonaparte's

Lady Hester Stanhope, Moore's close friend and
confidante, later incorrectly reported to have been engaged
to the General.

demands that she should declare war on Great Britain, and
Madrid apparently only awaited the arrival at Cadiz of a
treasure fleet from South America. Captain Graham Moore
had been given the task of intercepting these Spanish bullion
vessels and conducting them to Portsmouth – using force if
necessary. John Moore's brother had accomplished his mission
with startling success. His four frigates sighted four Spanish
ships off Cadiz, and he swooped upon them. The Spanish
admiral refused to come peaceably, and a vigorous sea-fight
followed: one Spanish frigate was blown from the water, and
the three others surrendered, and were conveyed to Spithead
carrying three and a half million dollars. John Moore had
written to his mother on 19 October: 'I think I see the spectacles

133

Graham Moore, rapidly rising to fame in the Royal Navy, who sailed with Sir John on the hazardous mission to Ferrol, Spain, in December 1804.

jumping off your nose, in reading the account of Graham's success. We shall hear no more of his being relaxed.' And the two Moore brothers were now to embark on an extremely hazardous venture – to Spain.

Late in November Sir John received a request for a meeting from Lady Hester's uncle, William Pitt, and he set off immediately for London. He arrived at his lodgings in a snow-storm, and was handed a sealed packet containing papers relating to the disastrous expedition to Ferrol undertaken by Sir James Pulteney in September 1800: troops had had to be re-embarked after the commander had found the place unassailable. Now

Ferrol was again the proposed target. Moore hastened to Downing Street, to meet Pitt, Lord Melville, the First Lord of the Admiralty, and Lord Camden, the Secretary for War.

Ministers had been strongly impressed by the argument, chiefly put forward by Rear-Admiral Sir Edward Pellew, now Commander-in-Chief East Indies, that Ferrol might be taken by a coup de main: up to 20,000 troops might be spared for such an expedition. Moore's opinion was requested. Moore was not enthusiastic: he needed to know much more about the defences. But, said Melville, the arguments in favour had been supported by Admiral Cochrane, who was commanding the squadron off Ferrol. Moore could see only one way to settle the question, and he asked if he might travel privately to Cochrane's squadron and undertake a reconnaissance. Ministers readily agreed; the First Lord added that Sir John might like to sail in his brother's frigate, the *Indefatigable*, which had been undergoing a refit at Plymouth and would now be ready to return to the Spanish station.

By Friday evening, 30 November, Sir John Moore had reached Plymouth docks, dressed in a civilian suit and travelling under the name of 'Mr Williams'. And on Monday 18 December a strange party strolled inland from the Spanish coastline, seven miles from Ferrol. Moore still wore his civilian dress; his brother and Admiral Cochrane wore blue jackets; servants carried fowling pieces and two dogs trotted at their heels. The unlikely hunting party had been landed by ship's boat in a deserted cove. They walked briskly up a nearby hill to gain a view of Ferrol's fortifications. Fowling-pieces were forsaken as they scribbled notes and sketches and scanned the Spanish defences through spy-glasses pulled from beneath their sporting gear. Admiral Cochrane's suspicions, already mentioned to Moore, were soon confirmed: the Spaniards had taken alarm at Britain's belligerent attitude, and reinforcements had been rushed into Ferrol; defences were being strengthened.

After only thirty minutes on the hillside, Sir John swung his glasses down towards the spot where they had left their boat: coming towards the landing place was another rowing boat, filled with Spanish soldiers. A man was told to hurry down to the sailors, to warn them and tell them to move to a sandy bay

Ferrol harbour,
Spain, where Sir
John barely
managed to escape
capture as a spy.
'We escaped
narrowly from a
most disagreeable
scrape,' commented
the General.

three miles behind the hill on which they now stood. Capture could be deadly: without uniform, the officers would be arrested as spies and probably shot. Then they ran down the hill and through the scrub to the bay, where they arrived panting – to find an empty beach. They stood impatiently on the sand and tried in vain to bribe some fishermen to take them off. Finally round the headland came the British sailors; the officers splashed out to join them, and the bluejackets bent their backs to row them away. Sir John learned that the boat had been intercepted by the Spanish sailors, but the British had managed to pull away and win the race round the coast.

The brief and almost disastrous visit had confirmed Moore's fears: an expedition against Ferrol would be suicidal with the Spaniards so wary and the garrison reinforced. And, as if to underline the dangers of attempting to disembark an army on this treacherous coast, a violent gale blew up, causing Sir John's warship to drag its anchor towards nearby rocks. Sailors slashed the cable to free the ship and fortunately she hove her head round towards the open sea. Safely back in London, Sir John emphatically declared that the idea of an expedition to Ferrol must be put aside. His report and Cochrane's despatches convinced Pitt, and Moore returned to Shorncliffe.

Preparations to combat invasion continued. Bonaparte had been crowned Napoleon, Emperor of the French, on 2 December. Early in the New Year, 1805, he sent peace proposals to George III, but Pitt intensified efforts to secure Russian and Austrian agreement for a full-scale military alliance, and emerged triumphant from diplomatic discussions. The allies would first destroy Masséna in Italy, then move westwards with overwhelming force on the northern side of the Alps towards the Rhine and France.

But Napoleon had perfected his military machine, and struck first. On 31 August the Grand Army, totalling over 200,000 men, began to move east from the Boulogne area, and on 26 September swept across the Rhine, reaching the Danube on 6 October. Eleven days later General Mack von Leiberich surrendered the 30,000-strong Austrian army at Ulm; on 2 December the Austro-Russian army collapsed at Austerlitz, and forty-eight hours later Emperor Francis of Austria agreed to unconditional surrender. The shattered Russian forces struggled back to their homeland. Napoleon had changed the political face of Europe, and British land forces had remained impotent. Only at sea had Britain made a contribution: late in October news reached Moore that the young naval officer whom he had met, and disagreed with, in Corsica, and whose behaviour he had so disapproved in Leghorn, had been slain at his moment of supreme glory. On 21 October Nelson's fleet had taken just five hours to destroy France's naval power at Trafalgar, and had established Britain as mistress of the seas.

Sir John Moore had continued to rot at Shorncliffe while these monumental events took place. Ironically, at the time when Nelson achieved his glorious victory another naval officer criticized Moore on the same grounds as Nelson had done in Corsica so many years before: over-caution. Admiral Sir Sidney Smith had escorted Moore on a reconnaissance voyage off Boulogne, to examine prospects of a combined operation against the French coastal positions. Moore believed that even if troops could be landed, they would have great difficulty in destroying the enemy lines and the flotilla in the harbour, and re-embarkation might be impossible. Smith declared in his report: 'General Moore, I am persuaded, would do his utmost to realise any plan laid down for him, with latitude and discretion in the execution; but he is too wary to undertake such a task voluntarily...' Smith's barbed comments were addressed to Lord Robert Castlereagh, handsome, formal and efficient Tory successor to Lord Camden as Secretary for War and the Colonies. And Castlereagh would perhaps remember Smith's judgement three years hence, when an energetic commander was required to lead the British bid in the Peninsula.

Meanwhile, Moore remained jaded. His promotion to lieutenant-general on 30 October failed to raise his spirits; so did his acquisition of the whole of the southern command in January 1806. Pitt, who had regarded Moore as 'a perfect officer', died in the same month; Lady Hester, who had nursed him through his last suffering, would soon set up house on her own, with Sir John a constant visitor. But the General still sought his escape. In March he begged the Duke of York to be allowed to serve in India, writing to his mother on the 27th: 'You know how tired I have for some time been of my employment here. I see little prospect in England of ever being occupied in any manner more important. I never believed much in invasion, and now less than ever.' His request had been refused – 'they do not wish me to go so far from this country'. Moore declined to appreciate the flattery. Instead he accepted the appointment of second-in-command in the Mediterranean, with his headquarters in Sicily and serving under the Foreign Secretary's brother, General Henry Fox. On 5 August he stepped ashore at Messina with Anderson; he would leave the island almost exactly a year later with some of the unhappiest memories of his career.

*

Chapter Seven

SICILY AND SWEDEN

Moore, always at his best in purely military situations, now found himself surrounded by political intrigues, diplomatic deviousness and personal rivalries. General Fox, who was also to be British minister in the Mediterranean, had arrived a mere fortnight earlier, and was to supersede General Sir John Stuart. The latter had succumbed to the same pressure from the Queen of Naples as that which Abercrombie had resisted when Moore last served in the area: from her court at Palermo in Sicily, she urged the British to send forces across the Straits of Messina to drive the French from Calabria and even from Naples itself. Stuart had managed to beat the French at Maida on 4 July, though more credit should have gone to his corps commanders. Full of his victory, he had now learned that General Fox was to take over his command, and he immediately suspected favouritism on the part of the Foreign Secretary in London. Further, Stuart had always believed that he, with his Corsican detachments, had performed greater feats than Moore at Alexandria. Instead of returning home, Stuart had remained in the area as commander in Calabria, and would clearly be under the influence of the Queen of Naples. The naval commander in the area was Admiral Sir Sidney Smith – with whom Moore had already clashed over the question of operations against Boulogne. The situation would indeed be complicated. Moore could only find one source of pleasure: the welcome he received from Mrs Fox, the delightful wife of his superior, and especially from Caroline, their dark-haired younger daughter: Moore came to look upon their home as his own.

Moore embarked upon a tour of inspection during August,

The Fox daughters: Louisa Emelia, later Lady Bunbury; and Caroline Amelia, whom Moore is believed to have loved, and who later married Lieutenant-General Sir William Napier.

during which he informed Sir Sidney Smith of Fox's intentions: the General refused to tie up forces in Calabria, where the people were divided and persons of property favoured the French; the Queen of Naples had been given a fair opportunity to guard the country; Sicily must remain the first priority. But Moore returned to Messina on 28 August to find his chief had weakened under pressure from Stuart, and had agreed to the

140

latter's plan for small troop demonstrations along the Calabrian coast to encourage the locals. Moore argued that from his own inspection of the coast the inhabitants would be incapable of taking advantage of any help. 'We should either march our whole force into Calabria, if its defence is a British object, or leave them to themselves.' He managed to strengthen Fox's resolve, and the latter left for Palermo to confront the Queen; on 4 September, Stuart returned to England. Fox arrived back in Messina on the 18th, disgusted with the Queen of Naples and her court, where he claimed he had witnessed more childishness, wickedness and stupidity than anything he could have imagined.

Sir Sidney Smith thought otherwise, and hurried to the court to lap up the delights the Queen offered. By the end of the month fresh nonsense had been concocted. Fox informed Moore that the Marquis of Circello, first minister at the Palermo court, had presented a plan for an attack by Neapolitan troops on Naples, supported by an offensive launched with British troops in Calabria. 'Nothing can be more absurd than the whole plan,' wrote Moore, 'or more false and erroneous than the data upon which it is founded. It is intersected with much impertinence, and even tho' from other circumstances it was not known, yet the language and general character of it would sufficiently discover it to be the joint production of Sir Sidney Smith and the Queen.' He persuaded Fox to turn down the scheme, although the language used by his superior in doing so did not seem to Moore sufficiently strong.

Further bad news came at the end of October, this time from England. Charles James Fox had died. Apart from his personal sadness General Fox – and Moore – feared the consequences: another Foreign Secretary would take office, and might take away General Fox's dual function of both commanding officer and minister. Gloomy predictions proved correct: in December the Queen of Naples received the new envoy, William Drummond, appointed by the latest Foreign Secretary, Lord Howick. Drummond wrote to Fox from Palermo, explaining that the Queen had already pressed him to support the idea of a military enterprise – could he have the military opinion? Moore, after discussions with Fox, set sail for his first meeting with the notorious queen, sister of the late-lamented Marie-Antoinette,

141

Maria Carolina,
Queen of Naples.
'She is a violent,
wicked person,'
wrote Moore – and
then crossed out
the last word to
substitute 'bitch'.

and he reached Palermo on 28 December 1806. He discovered Drummond to be diplomatic and apparently sensible,
but found the Queen to have all those taints of evil which he
had long suspected. 'She is a violent wicked person,' wrote the
normally charitable Moore in his journal, and then crossed out
the last word and substituted 'bitch'. Yet his audience with the
Queen during the first week of January 1807 had been out-
wardly civilized; conversation had been polite; Moore had

142

been impressed by the 55-year-old Queen Maria Carolina's good looks, although she used too much powder and rouge. But this was the woman who seemed determined to have British troops sent on an unprofitable mission to Italy, and who was prepared to lie about likely French opposition and the strength of local support in order to do so, and for this Moore could not forgive her. He noted that her lover, a Frenchman, had much influence. 'She . . . likes neither me nor the troops, and has already abused both very grossly. The King is a good-natured selfish man. If he had £3,000 a year, and a pack of hounds, he would be in his place; but as a King, and circumstanced as he is, to see him occupied with his amusements only is a little disgusting.' The whole atmosphere at Palermo stank in Moore's nostrils, and he fled back to Messina – and to Miss Caroline Fox. The 47-year-old battle-scarred general by now suffered the exquisite agony of being in love with a sparkling, 17-year-old beauty.

But Sicilian affairs kept him occupied, and these slid from bad to deplorable. General Fox – kindly, generous, and apparently unable to make his own decisions – relied increasingly upon his second-in-command. Word came from London that in view of increasing hostility shown by the Turks to Britain's temporary ally, Russia, Admiral Sir John Duckworth would lead a small expedition to the Dardanelles. In the event of war with Turkey, 5,000 troops would be detached from Sicily to occupy Alexandria. British strength on the island would therefore be drastically reduced. At the same time came news from Drummond at Palermo that Queen Maria Carolina seemed ready to betray the British to Bonaparte. Moore thought Admiral Sir Sidney Smith was closely involved: whether he had been privy to the Queen's plots or acted as a dupe, he would take advantage of any opportunity to assume a leading role in the Mediterranean. After urgent talks with Fox, Moore embarked across the gale-swept Mediterranean at the end of January to explain the situation to Admiral Sir John Duckworth at Malta.

From there he also wrote a letter to Brownrigg, the Duke of York's secretary and Moore's old friend. He declared it would be the height of folly to send Duckworth with a squadron but no troops to the Dardanelles, and to despatch troops but

no squadron to Egypt, leaving Sicily weakened. Moore's letter
to Brownrigg also admitted that General Fox had shown himself incapable of exerting the required authority; two months
ago Fox had received permission to retire, and Moore asked
Brownrigg to be informed whether the General was likely to
return home soon. If not Moore would like to be recalled. 'I
have great respect for General Fox, and considerable
attachment to him. He behaves to me in the kindest and most
confidential manner, and never decides on any measure without consulting me.' The words were all too true, but such a
commander could never accomplish the tasks which Moore
deemed necessary: Britain should take over the Sicilian government and should throw out the court of the Queen of Naples.

By March no reply had come from London, and the position
in Sicily had worsened still further. Drummond had proved
weak and had been 'humbugged' by Queen Maria Carolina.
'Mr. Drummond seems completely in the hands of the Sicilian
Court,' wrote Moore in his journal, 'at the same time that he
is flattering himself that he is directing them.' News arrived that
Duckworth intended to force his way to Constantinople – and
the troops for Alexandria were instantly embarked. Both
adventures were disastrous. General Mackenzie Fraser lost considerable numbers of men against the Turks in Egypt and had
to be reinforced by a further 1,600 troops from Sicily; Duckworth ran the gauntlet of the Dardanelles and returned with
nothing to show for his damaged ships. And in June instructions
arrived from Lord Castlereagh, now Secretary for War:
General Fox should employ troops as soon as possible for active
operations against Naples, or some other point on that coast.
The order clearly stemmed from reports sent by Drummond.

More despatches arrived from London, and on 9 July the
army commander showed the latest one to his subordinate:
General Fox had been recalled and should relinquish his post
to Moore. Sir John had never been more reluctant to accept
an appointment, but he immediately took action – even before
Fox had departed. He rushed over to Palermo to accost Drummond, and had a violent row with the British minister. Then
he obtained another audience with the Queen. The meeting,
potentially explosive, turned out otherwise. Moore found he
had to change his opinion of this remarkable woman, and wrote

Catania, Sicily,
visited by Moore in
March 1807.

in his journal: 'She is not herself a wicked or a bad woman,
rather the reverse, but she is guided very much by those about
her, and unfortunately she shows little discretion in the choices
she makes ... In private life she would have been a clever entertaining woman, violent in her passions, but upon the whole kind
and good.' Perhaps Moore himself had begun to fall under
Charlotte's spell; if so, the sooner he departed the better.

Moore's unhappy period on Sicily was fast drawing to a close.
General Fox had left on 3 August, with Moore's feelings for
his charming Caroline still unrevealed. Sir John had decided
that Caroline must be considered too young: if he had been
younger, and if he had not been constantly liable to be thrown
into a battle from which he might not return, the situation
would have been entirely different. As it was, any expression
of feeling must be out of the question – even though he had every
reason to believe his feelings might be returned. Moore, after
weeks of silence, had at last confided in Paul Anderson – who
had long suspected the state of affairs. 'She is so young, that
her judgement may be overpowered. My present feelings must
therefore be suppressed, that she may not have to suppress hers
hereafter, with loss of happiness.' A letter sent after the
departure of his previous superior had a note of special sadness:
'Farewell, my dear General. I beg you will remember me very

145

kindly to Mrs. Fox and to Caroline – for I believe she does not
like to be called Miss Fox . . .'

Moore's delivery from Sicily had now come. Instructions
arrived by fast cutter from Lord Castlereagh: Lieutenant-
General Sir John Moore was to embark with troops and proceed to Gibraltar where he would find further orders. On
Friday 30 October 1807, he sailed gladly from the island which
he had grown to hate, and his fleet of fifty-six sail reached
Gibraltar on Tuesday 1 December, where he opened fresh instructions.

Bonaparte, triumphant in western and central Europe after
his crushing victories over the Prussians at Jena and Auerstedt
fourteen months before, and his defeat of the Russians at Fried-
land in June – which had once more swung Russia away from
Britain – had instituted his counter-blockade against his sole
remaining enemy. Except for smuggling, only neutral Portugal
provided an access route for British trade with the Continent,
and Napoleon's gaze had become fixed on the Iberian peninsula; in November an army under Junot had crossed the Portuguese frontier. Moore was now told that if the royal family of
Portugal desired to escape to their territory in the Brazils, he
must land a corps to cover the evacuation and should accompany the royal persons as far as Madeira, which he was to
possess. But Moore had arrived too late: Lisbon had
fallen on the day he reached Gibraltar. The royal family had
already fled – and escorting their Highnesses was his brother,
Commodore Graham Moore.

Sir John wished him luck, and set sail for England to reach
Portsmouth on 1 January 1808. The year would begin with
more fresh orders, which would involve him in his strangest mission so far. And the year would end in the snows and knifing
winds of the retreat to Corunna, and the thundering climax
of his career.

*   *   *

Shouts sent sailors scampering up riggings, and stiff sails un-
curled with a tremendous flapping and crackling. Anchor
chains rattled onto fresh-scrubbed decks and bows were
brought round to face the open sea. Crowds lined the Yarmouth

beach to cheer the departure. The May sun shone on the Royal Navy's latest expedition against the French, 25 warships and 158 transports – the latter carrying about 12,200 soldiers, horses, food, ammunition, baggage, medical equipment, artillery pieces . . . For the past fortnight these ships had converged on the Yarmouth roads from Deal, Ramsgate, Harwich and Portsmouth, and among them lay HMS *Mars*, on which sailed the commander of the mission, Lieutenant-General Sir John Moore. Soon after dawn he had found time to scribble a letter to his 74-year-old mother. 'We expect that the whole of our convoy will be collected this forenoon, and as the wind is fair and the weather fine, I hope we shall be able to sail in the afternoon.' He had added: 'If the object of the expedition were more defined, it would be more agreeable . . .' The last words gave a hint of the unease which Moore already felt, and which would soon become amply justified.

Two months before, on 16 March 1808, London newspapers had declared: 'Bernadotte, to take charge of the French army to act against Sweden, is expected at Copenhagen.' Denmark and Prussia had declared war on Sweden twenty-four hours before. Russia, in alliance with France since the Treaty of Tilsit in July 1807, had invaded Swedish Finland without any declaration of hostilities. Despite all these pressures Sweden remained defiant; her king, Gustavus IV, refused to close the Baltic to his only ally, Britain. In London ministers had agreed that Gustavus must be helped; Sir John Moore had been selected to take this assistance across the North Sea and to use it to best advantage. But in which direction would this advantage lie? The question had remained unanswered after a meeting between Moore, the Duke of York and Lord Castlereagh on Sunday 19 April. 'It was plain from the whole of Lord Castlereagh's conversation,' wrote Moore in his journal, 'that Government had no specific plan, and had come to no determination beyond that of sending a force of 10,000 men to Gothenburg to be ready to act if occasion offered.'

Written instructions dated 20 April proved no more enlightening: 'It would certainly have been desirable before this Force proceeded on service,' declared these orders, 'that His Majesty's Government had been more fully apprised of the military views as well as the means of Sweden, and that a more

147

Gustavus IV, King of Sweden, described by Moore as 'without ability, and every now and then proposes measures which prove either derangement or the greatest weakness of mind'.

precise object could have been determined on to which the service of this Corps should on its arrival be applied.' But the orders did make some things clear: Moore must retain command of the British troops himself—he must not therefore put himself under Gustavus; nor must he embark upon any operation which would take him into the interior of the country without further orders from home; contact must be maintained with the British fleet. Subject to these stipulations, 'His Majesty is graciously pleased to confide altogether to your discretion to determine in which manner, consistent with military prudence the force under your orders can be most effectually employed to the annoyance of the enemy, and the support and protection

148

of his ally – you will consider the immediate security of Sweden as your first object.' In other words, Moore had the onus of responsibility. He would have to feel his way, and with extreme caution. He pondered the problem while the fleet sailed first through fine weather, then through clammy fog, before arriving at Gothenburg on 17 May, eight days after leaving Yarmouth.

Moore waited in Sweden's second city for a fortnight; the confusion surrounding his mission steadily increased. Letters from London and from Colonel George Murray, who had been sent on ahead to Stockholm, revealed difficulties being imposed by Gustavus: the King insisted on ambitious operations rather than defensive plans on Swedish soil; above all, he insisted upon command of the troops. Moore was also disturbed by the news that the Swedish regular army only amounted to 28,000 men, and he wrote in his journal: 'It is plain that Government in England were ignorant of the state of affairs in Sweden when they determined on sending this corps to act in concert with our fleet upon the enemy's coasts. They must have conceived that the Swedish force was more considerable than it is. It is so much inferior to that which is opposed to it, that they could take no advantage of any diversion we made.' From reports he had obtained from others, he believed Gustavus to be 'a man of honourable, upright mind, but without ability, and every now and then proposes measures which prove either derangement or the greatest weakness of mind. He has no Minister, but he governs himself.'

Already, Moore despaired of any hope of success. 'Our fleet, by guarding the sound and belts and by overawing the Russian squadron, will perhaps save him during the summer. Our troops, upon the plan proposed, can do him no service.' Only defensive operations should be considered; instead, Gustavus intended to launch futile and possibly disastrous attacks. Impatiently, but with his usual diligence, Moore studied the terrain around Gothenburg while attempts were made in London to clarify the situation.

While waiting, Sir John received other news from England to add to his displeasure. A full-scale French invasion of Spain had been launched in March: Murat had led 100,000 men into the country on the pretext of guarding the coast. Charles IV

149

and his son Ferdinand had been forced to renounce the throne; Napoleon's brother Joseph had been crowned king in Madrid. But the fiercely independent Spanish people had refused to co-operate, and insurrection had flared during May; Murat had been obliged to fall back to the Ebro, isolating Junot in Portugal. British money and equipment had begun to seep into the Peninsula, together with promise of more substantial help. Early in June Moore received a letter from Brownrigg at the Horse Guards. 'I heartily wish you had never gone to such a remote corner,' wrote his friend. It seemed as if the future Duke of Wellington would now have the job which Moore would have preferred above all others. 'Five thousand men are ordered from Cork to the Mediterranean . . . Three thousand are to go from hence, which, added to Spencer's corps, will form an effective army of 12,000 men, which report says is to be commanded by Sir Arthur Wellesley.' Brownrigg added: 'It is needless to say that I wish it were you.'

Early in June, Moore received further instructions from London which could only make the whole Swedish situation worse: the government had acquiesced in Gustavus's demand that he should command the troops – but the other orders that Moore should keep in contact with the fleet and stick to the defensive, remained in force. Moore's confusion resulted in a despatch to Downing Street on 11 June, in which he felt the need to describe the 'spirit' of his instructions, as he saw them. 'Except in the case of Zeeland, against which attack His Majesty's Government are quite decided, whatever other operation His Swedish Majesty may propose, if I cannot dissuade him from it, I am to place myself under his command, and follow his orders unless they should be such as I consider at variance with my instructions, and in their nature sufficiently important to justify such a step: in this case I am authorised first to remonstrate and finally to withdraw the corps.' Moore's next words amounted to a considerable understatement: 'I am fully aware of the delicacy of the situation in which I am thus placed and of the difficulties, of various kinds, in which I may be involved, but it is my duty to submit to whatever difficulties His Majesty's Government think it right to expose me . . .' He ended this despatch: 'I propose setting out for Stockholm tomorrow morning at daylight.'

Moore could hardly have been less fitted for the task which now lay before him. Superbly skilled on the battlefield, he had always been ill at ease in the diplomatic arena. And now he had to deal with a half-mad king, technically his superior officer. Leaving his army still on board the transports at Gothenburg, he set off in his open chaise, travelling across the flowery fields and through the harsh granite mountains to confront the thirty-year-old Swedish monarch, who had sat on the throne since the age of fourteen and had a fearful reputation for uncontrollable temper. After fifty-nine hours on the road, Moore's carriage clattered over the cobbles of Stockholm on the afternoon of Tuesday 14 June. He called on the British minister, Edward Thornton, to find no fresh developments, and two days later journeyed the one and a half miles from Stockholm to a pretty park surrounding the royal retreat.

Moore strode into the comfortable-looking white house to be presented to the King of Sweden, and found a neat, pale-faced young man who wore smart mustachios brushed upwards and whose cropped hair stood up from his forehead in a vain attempt to make him seem taller. Moore had constantly to bend to catch His Swedish Majesty's startling utterances.

Gustavus complained that he had only been given command of the British troops while they remained in Sweden, and he urged most strongly an attack on Zeeland – which he would undertake alone if necessary. Moore attempted to describe the immense difficulties and dangers, but without success. As he reported to London: 'His Majesty said he owned that he did not expect to hear from me, a General Officer, an advice not to attack, as it was well known that all those who had been satisfied with mere defence had been beaten. I forget all that His Majesty said upon this occasion, but the tendency was to state his forces and means as ample ... Whatever reasoning I offered, and I ventured to offer some occasionally, His Majesty never seemed displeased, but answered me as if I had not reasoned at all.'

Moore took this opportunity to complain over the treatment of his troops, still incarcerated on the ships. Why, he asked, had permission to land been refused? Gustavus replied that he had never asked for the troops to be sent to Sweden. 'His application had been for a corps of troops to act on the coast of Norway, and it was his surprise when he heard of their arrival at Gothenburg.' Sweden, a poor country, could not supply such a large body of men. 'The high pay of our soldiers,' wrote Moore, 'and our riches, would raise the price of provisions.' Besides, added the King, British soldiers were surely well acquainted with long periods on board transports. Gustavus then made his proposal, and one which shocked the cautious general. The British force should first threaten and then land on the coast of Livonia for an offensive operation in Finland. Moore asked for detailed plans to be drawn up, and quickly took his leave. He returned to his accommodation in Stockholm's New Town. The King must truly be mad, he declared, and he cursed the whole senseless situation.

Moore's opinion was confirmed when he received the details for the proposed Finnish operation next day. He only needed to take a cursory glance at the paper before informing the messenger, General Tibell, Swedish quartermaster-general, that the whole scheme seemed out of the question, and he elaborated on his reasons in a despatch to Castlereagh two days later. The Swedish king clearly flattered himself that affairs in Finland were more flourishing than they actually were. Estimates of Russian strength were highly optimistic, especially as the enemy had already disarmed pro-Swedish peasants. 'It would require very accurate information of the position of the Russian troops to justify a descent so near to Petersburgh, and in a state of things so vague it cannot be the wish of His Majesty's Government that I should take the corps I command to such a distance.' Moore's despatch of the 19th added: 'After what I have seen of the Swedish Government, and of the person who alone directs it, I should feel I was but a bad servant to my country, and very unworthy the trust the King has reposed in me, were I to place any part of the corps I command at his disposal.'

This report also described a second interview with Gustavus, at noon the previous day. Moore had explained his instructions. 'It was with great difficulty I was permitted to proceed, His Majesty constantly interrupting me by saying there was no misunderstanding on his part. He had never asked for troops but for offensive operations, and to act under his directive for the good of the common cause. Sweden had no occasion for foreign aid; she was, and always had been, quite equal to her own defence, and he would never submit to the disgrace of receiving foreign troops.'

Moore went back for a third interview with Gustavus at noon on the 20th. No fresh instructions had been received from London, so Moore took it upon himself to declare that a descent upon Russian-held territory was 'contrary to the views of the British Government in sending me to Sweden – it was an operation, in itself, so hazardous, and that promised at present so little advantage either to His Majesty's affairs or those of Great Britain, that it was out of my power to undertake it'. The King's reply was icy: 'Will you tell me then for what purpose you were sent here, since you will do nothing I propose?' Wearily, Moore repeated his instructions: his troops must be used for defensive purposes.

Moore's next despatch to Castlereagh seemed even more scribbled than usual. Ministers in London must have had difficulty in deciphering the angry scrawl, dated 23 June. 'I have the honour to inform your Lordship, that I am this moment returned from my audience with His Swedish Majesty, which proved one of the most painful interviews I ever had in my life...' This fourth meeting, unlike the others, took place in the company of leading Swedish officers, including Tibell – who had privately admitted his 'shame' at the Finland proposals.

The discussion was long and stormy, and Moore became so heated that he could not rely upon himself to write the subsequent report for despatch to London: Colonel Murray had to undertake this task instead. Moore told Castlereagh that his feelings had been wounded 'most severely'. Gustavus, in a storm of shouting, arm-waving and finger-jabbing, had accused the British general of deliberately misinterpreting words spoken at previous interviews, turning down all plans proposed, and being altogether thoroughly uncooperative.

Another spluttering accusation followed: the General had presumed to give the King of Sweden advice without being asked. To this charge alone Moore admitted guilt, but surrounded his confession with a heavy layer of sarcasm. 'I observe that I have committed an error. I should have confined myself upon the present occasion to receiving your commands and have asked leave to withdraw when Your Majesty had nothing further to add.' 'No!' exploded Gustavus. 'You would have

Colonel, later
General, Sir
George Murray,
who backed Moore
well in Sweden and
afterwards served
with him in the
Peninsula.

done very wrong. This interview was arranged for a clear statement of all that has passed – before witnesses – so that the King
of England may be correctly informed.' Moore kept his temper,
with difficulty, and declared that his orders were to sail home
if permission to land were refused; he now intended to sail, but
he promised to wait at Gothenburg until fresh orders arrived
from London.

Almost immediately, he regretted this agreement to delay
departure; back in his lodgings he wrote in his letter to Castlereagh: 'Not accustomed, My Lord, to such accusations, and
conscious of their injustice, I felt provoked, and irritated – diffi-
dent therefore of myself, and lest I should be wanting in that
respect to his Swedish Majesty . . . I made the promise hastily,
which upon reflection I wish I had withheld.'

His doubts soon increased. He had intended to leave Stockholm for Gothenburg on the morning of the 24th, but the weather turned wet and by now Moore was suffering from a cold; he decided to stay in the Swedish capital for a few more hours. During talks with Thornton, the British minister, he decided to start preparations for the departure of the troops, rather than wait for instructions from London; that afternoon Thornton communicated this decision to the Swedish government. Gustavus reacted with unprecedented pique.

Moore had retired to bed early that night, 24 June, still suffering from his cold; not long before midnight knocks sounded on the door of his lodging. On the doorstep stood the Swedish adjutant-general, attended by an armed officer, who demanded to see the British general. Despite protests that Moore had retired, he insisted upon delivering a message in person; Moore came from his chamber to be informed that he could not leave Stockholm without the King's permission. Gustavus had arrested the British general.

Early next morning Moore sought out Thornton to discuss the King's preposterous action, and the two men agreed that 'the reflection of the night might have sobered him sufficiently to see all its enormity'; General Hope, at Gothenburg, would be told to return to England with the troops if the King persisted. Murray was summoned to see Gustavus at noon and received confirmation of the arrest. Moore penned another angry letter to Castlereagh: 'Unless in the annals of French anarchy, there will not, I believe, be found elsewhere amongst civilised nations an example of such an act of violence as that now perpetrated upon my person.' Murray would travel to England at once, to present a full report of his commander's action, and Moore wrote: 'He has no interest, and if he had, he is not of a character to speak other than the truth – it is by that alone I wish to be judged ... if when everything is laid before the [British] King, His Majesty thinks I am in the wrong, he will order me to be punished. I shall well deserve it, for having brought by my misconduct such an insult upon the person and authority of the King, and the honour of the British nation.' Further abortive talks took place between Murray, Thornton and the Swedish authorities on 26 June. Moore could stand the situation no longer. 'It was my duty to make every effort to return to the post my sovereign had assigned to me at the head of his troops.' He decided to escape – and, as further defiance towards the King of Sweden, he would do so in full daylight.

Shortly before one o'clock in the afternoon of Monday 27 June, the first secretary of the British embassy drove his smart curricle to Moore's lodging, to take the general for an airing as part of his convalescence for his cold. The two horses trotted out onto the Stockholm–Gothenburg road; two miles beyond the first stage post, the curricle turned back towards the capital, but without one passenger. Moore hurried on, this time in the coach taking the courier from the British minister; provisions for two days were stowed beneath the wooden seat. On the evening of 29 June officers on board the famous *Victory*, anchored off Gothenburg, were entertaining local ladies to a ball when a battered fishing boat from the harbour bumped alongside. Out jumped one of the fishermen and clambered on board; officers exclaimed at the fellow's impudence as he stepped onto the deck, until General Sir John Moore flung off his peasant's cap. Four days later the fleet set sail for home, crossing with grossly outdated orders from Castlereagh to Moore dated 30 June and written in answer to the General's report of his first interview with the King on the 16th: 'His Majesty sees no other course... than that you should return.' Withdrawal should be accomplished in 'the most respectful and amiable manner'. The fleet made its way through thick fog to reach Dover on 15 July.

Fog also seemed to surround Moore's next step. He found no instructions or communication of any kind at Dover, and no one had even been sent to meet him. Moore had to make his way alone to London on Saturday 16 July, and he arrived to find the capital virtually deserted – all official personages had fled for the weekend, to escape the thundery, sticky weather. Again, no one had been instructed to receive him, and not until late Sunday did he receive an abrupt note that Lord Castlereagh would see General Moore at his office at 2 p.m. the following day. The atmosphere seemed strained; John Moore remembered Lady Hester's warning before he had sailed to Sweden: British ministers would play him false.

He did at least discover from the Duke of York's military secretary that arrangements had been made for his next task.

Sir John Moore would proceed to Spain, or Portugal, with the troops which he had brought from Sweden; they would be joined to others under Sir Arthur Wellesley, who had already sailed from Cork, and to those commanded by Brent Spencer now at the head of Cadiz Bay.

But Moore would only come third in the line of command, behind Sir Hew Dalrymple and Sir Harry Burrard; the choice of these two men seemed completely inexplicable – Moore had been deliberately passed over. Sir Hew had performed well as governor in Guernsey and Gibraltar – but he had last seen a battlefield over fourteen years before, and never as a general. A similar length of time separated Sir Harry 'Betty' Burrard, aged seventy-three, from active service. Yet Moore was in the prime of his life, and had been in the thick of battle only six years before, and as a general. He found it no consolation to discover that Sir Arthur Wellesley would be far further down the seniority list, coming beneath Dalrymple, Burrard, Moore, Sir John Hope, Sir Kenneth Mackenzie, General Fraser and Lord Paget.

Moore had rarely been a man to keep silent. Throughout his career he had felt it his duty to comment upon situations as he found them: Corsica, Holland, Egypt, Sicily and above all Sweden. Often his comments had been unpleasant; sometimes, as with Corsica, they had led him into trouble. Throughout his career he had had occasion to criticize expeditions which had been planned by ministers at home with no proper understanding of the problems involved, with inadequate information and insufficient preparation: this had applied to Corsica, Holland – and Sweden. Moreover, Sir John's politics were suspected by the Tory ministry under the Duke of Portland. It seems hardly surprising that Moore, though perhaps the soldier with the firmest military reputation, failed to find favour with ministers – and especially with another expedition being despatched, an expedition which would attempt to wipe out past failures – including the Swedish fiasco. The King of Sweden could clearly be called insane and Moore's actions could not be faulted, but Sweden remained an ally. All these elements had combined to bring about Moore's supercession, and his suspicions were confirmed during his conversation with the Duke of York's hesitant secretary.

'I understood from Gordon and from others that there had been much intriguing about the command,' wrote Moore in his journal. 'Ministers had done everything in their power to give it to Sir Arthur Wellesley; but he was so young a lieutenant-general that the Duke [of York] had objected to it, and afraid of disgusting the army and the nation by such an appointment, they had given it up. Disappointed in their favourite object, they were determined it should not be given to me, and, to prevent the possibility of its falling to me, Sir Harry Burrard was named as second.'

Moore saw Castlereagh the following afternoon as requested. Strangely, the Secretary for War made no mention of Spain or Moore's next employment. Apparently reluctant to broach the subject, Castlereagh confined discussion to the Swedish upset and remained as smooth and diplomatic as ever. The cabinet had been fully sensible of Moore's position in having to deal 'with a King mad and impracticable', and the General had conducted himself 'perfectly to the satisfaction of the Government'. Only one slight criticism might be made, concerning the propriety of Moore's escape: it would have been better to have left earlier or to have remained. Moore replied that one of the reasons for his escape had been his wish to 'leave Government more at liberty to act as they thought proper, not embarrassed by any consideration for my person'. Only once during the conversation did Castlereagh hint at larger matters for discussion. 'As I was leaving,' wrote Moore in his journal, 'he said he would probably wish to see me tomorrow, when he would speak with me on another subject.'

When Moore left Castlereagh's office he called on the Duke of York; the commander-in-chief received him with his usual kindness, and assured him 'that the King and he perfectly approved all I had done'. Unknown to Moore, rumours were already circulating that George III had expressed the opinion that Moore had been involved in a political plot to get his troops away from Sweden, so he could command them in Spain. The Duke of York asked his visitor if Castlereagh had spoken about any other subject than Sweden. 'I said he had not. His Royal Highness seemed much embarrassed. I knew very well what was going on was not his doing.'

Later in the evening, after Moore had retired to bed, a note

came from the Secretary for War's office: Lord Castlereagh
wished to see him at 3 p.m. the following day, Tuesday, and
Moore was asked to make arrangements to leave town as soon
after that time as possible. He ordered a chaise to be at the
door at 4 p.m. and packed the single portmanteau which he
had brought with him from Dover: all his heavy baggage would
be going round to Portsmouth on the vessel in which he had
come from Sweden. Thus prepared, he stepped briskly into
Castlereagh's room at the appointed time and accepted a chair
before the Minister's huge desk.

Castlereagh apparently still found it difficult to come to the
point: he talked at length about Spain in general, and about
the departure of Sir Arthur Wellesley from Cork – his force
might be expected off the Tagus on the 20th, and he had been
ordered to land if he felt himself strong enough to attack; if
not, Sir Arthur was to await Sir John Moore's arrival. Castlereagh prattled on, avoiding Moore's quizzical gaze, and
seemed to throw in the names of Sir Hew Dalrymple and
Sir Harry Burrard almost as afterthoughts. 'It was thus by
inference only,' wrote Moore afterwards, 'that I was to understand that I was to proceed on this service as a lieutenant-
general under Sir H. Dalrymple and Sir H. Burrard. This I
thought a most extraordinary manner of behaving to me ... It
was evident from Lord Castlereagh's manner that he was
ashamed of himself.' Moore sat in silence as Lord Castlereagh
spoke; an awkward pause followed the end of the Minister's
monologue. Then Moore began his reply.

'My Lord,' he declared, 'the chaise is at my door, and upon
leaving your Lordship's I shall set out for Portsmouth to join
the troops with whom I perceive it is intended I should proceed
as lieutenant-general. It may perhaps be my lot never to see
you again. I, therefore, think it right to express to you my feelings of the unhandsome treatment I have received from you.'
Lord Castlereagh protested that he failed to understand
Moore's meaning. Sir John immediately referred to his non-
reception at Dover and in London. 'Had I been an ensign it
would hardly have been possible to treat me with less ceremony ... You have told me that my conduct in Sweden was
approved, but from your actions I should have concluded it
was the reverse. I am at a loss to conceive the cause.' He

continued: 'I have a right, in common with all officers who have served zealously and well, to expect to be treated with attention, and when employment is offered to me, that some regard should be had to my former services.' Castlereagh sat mute, apart from one or two muttered protestations. Moore finished, rose abruptly and walked from the room; halfway through the door he turned to give a slight bow. 'Remember, my Lord, I protest against the expedition and foretell its failure.'

The post-chaise rattled down the road to Portsmouth, stopping twice on the way: he called at Marshgate House, Richmond, to dine with his brother Frank and family, then journeyed to Brook Farm, Cobham, Surrey, to spend the night with his mother. He left next morning in the pouring rain, with his mother and sister Jane weeping on the steps – something they had never done before, and which worried him sufficiently to make him write a letter from Portsmouth, despite the bustle of imminent departure. 'I am going on the service of my country, and shall hope to acquit myself as becomes me of whatever part is allotted to me. God bless you, my dear Mother. I shall write to you whilst I continue here, and hope for the time when I shall be allowed to pass the rest of my days quietly with you, my brothers, and Jane.'

One more loose end received a tidy knot. On 23 July a special messenger arrived at his Portsmouth headquarters bearing a letter in Castlereagh's hand. The Minister felt it right that Moore should not leave England without hearing that he had told the cabinet, and the King, of the General's complaints. While ministers insisted the criticism was unfounded, 'I have to assure you that had not the arrangements of the army been so far advanced as that they could not be undone without considerable detriment to His Majesty's service, there would have been every disposition on their part humbly to have advised His Majesty to relieve you from a situation in which you appear to consider yourself to have been placed without due attention to your feeling as an officer.' Moore, believing the letter had been intended to irritate him, replied within the hour. 'I am about to proceed on the service on which I have been ordered, and it shall be my endeavour to acquit myself with the same zeal by which I have ever been actuated when employed in the service of my country.' And Moore declared his complete faith in 'His Majesty's justice'. He refrained from expressing similar confidence in the cabinet. As he confided in his journal: 'I sent them a very calm answer, in which I gave them a wipe which they will feel but cannot resent...I am in hopes now to be allowed to go quietly...Sir Harry Burrard arrived yesterday, and I gave up the command to him.' Sir Hew Dalrymple had still to appear.

After a delay caused by south-westerly winds, the fleet sailed on the last day of July. By noon the mists had swept down from the lowering rain clouds, to curtain Sir John Moore's last sight of England.

Chapter Eight

ADVANCE INTO SPAIN

Events in Spain now sent ripples across all Europe. British troops were at last striking back against the French, after a seven-year absence from the battlefield. European capitals seethed with rumour and counter-rumour. Fast frigates cut north under all sail to bring the latest news to London and to 10 Downing Street; a momentous campaign had opened. Yet Sir John Moore had to stand to one side for the moment: the war was to be waged by Sir Arthur Wellesley, simply because this general, who had won his honours in faraway India, had reached the arena before him.

The first target would be Andoche Junot, stranded with 5,000 men in Portugal after the Spanish insurrection. On the day before departure from Portsmouth Sir Harry Burrard had received a message from Castlereagh informing the British commander that Sir Arthur had arrived at Corunna. Sir Arthur continued south, sailing from Oporto on 21 July. Burrard's fleet made land at Cape Finisterre on 16 August and another frigate brought him further news: Sir Arthur had disembarked with his troops in the Mondego River, halfway between Oporto and Lisbon. Sir Harry Burrard, gallant for his age, clambered into a frigate and sped south to be in closer contact, leaving Sir John Moore with orders to lie off Vigo and await further instructions.

The fleet sighted Vigo on the 17th, but Moore decided to go further, believing Burrard would be unable to send the next orders because of the contrary wind blowing fresh from the north-east. The warships and transports accordingly reached Oporto on 18 August. There Moore discovered that Burrard had proceeded the evening before to Mondego; he also received

the inspiring news that General Pierre Dupont had surrendered his French army of 30,000 men to Spanish forces under Castaños, after a muddled encounter on 23 July. Both commanders had behaved with considerable incompetence, but the Spaniard had managed to hang on to the advantage, thus bringing about the first capitulation of a Napoleonic army and increasing Junot's isolation. In addition to this excellent report, Moore heard that Sir Arthur Wellesley had begun his march from Mondego towards Lisbon, where Junot had the bulk of his troops, and that Sir Arthur had been joined by General Brent Spencer's corps from Cadiz. Events were clearly quickening, and Moore ordered the fleet to hasten for Mondego, which was sighted on the 19th. And then the winds dropped and the fleet lay becalmed. The men sweated beneath the Spanish sun, and Moore fretted.

British troops under Sir Arthur Wellesley land in Mondego Bay, August 1808, to begin British participation in the Peninsular War.

Waves idly slapped the warships and ugly troop transports; to the east shimmered the Spanish horizon. Sir Arthur Wellesley and his 18,000 men were believed to be somewhere near Obidos, and a letter from Burrard to Moore revealed the commander's fear that Sir Arthur had advanced too far. Burrard therefore instructed Moore to land as soon as possible and proceed to Leiria to cover a possible retreat. Not until 8 a.m. on 22 August could the landing begin.

163

General Sir Hew 'Dowager' Dalrymple, Commander-in-Chief of the British Expedition to Portugal, who had last seen active service fourteen years before.

On this same day 100 miles to the south the sun rose upon a scene of terrible destruction, with screeching vultures quarrelling over the bodies of thousands of dead and dying British and French soldiers. The first British battle of the Peninsula War had been fought the previous afternoon. Another forty-eight hours would pass before Moore received news of the battle and its result. Meanwhile instructions from Sir Harry told him to cancel his disembarkation: troops who had not yet been put ashore should be sailed further along the coast ready for use closer to Lisbon.

On the morning of 24 August Moore reached Maceira Bay, and learned from Captain Bligh of HMS *Alfred* that the French had been thrashed at Vimeiro on the 21st. Junot had been out-manœuvred by Sir Arthur; French troops had been out-fought by the British; the enemy had retired in confusion to Lisbon leaving 2,000 slain and wounded. Sir Harry Burrard had landed during the action, and Sir Hew Dalrymple had arrived to take over command on the 22nd.

Sir John immediately wrote a note of congratulation to Sir Arthur Wellesley; his rival general sent a gracious reply from his camp at Ramalhal on the same day, still flushed with success and still irked by Burrard's refusal to allow the British to pursue the French while they remained disorganized.

'I wish that you had arrived a few days sooner,' wrote Sir Arthur, 'that you might by your influence have prevailed with those who prevented me from making all the use in my power of the victory which the troops had gained. But you are not now too late, and I hope that you will soon come to head-quarters and ascertain the state and means of this army, and state your opinion to the Commander-in-Chief respecting the means to be adopted.' Winter weather would soon set in, warned Sir Arthur, and he added: 'We have done nothing since the 21st. I am therefore very desirous indeed that you should come over here ...' Clearly the victor of Vimeiro remained dissatisfied with the attitudes and abilities of his commanders; equally obviously Sir Arthur believed he would have an ally in Sir John.

Meanwhile, Moore's men continued to disembark, stiff and jaded after their long confinement on board – some of them now set foot on dry land for the first time since the start of the

General Jean Andoche Junot, Commander of the French troops in Portugal.

Swedish mission. An eye-witness described the scene: 'There were soldiers, horses, sailors, guns, wagons, some of which were being fitted together, mountains of ship's biscuits, haversacks, trusses of hay, barrels of meat and rum ... dragoons busy catching and saddling their horses. But the latter could not be mounted for, owing to their long sojourn in the ship, during which they had been standing, they had lost the use of the legs, and the moment a trooper mounted one of them, the horse folded up.' Some men jumped into the boats, happy with the prospect of dry land at last, only to drown in the surf.

Moore supervised the landing, and at the same time sought further news. He learned that General Junot had sent a flag of truce on the 22nd, and a suspension of hostilities had been agreed. Moore reached the British headquarters on the evening of the 25th – and the whole situation appalled him: Sir Arthur, absent from the camp at that time, had been absolutely correct in his criticisms. 'I was sorry to find everything in the greatest confusion,' wrote Moore, 'and a very general discontent. Sir Hew, though announced to the army, had not as yet taken the direction of it; much was still done by Sir Arthur Wellesley, and what was not done by him was not done at all.' Having learned details of the battle of Vimeiro, his admiration for Sir Arthur grew – and he agreed with the latter's sentiments over the need for rapid pursuit. 'Sir Arthur's views ... were extremely right.' But the French had been allowed to retreat; negotiations for peace in Portugal had now begun. Almost immediately it became evident that Junot was insisting upon terms extremely favourable to the French. Sir John Moore noted in his journal on 28 August that the French commander was demanding that his defeated troops should not be treated as prisoners of war, but should be embarked with arms and baggage for France.

But Sir John, like Sir Arthur, believed the terms should be accepted – even though the French would sail home in vessels provided by the British. The terms might be dishonourable to the British, but, now that the opportunity for total defeat of the enemy had been let slip, the alternative prospects were depressing. 'I hope the negotiations will terminate favourably,' commented Moore on the 28th. 'It is evident that if any operation is to be carried on it will be miserably conducted, and that seniority in the Army List is a bad guide in the choice of a military commander. Sir Arthur Wellesley seems to have conducted his operations with ability, and they have been crowned with success. It is a pity, when so much has been thrown into his hands, that he has not been allowed to complete it.' Moore thanked his good fortune in not being involved; now the battle had been fought, he would insist on remaining a spectator in the inevitable wrangle. 'I have told both Sir Hew and Sir Arthur that I wished not to interfere; that if the hostilities commenced, Sir Arthur had already done so much that I thought it but fair he should have the command of whatever was brilliant in the finishing . . . I considered this as his expedition . . . For my part I wished I could withdraw myself altogether.'

His desire to stand aside for the moment was to be fulfilled; but his wish to pull out completely would not be met. Sir John Moore avoided the controversy which was about to break out over negotiations with the French; but his very abstinence from this argument would result in the situation which the government had apparently sought so hard to avoid. Sir Hew, Sir Harry and Sir Arthur would be involved, and would be obliged to return home – leaving Sir John as the only possible choice for the next fatal operations against the French over the border in Spain.

Terms of a convention were ratified on 31 August by Sir Hew at Torres Vedras and by Junot at Lisbon; on 1 September the British HQ moved to Cintra, nearer the Portuguese capital, and the notorious convention therefore received the name of this latest British headquarters. The French were to abandon intact all forts, arsenals and military stores, and to sail home – but in British vessels and with no time specified for their exclusion from further conflict. Immediate opposition to the Cintra Convention erupted in Lisbon and London, even though no other means could have been found to effect the departure of the French, short of another battle, and even though the British aim of clearing the French from Portugal had been fulfilled. The Portuguese, appalled by the amount of loot the French were collecting to take with them, read of the agreement in newspapers which displayed black borders of mourning. Before long the Tory ministry in London would be forced to institute a court of inquiry.

The young Sir Arthur Wellesley, painted by J. Hoppner at about the time of the Peninsular War.

Meanwhile, plans were despatched from Downing Street for taking the war into Spain. Moore called upon Sir Hew Dalrymple on 7 September and emerged distraught from the meeting. The commander had revealed the contents of a letter from Castlereagh, which suggested future operations in north Spain 'upon the flanks and rear, as he called it, of the French from Santander or Gijon, whilst the Spanish pressed them in front'. Moore condemned the plan in the privacy of his journal as the usual 'plausible verbose nonsense . . . a sort of gibberish which

169

men in office use and fancy themselves military men'. He added: 'It does not appear that our Ministers are in communication with the leading men in Spain, or are acquainted with their means or designs. Without a knowledge of these, and a perfect concert with the Spaniards, I cannot see how it is possible to determine where or how we are to act.' Moore revealed his fears to Sir Hew at the interview on the 7th: Sir Hew replied that he did not even know who the leading Spanish generals would be. Moore's opinion of his commander sank even lower: 'Sir Hew, having never had the experience of command, seems quite at a loss how to work with the different heads of department; the troops suffer.'

Sir Arthur Wellesley agreed, and hastened to enlist Sir John Moore as an ally. The latter, after a depressing visit to Lisbon on the 9th, established his camp outside the city at Quelus on the 17th. Within an hour of his arrival he received a startling letter from his fellow general. 'It appears to me to be quite impossible that we can go on as we are now constituted,' wrote the blunt Sir Arthur. 'The Commander-in-Chief must be changed, and the country and the army naturally turn their eyes to you as their commander.' He continued with a reference to Moore's private upset following his return from Sweden. 'I understand, however, that you have lately had some unpleasant discussions with the King's Ministers, the effect of which might be to prevent the adoption of an arrangement for the command of this army which in my opinion would be the best, and would enable you to render those services at this moment for which you are peculiarly qualified.' Sir Arthur asked Moore if he would agree to a meeting, and he offered himself as a go-between in discussions between Moore and the ministers. 'I am no party man, but have long been connected in friendship with many of those persons who are now at the head of affairs in England; and I think I have sufficient influence over them.'

Moore, studying the letter at his HQ in the pretty pink palace of Quelus, puzzled over Sir Arthur's motives, and wrote: 'This letter surprises me the more as I have little previous acquaintance with Sir Arthur, and have had very little communication with him since I joined this army.' Nevertheless an affirmative reply to the request for a meeting left Quelus the same night.

Sir Arthur cantered over from his own HQ the following day.

THE XVth,

OR,

King's Regiment of Light Dragoons.

THE

Highest Bounty

WILL BE GIVEN

For a few Heroes,

NOW WANTED

To complete this gallant Regiment.

VOLUNTEERS will be genteelly treated, and have many Advantages pointed out to them, on Application to

SERG. COOKE, *White Horse, Oxford-Street.*

SERG. WILLIAMSON, *Flying Horse, Borough.*

SERG. MATHEWS, *Ship, Croydon.*

CORP. WILSON, *King's Arms, Little Chelsea.*

N. B. BRINGERS well satisfied.

Recruiting card dated 1804, issued in an attempt to swell cavalry ranks for the accelerating war with the French.

171

Moore stood to receive him as his guest brushed the dust from his uniform. The two men, almost strangers, started to size each other up. Sir John intended to display caution – he wanted no part in any plotting – and immediately made his position plain. He admitted he shared Sir Arthur's opinion about the present command in the Peninsula: Sir Hew had clearly proved unfit. 'But it is the business of Government to remove him if they think proper. I can enter into no intrigue upon the subject.' He agreed that he had been shabbily treated, but Castlereagh knew his feelings already. Sir Arthur refused to be deterred, begging to be allowed to speak on Sir John's behalf, and he disclosed that he intended to sail for England the following day. He would champion Moore's cause in London. Moore's account in his journal continued: 'If he is sincere, and I have no reason to doubt him, his conduct is very kind. If he should be otherwise, I am no worse than I was, for I said nothing to him that I would not have said to anybody with whom I had conversed upon this subject.'

Sir Arthur Wellesley would reach Plymouth on 4 October. On the same day, Sir Hew Dalrymple left for England, summoned to explain himself before the court of inquiry into the Cintra Convention. Sir Harry Burrard would follow him later. But Sir Arthur's intercession on Moore's behalf would be unnecessary: his ship had crossed a frigate heading for Lisbon with instructions from Downing Street to Moore. Sir John broke the seal and ripped open the waxy envelope on the afternoon of 6 October, to pull out a foolscap sheet dated 26 September.

'His Majesty having determined to employ a corps of his troops of not less than 30,000 infantry and 5,000 cavalry in the North of Spain to co-operate with the Spanish armies in the expulsion of the French from that kingdom has been graciously pleased to entrust to you the command in chief of His Forces.' At last Moore would command an army in the field. His excitement bubbled into his battered journal. 'There has been no such command since Marlborough for a British officer.' He continued: 'How they came to pitch upon me I cannot say, for they have given sufficient proof of not being partial to me.' A private letter from Castlereagh accompanied the despatch, assuring Moore of his personal assistance and begging him to write 'confidentially and privately on all subjects connected with my command. I have answered in the same strain of civility, and mean to write to him as cordially as if nothing had before passed to prevent it. This the good of the service requires.' Moore added: 'I think of nothing else.' The prologue in the Peninsula had ended; now Sir John Moore could wage the real war.

*　　*　　*

Yet Moore remained the canny Scot. He fully appreciated the difficulties and dangers involved, not least being the lack of proper planning at home and the absence of any groundwork to secure Spanish co-operation. His orders left this vital project very much in his own hands; Castlereagh had merely written: 'I shall lose no time in forwarding to you from hence such information as I may have been enabled to collect, and I am to recommend that you will take the necessary measures for opening a communication with the Spanish authorities for the purposes of framing the plan of the campaign, on which it may be advisable that the respective armies should act in concert.' Yet with which Spanish army should Moore co-operate? And how would the problem of respective Anglo-Spanish command be settled? Castlereagh's instructions remained vague, and a further letter dated 30 September offered no help: 'I shall write to you at an early period upon the subject of relative command with the Spanish Generals. It is a point of considerable delicacy – but I hope will be less embarrassing as the magnificence and composition of your corps secure to you a preponderating authority in all operations.'

But no time could be spared. Moore's orders meant that all preparations must be completed as soon as possible: winter weather would soon terminate the campaigning season, and it would be folly to be stranded in Spain without adequate provisions to last until spring. Moore's army would total 40,000 men: 20,000 infantry, two regiments of cavalry and artillery already in Portugal, plus 10,000 infantry, five regiments of cavalry and the proportionate artillery sailing from Falmouth direct to Corunna. About 10,000 troops were to remain in Portugal, initially commanded by Burrard. According to Moore's orders of 26 September: 'It has been determined to assemble

French sentinel of Napoleonic times: army surgeons
preferred white uniforms to be worn by the men to
encourage cleaner cloth, so reducing risk of wound
infections.

this force in the north of Spain as the quarter where they can
be most speedily brought together and that to which the operation of the enemy appear at present to be principally
directed.'

Although the need for speed was emphasized, much had once
again been left to Moore. 'It will be for you to consider on what
points in Galicia or on the border of Leon the force can be most

advantageously assembled and equipped for service, from whence they may move forward as early as circumstances shall permit.' Moore had to make one of two choices: he could either march the army by land into Spain from Portugal, or go by sea to Corunna. Within three days after receiving his orders on the 6th he had written to Castlereagh to inform him that he intended to march direct. The passage by sea to Corunna would be precarious, especially at this season, and the country around Corunna would probably not be able to supply the force coming from Falmouth under Sir David Baird and his own contingent. Moore said he would unite with Baird later, and would lead his own army from Lisbon using three routes: Coimbra, Guarda and Alcantara. But he warned he could give no estimate for the date upon which the Spanish frontier would be crossed. 'It depends upon a knowledge of country which I am still without, and upon Commissariat arrangements yet unmade.'

On 9 October Moore also wrote privately to Castlereagh: 'The great object at present is to get the troops out of Portugal before the rains set in; but, at this instant, the army is without equipment of any kind, either for the carriage of the light baggage of regiments, artillery stores, Commissariat stores, or other appendages of an army; and not a magazine is formed in any of the routes by which we are to march...I mention this circumstance in the first place, because it is a truth, and in the next, to prevent your Lordship from being too sanguine as to the probable period of my reaching the North of Spain.'

Moore's difficulties were indeed immense; nor did he find the army in Portugal in peak condition. The troops had been inactive since Vimeiro: cold weather had already crept down from the mountains, and the drop in temperature was very noticeable in contrast with the sweltering summer campaign. Sickness had steadily soared; morale had dropped. One officer described the situation at Quelus: 'What with the great heat, the cold nights, the eating of fruit and the drinking of young wine, the health of the army became so much impaired that typhus and dysentery broke out and spread rapidly, affecting even the inhabitants of villages lying close to the camp. The pestilential stench of our slaughter-house refuse, also contributed somewhat to the trouble; while, in addition, a huge hospital was installed in one of the wings of the castle, not far behind and below our stores depot, and separated from it only by a long ditch which was used as a latrine by dysentery patients, and was not 500 yards away. Infection was bound to occur...'

But the men were prodded from their inertia by Moore's first General Orders, posted on the 9th: 'The Troops under Lieutenant-General Sir John Moore will hold themselves in readiness to move on the shortest notice. Directions will be given with respect to the sick. The Lieut.-General sees with much concern the great number of this description, and that it daily increases. The General assures the troops, that it is owing to their own intemperance, that so many of them are rendered incapable of marching against the Enemy: and having stated this, he feels confident that he need say no more to British soldiers to insure their sobriety.' These General Orders also declared that all heavy baggage would have to be left in Lisbon; and on 10 October Moore informed his army that women and children would be classed in this category, much to the chagrin of the men and the 1,200 females now with them in camp. Commanding officers were ordered to prevent as many as possible from following the troops, 'as in the course of the long march which the army is about to undertake, and where no carts will be allowed, the women would unavoidably be exposed to the greatest hardship and distress...' Yet many managed to slip after their men. Few would survive.

The army began to stir and shake itself ready for the march to war. In thousands of tents, rough bivouacs and billets scattered over the countryside north of Lisbon, men began to collect their belongings, check their equipment, and scrounge or steal those items which they found themselves without. Messengers rode from one section of the camp to another; from dawn to dusk the camps echoed with commands, shouts and the clatter of weapons. Hundreds of fires sent blue smoke wisping upwards until a pall hung over the whole area, and the fuel used – rock-rose, rosemary, myrtle and other shrubs – filled the air with a fragrance which mingled with the stink of sweat, musket grease and cooking smells. Pile upon pile of biscuits were baked from bolted wheat flour, as large as pancakes, their outsides a glossy golden colour with insides as white

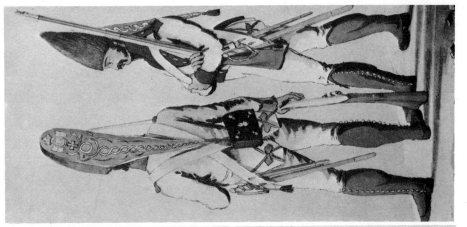

Portuguese and Spanish soldiers at the time of the Peninsular War.

as snow. Commissariat officers sat behind trestle tables littered
with lists of essential supplies, and tried to collect sufficient
transport.

Increasingly, a strange and irritating screeching noise could
be heard as dozens of Portuguese bullock carts were assembled:
these primitive vehicles had solid wheels and ungreased axles,
attached by leather straps to a wooden yoke behind the bullock's horns, and they made a persistent din which men swore
would drive them crazy. 'The scratching of a knife on a pewter
plate is like the sweet sound of a flute beside them.' All the hack-
ney carriages in Lisbon had been requisitioned and their super-
structures removed, but still the supply officers scoured the
country to find more vehicles.

And despite all the frantic activity, much remained to be
done. 'I wish I could announce to your Lordship greater progress,' wrote Moore to Castlereagh on 10 October, 'and that
this letter had been addressed from anywhere but from Lisbon... In none of the departments is there any want of zeal,
but in some of the important ones, there is much want of experience, and perhaps even of ability. This applies particularly to
the Commissariat, few of whose members have ever seen an
army in the field... I have no hope of getting to march at
present with more than the light baggage of the troops, the
ammunition immediately necessary for the service of the artillery, and a very scanty supply of medicines.'

Each day was precious; each dawn the further slight drop
in temperature indicated the approach of winter. 'Pray for good
weather,' wrote Sir John to Lady Hester. 'If it rains the torrents
will swell, and be impassable, and I shall be accounted a
bungler.' He added: 'I wish you were with us... we should give
you riding enough, and in your red habit, *à l'Amazone*, you
would animate us and do us all much good.'

Within a week Moore received unsettling news: the British
officer sent to confer with the Spaniards reported that the
enemy would be much greater in numbers than had been
expected. A despatch from Moore to Castlereagh on the 18th
declared: 'I have received letters... from Lord William Bentinck from Madrid, in which he mentions that the Madrid
Government had been thrown into a considerable degree of
alarm, in consequence of a letter intercepted from the Governor

of Bayonne to Marshal Jourdan, informing him that between 16 October and 15 November 66,000 infantry and from 5–7,000 cavalry would be entering Spain.' Moore continued: 'It is impossible to be more anxious than I am to get forward, but it is useless to take forward troops without the means to enable them to act . . . I am hurrying as much as possible. The greater part of the troops are in motion in the course of this week . . . I have received no report yet of the arrival of Sir David Baird [at Corunna]. I expect it daily . . .'

Moore, working sixteen hours a day – visiting units, checking lists, issuing orders, studying maps, sending despatches and letters – was acutely aware of the defects stemming from lack of preparation undertaken before he received the command. 'The arrangement for supplies should have been made,' he wrote angrily to Bentinck, 'and the information respecting roads should have been got before the march began – but when I got the command nothing of this sort had been done. They talked of going into Spain as if going into Hyde Park.' The army commander even found himself without finance. His military chest contained a mere £25,000, insufficient even for hiring transport. Some stores were obtained on credit from a Lisbon merchant – who went bankrupt. 'It is impossible to describe the embarrassment we are thrown into,' reported Moore to London. 'Nothing but abundance of money, and prompt payments will compensate, when we begin to move, for the want of experience and ability of our Commissariat.' The troops were to have an additional burden: 'It is my intention to make the troops find their own meat, and to call upon the Commissary for bread and wine and forage only.'

Yet skimping and saving could only be taken so far, and some problems could not be overcome by mere diligence: chief among these loomed the choice of routes into Spain. Moore had studied all maps available and originally planned to take two routes from Lisbon to Almeida, one via Coimbra and Celorico, the other to Abrantes and then through Castelo Branco, while two brigades under General Hope would advance from Elvas through Estremadura. The three would converge somewhere in the plains of Old Castile for a move to Salamanca and the junction with Baird's corps from Corunna. Moore would then strike for Valladolid or perhaps even Burgos: the latter was the most Moore would concede to his instructions for operations in 'the north of Spain'.

But now his plans received the most serious setback to date, one serious enough to make him curse with renewed vigour the ministers in London who had thrown him and his army into such an ill-prepared mess. The maps seemed virtually useless. Portuguese engineer officers advised him that the two routes from Lisbon were unsuitable for cavalry and out of the question for artillery. All but the lightest guns would have to be hauled south to join Hope's detour through Estremadura, together with Moore's two cavalry regiments. For an officer so conscious of the need for careful reconnaissance, this lack of essential information seemed almost intolerable; and for a commander so aware of the importance of balanced forces, the necessity to detach his artillery and cavalry from his infantry rendered the situation infinitely worse. His army would be split hither and thither, with forces moving from Lisbon, Elvas and Corunna, over country noted for its deplorable communications, and with rains liable to wash away bridges and whole sections of roads – and against a concentrated enemy having the advantage of interior lines. Moreover, he could expect little help from the Spanish ally. The Madrid government, known as the Central Junta, had been reported by Bentinck to be sluggish and apathetic; the Spanish armies were fragmented, and rivalry seemed rife between the leading generals – General Castaños in Astorga, Cuesta moving down from Salamanca, Llamas moving up from Valencia, Joachim Blake, a dashing Irish soldier of fortune now in Leon, and Palafox – who had limited military experience – in Aragon. Bentinck had hoped the news of French reinforcements might stir the Spaniards to greater effort; only time would tell, and time was fast running out. Moore could wait no longer.

'*Arrivo! Arrivo!*' screamed the Portuguese cart drivers at their animals. Scores of British officers shouted the orders to march. Steady, insistent rolls were beaten on taut drumskins. Dust swirled high in the thick air. Abandoned bivouacs littered the deserted camps. Bullocks bawled and horses whinnied and men swore as their knapsacks bit into their unaccustomed backs. Moore's regiments were on the move with all the confused cacophony which announces an advancing army. Sir John attended

to one last duty: finding a sheet of paper on his desk, he wrote his last despatch from Quelus, dating the report 27 October 1808. 'Everything is now clear of Lisbon except two regiments which march tomorrow and the day following.' He told Castlereagh: 'I shall myself leave in a couple of hours.' He scattered sand over his bold signature and folded the paper, smudging wet words as he did so.

Lisbon, viewed from the north.

Sir John Moore walked to his horse to lead the stab into enemy territory: with too few men, too late in the year, along unfit roads, with his forces scattered, hampered by lack of finance and heavy equipment, unable to rely on his Spanish ally – and against an experienced enemy far superior in numbers. 'If we get over this march,' Moore had admitted to Bentinck, 'nothing after will appear difficult.'

181

*

Chapter Nine

RETREAT

Moore hurried after his advance regiments along roads which at first were found to be good – and quite suitable for artillery. Late on the day of his departure he reached Villafranca, where he opened his journal to jot down his thoughts. 'I go to meet the troops as they arrive by their different routes at Almeida, and shall collect them at Ciudad Rodrigo and Salamanca, and wait until Hope's and Sir David Baird's corps get to Astorga and Espinar, when, according to circumstances, I can direct the junction of the whole at Valladolid, Burgos, or wherever else is thought best.' He crossed the Tagus and into Spain on 1 November, still finding the road suitable for artillery. Around lay desolate countryside, uncultivated except for occasional oaks, olives and cork trees. By 4 November the sandy gravel road had taken him to Castelo Branco. 'One brigade of ours has gone this way; the whole country is dreary...This is a miserable place.' He received a letter from Hope at Elvas, dated 30 October: Hope was to begin his march on 2 November, and expected to reach Valladolid by the end of the month, travelling via the Spanish capital.

But twenty-four hours later as Moore rode from Castelo Branco, despatches were handed to him which contained ominous information. The French were believed to have received an extra 10,000 men, and General Castaños and the army of Aragon were making movements towards the enemy right, which Moore judged would precipitate battle with the French. 'This has made me rather uneasy at my separation from General Hope, the more so, as I now find I could have brought the artillery by this road.' Moore had sent a messenger hurrying over to Hope with orders for him to rush his artillery forward,

General Sir John Moore points the way into Spain: one of
the few portraits depicting Moore on horseback.

if possible finding a way to avoid Madrid, both for reasons of
speed and security: the French would be bound to make the
capital their primary target. And on 5 November, unknown
to Moore, a small figure rode into the main French camp, head
uncovered to allow all to see him – Napoleon Bonaparte, conqueror of Europe, had come to lead his regiments.

Winter rain-clouds had gathered over the black mountains.
Thunder rumbled to the north, and inexperienced men in
Moore's army believed the noise came from distant artillery
fire. Daylight grew dimmer, and the ochre plains dulled to grey.
Rain sluiced upon the troops at dawn on 6 November and continued unabated for the next forty-eight hours. 'I never saw
a worse day,' wrote Moore on the 7th. He added: 'I received
letters from Madrid ... which do not describe the affairs in

183

Spain as prosperous. The Junta are very inefficient, the armies weak, and the French getting reinforcements daily.' In answer to a request made via Bentinck, the Central Junta had informed Moore that he should concert his movements with General Castaños. The sodden soldiers struggled on, and most behaved extremely well. But occasional looting had been reported. Moore, of whose methods one officer had written 'the cat-o'nine-tails is never used and yet discipline is there seen in the highest state of perfection', now had to react with severity. A soldier found guilty of marauding and robbing at Almeida on 10 November failed to receive the commander's pardon. Moore, in his orders on the 11th, declared the crime to be 'deliberate villainy' and stated: 'He must therefore suffer the awful punishment to which he has been condemned.' The man was shot, with Moore's words ringing about his army's ears: 'The army is sent by England to aid and support the Spanish nation, not to plunder and rob its inhabitants.' On the same day he advanced to Ciudad Rodrigo, and on the 13th he travelled a further 27 miles to Salamanca, his immediate objective. To escape the Spanish reception committee provided by the mayor and corporation, Moore dodged down a back road; he entered the ancient city, prominent with its towers and cupolas on the brown hillside, unseen.

Bad news awaited him. The French had moved on to the offensive, and with customary boldness. Burgos had been taken. And during the night of the 14th a dishevelled courier brought further ill-tidings to Moore's lamp-lit headquarters: the French had advanced and entered Valladolid, only seventy miles from Salamanca and within a four-day march. British troops could not be assembled before the 25th at the earliest. 'I have thus no option, if the French advance, but to fall back on Ciudad Rodrigo, which is a poor country, not able to subsist such a corps for any time, and if I am afterwards obliged to go into Portugal, I do not mend the matter.' Moore's journal entry for the 15th continued: 'I always foresaw this event as a possible one, that the French would move upon us before our junction. I, however, always hoped that we should not be so unfortunate.' It seemed that only the Spanish could stop the French from arriving before Baird's men from Corunna and Hope's column from the south, yet Moore increasingly despaired of allied support: 'the positions of the Spanish armies I have never been able to understand'. Spanish forces remained widely separated and seemed content to move on the French flanks, leaving the whole country open to enemy incursion and the British army liable to attack. 'It is singular that the French have penetrated so far,' commented Moore.

As usual, ministers in London remained totally incapable of realizing the true situation. A despatch to Moore from Castlereagh, dated 14 November, would arrive too late, its contents already rendered nonsensical by events. 'Should the Spanish Government appoint a Commander-in-Chief of all the armies . . . you will consider yourself as placed under the orders of that officer . . . It will be most gratifying to His Majesty to find that the intercourse between the British Army and the Spaniards has been invariably distinguished by marks of reciprocal confidence and kindness.' As these instructions were being despatched, Moore was addressing the Junta in Salamanca: if the enemy attacked before his troops could unite, warned Moore, he would have to retire and leave the Spaniards to their fate. Salamanca's leading citizens heard him in silence. And as his troops continued to arrive at the city from the Lisbon road, he ordered them to be ready to march again with provisions for three days. He had no faith in the Spanish people. 'It is said that the peasantry and lower orders are enthusiastic and determined never to submit to France, but the enthusiasm is less as the class ascends.' John Hookham Frere, British envoy extraordinary in Madrid, believed otherwise, and the diplomat and the General would soon clash. Frere wrote to Moore on the 13th: 'The fixed spirit of resistance, which, without calculation of danger or of means, seems to have rooted itself in the minds of the people, appears superior to any reverse.'

Moore, surrounded by anxious officers as he studied tattered maps, could find no reason for optimism. Baird had still many mountainous miles to travel before he could reach the comparative safety of Salamanca; Hope had still to manoeuvre round Madrid. Thick black arrows on the maps strewn across the General's desk indicated the French threats; Moore, with his force of about 10,000, risked annihilation at the hands of an enemy twice or three times his strength. Frere must be mad, or totally deceived; Moore replied on the 16th that the Spanish

185

John Hookham
Frere, British
Envoy
Extraordinary to
the Spanish
Government, who
fed Moore with
misleading and
dangerous
information.

armies seemed to be much too far apart, risking destruction
piecemeal. 'Until my force is united, I must be covered and
protected. As the corps come to me from such opposite directions, Corunna and Madrid, I cannot move towards one, without increasing my distance and forsaking the other; and whilst
they are each marching towards me, if I am forced to fall back,

they will both risk to be destroyed.' Moore had therefore decided to take the only step he thought open to him, short of withdrawal: the corps from Corunna must not move further into danger. 'I shall direct General Baird to collect the whole of his corps at and about Astorga, when his retreat to Corunna is safe; but not to come towards me, until I give him notice.' Rumours had reached the British HQ that General La Romana had been appointed virtual commander-in-chief of the Spanish forces, but Moore did not know where this gentleman could be contacted; he asked Frere to pass on the military information contained in his letter.

Two or three hours later Moore received a shattering message from General John Leith, liaison officer with the Spanish forces. 'I regret to inform you that the army of General Blake ... has been defeated in several attacks since the 5th instant, and is entirely dispersed.' All other armies had suffered serious losses; most units had disintegrated; Spanish soldiers were weakened and starving. Only one Spanish force of any size now survived which could give the British support; this, under Castaños, consisted mainly of peasantry, while Romana, attempting to scratch together another army, had disappeared. 'God knows where,' wrote Moore to Frere, on the 19th. 'The imbecility of the Spanish Government exceeds belief... I am in communication with no one Spanish army; nor am I acquainted with the intentions of the Spanish Government, or of any of its Generals ... In the meantime the French are within four marches of me, whilst my army is only assembling: in what numbers they are, I cannot learn...' 'If things are to continue in this state,' he added, 'the ruin of the Spanish cause, and the defeat of their armies, is inevitable; and it will become my duty to consider alone the safety of the British army, and to take steps to withdraw it from a situation where, without the possibility of doing good, it is exposed to certain defeat.'

Yet Moore still stayed at Salamanca, despite all the pressures for withdrawal. The days passed amidst increasing tension: rumour fed upon rumour; the troops remained at immediate notice to move, and unease multiplied; rain and perhaps snow would soon destroy the escape route. Each hour Moore anxiously awaited further news: from Hope, Baird, the Spaniards, Frere; but firm information seemed unobtainable. Baird, who had arrived at Astorga on 19 November with part of his infantry, had experienced a complete lack of co-operation from the Spaniards during his advance from Corunna, and admitted to mounting apprehension. 'My dear Sir John,' he wrote on 23 November, 'the more I consider our situation, the more I am convinced of the danger that would attend my making, at the present moment, any movement in advance, or attempt to join you, until my force is more collected.' No Spanish support could be expected, and the French were probing his front. 'As it could never be intended by the British Government that our army should engage in the defence of this country unaided and unsupported by any Spanish force, I confess, my dear Sir John, I begin to be at a loss to discover an object at this moment in Spain.'

Even Moore found it increasingly difficult to justify his continued presence in Salamanca. Two despatches left for London on 24 November: in one, Moore warned that 'the junction of this army becomes exceedingly precarious', and in the other he detailed the whole lamentable state of affairs. 'If I had had a conception of the weakness of the Spanish armies, the depleted state of the country, and the apparent apathy of the people, and the selfish imbecility of the Government, I should certainly have been in no hurry to enter Spain, or to have approached the scene of action, until the Army was united.' His advance 'may prove the worst thing I could have done' and he repeated the warning already given to Frere that he might soon have to withdraw.

But Moore tarried, despite news from Frere that the government in Madrid would soon flee to Cordova. Frere still insisted that the British should stay and fight. 'What they [the Spanish government] most deprecate, and I think with most reason, is a retreat upon Portugal. It would sink the hearts of the whole country...' This letter from the British envoy reached Moore's headquarters late on 26 November; the British commander read and re-read the words and could find no grounds for agreeing with the British minister. Seven hours later, as dawn spread over Salamanca's steeples and his soldiers were roused for another day of anxious waiting, Moore took up his pen. Once again he described to Frere the dangers besetting him; he said he must make one of two choices. 'I must ... throw myself into

Major-General Sir David Baird, later described by Wellington as 'a gallant, hard-headed, lion-hearted officer, but he had no talent, no tact'.

the heart of Spain, and thus run all risks, and share the fortunes of the Spanish nation; or I must fall back upon Portugal.' He made clear which he preferred without actually saying so: all his military training and experience rebelled against the hopeless march forward. 'By marching into Spain, I detach myself from my resources, and should, probably, be able to take with me but a small portion of the military stores I have brought

189

forward.' And even these stores were inadequate, owing to lack of resources back in Lisbon.

But Moore added another sentence, and this altered the whole situation. 'The question is not purely a military one; it belongs at least as much to you, as to me, to decide upon it.' Diplomatic considerations must also be taken into account, based upon the need to support the Spanish ally: and Frere had already made his opinion plain. Moore therefore pulled another sheet of paper towards him, this time to write to Sir David Baird. He overruled all Baird's sound arguments, and his own previous order, for halting the northern column at Astorga. 'I see my situation, and that of the army I command, in as unfavourable a light as you or any one can do. But...it is our business to make every effort to unite here, and to obey our orders and the wishes of the country to aid the Spaniards as far as it lies in our power. It would never do to retreat without making the attempt. If the enemy prevent us, there is no help for it; but if he does not, I am determined to unite the army.' The next step after the junction would depend upon circumstances, but Moore fully realized that by then he would be committed.

Yet while the courier galloped north from Salamanca with this letter to Baird, another messenger reined his horse before Moore's headquarters. Moore read news conveyed in the spidery handwriting of Mr Charles Stuart, acting minister in Madrid. The army under Castaños – the sole remaining Spanish force with any semblance of strength – had been crushed. Defeat had been inflicted five days before at Tudela, north-east of Madrid. The door to the capital and to Salamanca gaped wide. 'The French have 80,000 in Spain,' wrote Moore in his journal, 'and 30,000 were to arrive in twenty days from the 15th of this month. As long as Castaños' army remained there was hope, but I now see none.' Within an hour of receiving this news on the evening of the 28th, Moore summoned his staff for an urgent meeting. Officers sat silent at the long table; Moore stood before them and gave his decision. 'I have determined to withdraw the army.' The officers murmured in protest; Moore showed them the intelligence he had just received and allowed no opposition. 'I have not called you together to request your counsel, or to induce you to commit yourselves by giving any opinion on the subject. I take the responsibility entirely upon myself. I only require that you will immediately prepare for carrying it into effect.'

Moore began to write the necessary orders. First came a brisk, business-like despatch for Baird. 'It certainly was much my wish to have run great risks in aid of the people of Spain; but, after this second proof of how little they are able to do for themselves, the only two armies they had having made so little stand, I see no right to expect from them much greater exertions; at any rate we should be overwhelmed before they could be prepared. I see no chance of our being able to form a junction; as certainly at Burgos the French have a corps which will now move forward.' If possible, Hope would join Moore by forced marches; meanwhile Baird would fall back on Corunna. Similar orders left for Hope, and a brief despatch to Castlereagh was sent the following morning, 29 November.

But while Moore waited for Hope to struggle over to join him, and while his troops prepared to leave Salamanca, the situation once again began to change. Stuart wrote on the 30th to say that reports of enemy strength around Madrid were probably exaggerated, and that according to Spanish accounts a small force had inflicted considerable losses upon the French near Sepulveda. Romana was attempting to bring together remnants of Blake's defeated army, and wrote from Leon on the 30th, urging an early junction with Moore's army. 'I hope we shall soon be in a condition to make some movement. I wait for nothing but shoes to begin my march; for my troops are in the most complete state of nakedness that is imaginable, but their spirits are not depressed; and, by nourishing them well, they will do their duty.' Such a military appeal meant more to the British commander than the offensive letters which now began to arrive from Frere, but Moore told Stuart on 1 December that he would still retire. 'There is nothing so easy, as for the Junta, with their pens, to form armies; and they have I see in this manner collected one of 80,000 men in Leon. But Romana, who they have put down at 20,000, has only 5,000 fugitives from Blake, without arms, clothing, stores, or ammunition; without organisation, or officers to make any; the soldiers neither disciplined, nor susceptible of taking any; when checked, they go off...'

191

Pressures persisted. On 2 December two aged Spanish officers were shown into Moore's room, sent by Frere: Don Ventura Escalante, captain-general of the armies of Granada, and Brigadier-General Don Augustin Bueno. Both urged him not to retire and abandon Spain to the enemy, and tears glistened in their rheumy eyes. Fresh appeals arrived from Madrid. Reports flooded in, doubtless grossly exaggerated, of Spanish resistance elsewhere. Moore's officers sat at his dining table, and instead of their usual cheerful chatter they ate in silence. On 4 December the British troops under Hope reached Alba, just down the road, and Moore rode off to see his subordinate. Now he had artillery and cavalry within reach. He returned early on 5 December, perhaps the most fateful day of his life.

First he received a renewed appeal from the Central Junta, dated 2 December and containing 'a true and just representation of affairs at this moment': Castaños, with 25,000, would fall back on Madrid to join with 40,000 already at the capital and with 10,000 previously in the Somsierra region. 'With this number of troops the Enemy's army which has presented itself, is not to be feared.' The appeal continued: 'But the Junta, still apprehending an increase of the Enemy's force to unite with that at hand, hope that your Excellency, if no force is immediately opposed to you, will be able to fall back to unite with our army, or take the direction to fall on the rear of the Enemy.' Moore put the paper aside and continued his preparations: he placed no trust in Spanish words.

At 7.30 p.m. came an emissary from Frere. This messenger, Colonel Venault de Charmilly, had previously called at Moore's HQ and had been viewed with some suspicion – with justification: Charmilly had been involved in corruption, and so far in his career had been a coal-merchant, distiller, money-lender and bankrupt. Now he had been entrusted with an important letter. Frere at Talavera had clearly been influenced by a report of the state of affairs in Madrid brought to him by Charmilly. The capital had risen in opposition to the French; at last the people of Spain were taking up arms. Frere told Moore: 'I consider the fate of Spain as depending absolutely for the present upon the decision which you may adopt. I say *for the present*; for such is the spirit and character of the country, that, even if abandoned by the British, I should by no means despair of their ultimate success...' Moore read the letter in silence. His mind revolted at the manner by which it had been sent – in the hands of an untrustworthy, unofficial, and probably dishonest gentleman of fortune. Charmilly attempted to enthuse over the Madrid insurrection. 'It is now too late,' snapped Moore. Charmilly protested; Moore silenced his visitor with another terse sentence: 'I am very busy tonight.'

Hour after hour through the night Moore's anxious aides could see light from beneath his door. Then came an abrupt command; the General handed out a despatch to be rushed to Baird and closed the door again. He snuffed his candles; the decision had been made. 'My dear Sir David. The city of Madrid have taken up arms, have refused to capitulate to the French, are barricading their streets, and say they are determined to suffer everything rather than submit. This arrests the French; and people who are sanguine entertain great hopes from it – I own, myself, I fear this spirit has arisen too late.' But he added: 'There is, however, no saying...' Baird must therefore halt his withdrawal and prepare to move forward again to Astorga. Moore also detailed this plan in a despatch to Castlereagh. Earlier in the day he had written to the Minister informing him of his decision to retire, despite rumours of a Madrid insurrection; now the withdrawal would be delayed, though he held frail hopes for the Madrid rising, 'unless the spark catches and the flame becomes pretty general – and here [in Salamanca] the people remain as tranquil as if they were in... peace'. Moore rose from his couch before dawn and scratched another letter to Sir David. 'I wrote to you last night, to suspend your retrograde movement. I now write to you, to beg that you will put to the right about, and return bag and baggage to Astorga.' The British army would unite, and strike. The immediate line of advance would be northwards towards Benavente. 'The enemy have nothing to present in that direction; we must take advantage of it, and by working double tides make up for lost time.'

At last there would be action; despite the dangers Moore felt his spirits surge. But he needed all his good humour to see him through another meeting with Charmilly, who called to see him at noon on the 6th saying he had another message from Frere.

'And why did you not give it to me last night?' demanded Moore. Charmilly gave a hesitant reply: Frere had told him not to hand it over unless it seemed necessary. Now, ignorant of Moore's plans, he believed the time had come. Moore took it from his hands, and when Charmilly stammered more explanations he received the curt command: 'Sir, will you be so good as to go near the fire, and let me read that letter?' The message proved short and extremely insolent: Frere threatened Moore that his decision to withdraw would be taken to higher authority. 'In the event which I did not wish to presuppose, of your continuing the determination already announced to me of retiring with the army under your command, I have to request that Colonel Charmilly, who is the bearer of this, and whose intelligence has already been referred to, may be previously examined before a Council of War.' Moore frowned, then grinned – the impudence, and the irrelevance, appealed to his humour. Once again Charmilly scuttled from the room, with the General's laugh following down the corridor.

Moore sat down and took up his pen. He told Frere that he had already decided to halt the withdrawal and orders had been despatched. He made no direct reference to the content of Frere's threatening letter, but concluded: 'If Mr Charmilly is your friend, it was, perhaps, natural for you to employ him; but I have prejudices against all that class; and it is impossible for me to put my trust in him. I shall, therefore, thank you not to employ him any more in any communication with me.' Later he sent another scathing note. 'I neglected to mention to you . . . that the General Officers Escalante and Bueno had been with me.' The British commander dismissed these two Spanish veterans, whom he had seen on the 2nd, as 'two weak old men, or rather women, with whom it was impossible for me to concert any military operations, had I been so inclined'. He added: 'I shall be obliged to you to save me from such visits, which are very painful.'

Moore plunged thankfully into his military tasks. His young staff officers reacted with enthusiasm to the prospect of battle. The army would move as soon as possible. Yet Moore knew this advance could be towards complete destruction. He told Castlereagh: 'Your Lordship may depend upon it that I shall never abandon the cause as long as it holds out a chance of succeeding – but you must be sensible that the ground may be, in an instant, cut from under me. Madrid may fall, and I shall be left to contend with very superior forces indeed.' He had confided to Baird in his letter written early on the 6th: 'I mean to proceed bridle in hand; for, if the bubble bursts, and Madrid falls, we shall have a run for it.' Unknown to Moore, the French had issued a bulletin forty-eight hours before. 'The town of Madrid has capitulated; our troops entered it today at noon.' Even before his decision to advance, Moore had sent a strong warning to Lady Hester: 'We are in a scrape; but I hope we shall have spirit to get out of it. You must, however, be prepared to hear very bad news.' His closing words would cause terrible anguish to the reader. 'Farewell, my dear Lady Hester. If I can extricate myself and those with me from our present difficulties, and if I can beat the French I shall return to you with satisfaction; but if not, it will be better that I should never quit Spain.'

*   *   *

Not until 13 December could preparations for the advance be completed. Moore had waited as long as possible in his attempt to achieve some liaison with the Spaniards, but late on the 12th he told Castlereagh that he intended to move the next day. 'I have not heard from the Marquis of Romana, and must give up the co-operation of his corps for the present. Sir David Baird will not be at Astorga for some days, but he will advance to Benavente when ready, and as he will be in my rear he can come up, or I can fall back upon him, but I do not think it advisable longer to delay moving forward.'

By now Moore had learned that Madrid had fallen: an officer sent to the city had returned on the night of the 9th with the expected but nevertheless frightening news. Yet Moore believed that French troops would still be tied down in the Madrid area; insurrection apparently continued at Saragossa. He explained his plans in his letter to Castlereagh. 'I shall threaten the French communications, and create a diversion, if the Spaniards can avail themselves of it.' But he warned the Minister that he would be very heavily outnumbered, and would have to pull back if the enemy turned towards him.

British advance troops had begun to file from Salamanca on the 11th, and now the numbers swelled. Men were fit and rested; the weather remained clear and bright, though each night brought frost and the horses slithered on the hard-packed roads. Once again the infernal screech of the Portuguese carts filled the air, and squealed for miles across the bleak plateau north of Salamanca. For hours the men trudged across the plain, seeing few trees, hearing no birds, and with only occasional peasant mud hovels to break the monotony. Moore's headquarters staff rode from Salamanca at dawn on the 13th and soon caught up with the army. The British would move in two main columns, with the left heading to Toro for the junction with Baird's force, and the right making for Alaejos behind a thin cavalry screen. No sign could be seen of any enemy. After Alaejos would come Valladolid, if the French were not in the area, and from there Moore hoped to threaten enemy communications while keeping his own link open with Astorga and Galicia. But now came an abrupt change of plan.

A few days before, a French officer had been hacked down by peasants at the small village of Valdestillos near Segovia. Soon afterwards a British captain, Waters, had paid the partisans twenty dollars for the contents of the murdered man's sabretache; among the documents lay a letter from Berthier to Marshal Soult, who was in command of the 2nd French Corps at Saldaña. The message described Madrid as quiet; French troops were marching towards Badajoz. Soult was asked to clear the country between the Galicias and the Douro, and Berthier claimed that no Spanish troops could oppose this operation. And the English had withdrawn.

Sir John Moore leaped upon the opportunity now offered: the enemy apparently knew nothing of his whereabouts, while he had full details of theirs. Orders were immediately issued for a dramatic change of direction: all forces would march north-west towards Toro. Moore intended to slash direct at the unsuspecting Soult – no longer would he be content with merely threatening French communications. He dashed off a note to General John Cradock, who had been named commander in Portugal: 'Bonaparte takes for granted that the British are retiring on Lisbon – as soon as the army is united, I shall see what can be done against Marshal Soult.' But Moore added: 'If any

196

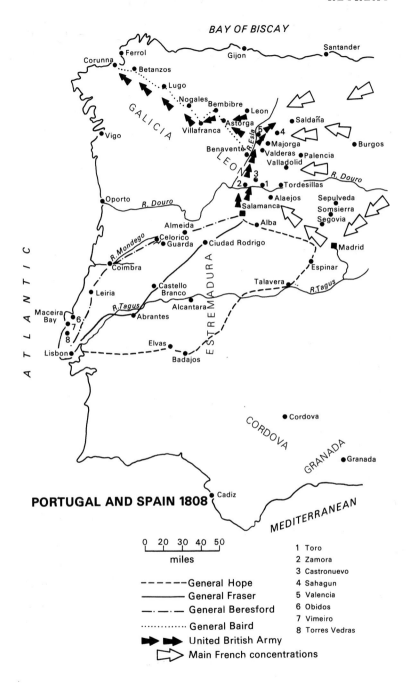

BAY OF BISCAY

PORTUGAL AND SPAIN 1808

```
0  20  30  40  50
      miles
```

-------- General Hope
———— General Fraser
—·—·— General Beresford
············ General Baird
▶▶ United British Army
▷ Main French concentrations

1 Toro
2 Zamora
3 Castronuevo
4 Sahagun
5 Valencia
6 Obidos
7 Vimeiro
8 Torres Vedras

circumstances oblige me to retreat, it will be on the Galicias.'
All available transports should therefore be sent to Vigo.

Moore reached Toro on the 15th and explained his change
of plan in a despatch to Castlereagh next day: Baird's first brigade had reached Benavente and the second would arrive
shortly. 'I shall march from this [place] tomorrow, to some villages within two or three leagues of Benavente. I shall there
be so close, as to be able to protect Sir David's junction... It
will be the 20th before all his Corps are up. If then Marshal
Soult is so good as to approach us, we shall be much obliged
to him, but if not, we shall march towards him. It will be very
agreeable to give a wipe to such a Corps.' He read through
this sentence, then changed the word 'wipe' to 'blow', making
the alteration with one of the newly invented pencils which
made writing in the field so much easier.

Moore allowed himself a moment of elation: Soult would
have about 18,000 men, while the united British army would
total twice as many; if he could strike first, then retire, he might
pull off a considerable victory and divert enemy attention from
the south, thus allowing Spanish forces to re-assemble. But the
British commander knew he would be placing his army in even
greater danger than before: he must avoid uncovering Astorga
hence jeopardizing his communications back through the
Galicias to Vigo or Corunna. And the risk might be in vain:
Soult might retire to join Junot, in which case the British would
be 'forced to desist'. Moore told Castlereagh: 'In short, unless
some great efforts, of which there is now but little probability,
are made by the Spaniards, it is evident how the business must
terminate. For, even if I beat Soult, unless the victory has the
effect to rouse the Spaniards, and to give their leaders ability,
it will be attended with no other advantage than the character
it will attach to the British arms.' And almost immediately
Moore learned that Romana, whom the Junta had claimed had
22,000 men, would be of minimum value: the Spanish general
sent a message to Moore saying he intended to retire into the
Galicias. If the British had to use the same roads, provisions
would be even more scarce.

Nevertheless the British moved on, deeper into enemy territory. Infantry regiments crossed the chilly Douro at Zamora
and Toro, with a cavalry screen fanning out to the east. The

Helmet belonging to Lieutenant-Colonel, later General, Rowland Hill, one of Moore's subordinate officers in Spain.

troops marched in dense columns to enable the army to proceed as quickly as possible. The pace increased. At each halt the men flung themselves to the frozen ground, until the sergeants shouted the advance again, then they staggered to their feet and began to march, 'looking neither to the right nor to the left'. Each halt became shorter; eleven-hour marches became common. By 17 December the British HQ had moved to Castronuevo. During the day Sir David Baird rode over from

199

Benavente to confer with Sir John. Baird, who had served in India with Sir Arthur Wellesley, was later described by the Duke of Wellington as 'gallant, hard-headed, lion-hearted, but he had no talent, no tact' and was inclined to be sulky; he now received a warm welcome from Sir John Moore. By the 19th the headquarters had shifted to Valderas, and next day stepped forward to Majorga. Men now had to shuffle through ten inches of snow. But at last Moore's units could join with Baird's – and Soult lay almost within reach.

On 21 December the army lumbered north-east towards the enemy at Sahagun, beneath skies which dawned grey and full of snow and which soon turned to black thunder-clouds. By early afternoon raindrops began to drum on the soldiers' capes; within an hour men were enduring sweeping sheets of rain, and lightning cracked overhead. Snow turned to slush and the horses and baggage carts churned the mess into mud; saturated soldiers hauled guns from ditches – and always came the command to keep moving. In front trotted the cavalry.

Lord Henry Paget and his hussars had the task of driving the enemy from Sahagun, and in doing so they brought about the first major clash of the campaign. Enemy scouts had given the alarm, and trumpets could be heard shrilling from the Sahagun streets as Paget's men came close. French dragoons burst from the houses to form line 400 yards from the advancing British cavalrymen, and down swooped Paget allowing no time for the enemy to organize. One officer described the shock of impact: 'Horses and men were overthrown and a shriek of terror, intermixed with oaths, groans, and prayers for mercy, issued from the whole extent of their front.' The French broke and fled with the 15th Hussars hard on their heels, firing as they went – one British cavalryman shot his own horse in his excitement. The army moved on into Sahagun, and Moore sat to write his journal: 'Lord Paget with the 10th and 15th Hussars by a night march surprised and defeated 600 or 700 of the French cavalry, took two lieutenant-colonels and 11 officers and 140 men. It was a handsome thing, and well done.'

Snowflakes were again floating down outside Moore's window and fog had fallen to muffle even the Portuguese carts. Moore had to permit a day's rest for his men, and to bring up provisions. He found time to write a letter to Frere. 'The movement I am making is of the most dangerous kind. I not only risk to be surrounded every moment by superior forces, but to have my communication intercepted with the Galicias. I wish it to be apparent to the whole world, as it is to every inhabitant of this army, that we have done everything in our power in support of the Spanish cause, and that we do not abandon it until long after the Spaniards have abandoned us.' During the afternoon of the 23rd, still at Sahagun, he brought his journal up to date. 'This night we march in two columns to Carrion, where I believe some of the French are. Next night I mean to march to Saldanha so as to arrive and attack at daylight; we start at eight this evening.' He closed his notebook and turned to final preparations for battle.

But disturbing reports were reaching the British head-quarters. Paget's brilliant action against the French cavalry had alerted Soult to his danger. Reinforcements were believed to be reaching his camp: provisions and forage were being pre-pared for the enemy in the villages in front of Palencia. It seemed Soult had determined to fight, and was gathering extra strength. Moore continued his arrangements. Then at 7 p.m., an hour before the army would begin to march, a Spanish peasant brought a message from Romana. Moore read the note as he sat on his horse in the pouring rain: the Spanish com-mander warned that agents had reported a mass movement of French from Madrid. Napoleon was leading his whole force north against the puny British army – and was already three marches along the road. Moore hurriedly dismounted and re-entered his headquarters; he tossed aside his dripping cloak and issued orders to countermand the advance. He had achieved his object of drawing the French from the south – with a success even greater than he had dared to hope – but this very success had brought tremendous peril to the British army. Now Moore must withdraw, if he could: the luxury of a 'wipe' at Soult could no longer be afforded.

Moore took up his journal again next morning, 24 December, as his troops began to leave the town, and he set out his reasons for his thrust north. 'For this, I was aware that I risked infinitely too much; but something, I thought, was to be risked for the honour of the service and to make it apparent that we stuck to the Spaniards long after they themselves had given up their cause as lost.' Troops could be heard marching beneath his window as he added: 'If we can steal two marches upon the French we shall be quiet; if we are followed close, I must close and stop and offer battle. At this season of the year, in a country without fuel, it is impossible to bivouac; the villages are small, which obliges us to march thus by corps in succession. Our retreat, therefore, becomes much more difficult.' Moore closed his journal; the remaining pages would stay blank, unmarked except by smeared mud and snow from the dreadful road to Corunna.

Chapter Ten

FIELD OF HIS FAME

'If only these 20,000 were 100,000!' gloated Napoleon. 'If only more English mothers could feel the horrors of war!' The Emperor believed the British to be trapped: outnumbered three to one, they would be encircled and annihilated.

Moore considered such a fate to be very possible, and at the same time had to contend with grumbles from those in his army who felt deprived of the expected clash with Soult, Duke of Dalmatia – known to the men as the 'Duke of Damnation'. A sixteen-year-old officer in the 42nd described the reaction among his Highlanders when Sir David Baird announced the retreat. 'The effect of the counter-order on our soldiers was the most extraordinary; and from the greatest pitch of exaltation and courage at once a solemn gloom prevailed throughout our ranks. Nothing was heard on every side but the clang of firelocks thrown down in despair, which before they guarded as their dearest treasure.' Troops filed sullenly from Sahagun at noon on Christmas Eve, ice crackling beneath their heavy feet. The young Scottish officer added another paragraph to his description: 'What a difference exists between the humour of an advancing and retreating army, especially when composed of English.' Not even Sir John Moore's skill at controlling men would be able to overcome this difference, and his failure to do so brought him terrible personal anguish – although no other British general would have been able to achieve even his limited success.

Generals Hope and Fraser led the way, heading their divisions towards Benavente and Majorga; next came Moore with the reserve, taking the same route and with Paget's cavalry acting as rearguard; meanwhile Baird would cut further north

Marshal Soult,
Duke of Dalmatia –
known to the
British troops as the
'Duke of
Damnation' –
Moore's immediate
enemy in Spain.

across to Valencia before proceeding to Astorga, where the two elements of the army would reunite. The first obstacle would be the Esla, to be crossed at Valencia and Benavente. The French were thrusting forward to intercept. On Christmas Day Napoleon rested his army at Tordesillas, fifty miles to the south, but Soult's cavalry pressed down the road behind Baird's infantry and began feeling out British strength.

Baird's first regiments reached Valencia and the Esla on the 26th; rain had now become continuous and the river appeared to be rising fast, but the men plunged across the ford and up the far bank, some soldiers sinking to their cross-belts in the icy mud. Further south, Moore and the rest of the army reached the Esla outside Benavente, and clattered across the stone bridge. Squadrons of enemy light cavalry had managed to slip through the screen provided by Paget, and the French horsemen could be glimpsed through the curtains of torrential rain. Two privates of the 43rd had been posted on high ground before the bridge, with orders to give the alarm should they see the enemy, but the day had become so dark that the French were on them before they knew it. One of the pair, John Walton, ran to warn his regiment, but the riders cut him down with no less than a dozen sabre slashes; yet he still managed to crawl on, half-alive. His companion stood and fought until the French withdrew, and he emerged unhurt with his uniform in ribbons and his red bayonet bent double, nicked like a saw. Men from Robert Craufurd's Light Brigade had been detailed to hold the bridge until the last stragglers had crossed, after which the structure would be blown up; enemy horsemen hovered like birds of prey, and Craufurd glowered back from above the turned-up collar of his drenched great-coat. For over a day the Light Brigade held the bridge; and it took the French a similar length of time to repair the stonework after they had gone.

Moore used the respite to rest his men at Benavente, and to condemn their behaviour so far. Discipline seemed to be breaking fast beneath the strain of the French pursuit, the discomfort of the weather, and the demoralization caused by retreat; men sought alcohol with a lust which almost made them berserk. 'The commander of the forces has observed with concern the extreme bad conduct of the troops,' declared the General Orders on 27 December. 'The misbehaviour of the troops in the column which marched by Valderas to this place exceeds what he could have believed of British soldiers.' The notice continued: 'It is impossible for the General to explain to his army the motive for the movement he directs... When it is proper to fight a battle, he will do it.'

'Today or tomorrow,' scribbled an over-confident Napoleon to Josephine, 'it is probable that great events will take place. If the English have not already retreated, they are lost; even if they have already moved they shall be pursued to the water's edge, and not half of them shall re-embark.' He demanded

Major-General Robert Craufurd, fiery and famous
commander of the Light Brigade, who relied upon
maximum discipline to keep control.

exaggerated publicity: 'Put in your newspapers that 36,000
English are surrounded, that I am at Benavente, in their rear,
while Soult is in their front.'

Moore's regiments began to pull out from Benavente, while
Baird continued along the road from Valencia in the north.
Ahead lay Astorga and possible battle. The British commander
outlined his plans in a despatch to Castlereagh from Benavente
on the 28th. He would leave with the reserve the following day,
while Lord Paget, of whom Moore spoke highly, would remain
to cover the retreat. 'The roads are very bad, and the means
of carriage scanty. If I am pressed . . . I may be forced to fight
a battle. This however I shall endeavour to avoid, for certainly
in the present state of things it is more Bonaparte's game than
mine. It is said that he comes himself, with 10,000 of his Guards.
The force moving against us cannot be less than 50,000 – we
should, when at Astorga, be about 27,000 . . . The country

about Astorga offers no advantage to an inferior army. I shall therefore not stop there longer than to secure the stores, and shall retreat to Villafranca, where I understand there is a position. But if the French press me, I must hasten to the coast.' The men poured out of Benavente, with smoke spiralling into the dark sky from burning buildings: even stores were having to be burned to prevent them falling into enemy hands – no time could be allowed for full distribution, but clothing and food lay piled by the roadside for the men to help themselves. Back in the town on 29 December the streets were deserted; civilians had fled indoors. Litter lay everywhere: priceless panellings and paintings, pulled out and half-burned to provide warmth, were jumbled with elegant tapestries, crumpled and torn after being used by men for blankets.

On the French side of Benavente the British cavalrymen waited. Enemy *chasseurs* trotted from the trees on the far side of the Esla ford and down to the river; one by one they started to cross and urged their horses onto the flat ground in front of the British cavalry. John Colborne, Moore's military secretary, had slipped away from the General's staff to observe the scene. 'Lord Paget galloped up twirling his moustachios, and said: "You see, there are not many of them!"' But the French continued to cross until up to five hundred had reached the near bank and formed into line. The first British charges were repulsed; on came the menacing Imperial *chasseurs* towards the Benavente suburbs. Paget rallied his straggling cavalrymen and took them behind the cover of nearby houses; he waited calmly while the French advanced two miles from the river. Enemy harness jingled louder and the British hussars and dragoons could hear Frenchmen calling to one another.

Then Paget gave a massive bellow, heeled his horse forward, and charged, with 450 men of the 10th Hussars and 200 men from the 18th Light Dragoons and the King's German Legion surging around him. The two lines crashed, sabres rising and falling, French and British fought knee to knee, horses and men screaming and dropping together; but the French broke first, reining round and spurring their mounts back towards the river. Paget's men swept after, cutting down the retreating enemy until survivors plunged into the flood to reach the far bank. They left fifty-five men dead or wounded; among the prisoners was their commander, General Comte Charles Lefèbre-Desnouettes, the Empress Josephine's 35-year-old nephew.

Moore received his illustrious captive with kindness and courtesy, washing and binding the Count's forehead which had been slashed by a British sabre, and lending his own clothing to replace his opponent's spoilt uniform. A flag of truce went across the river to seek the Count's baggage, and this returned in time for Desnouettes to change for supper. Moore asked him if he still lacked anything, and Desnouettes glanced at his side, missing his sword. Moore unbuckled his own and handed it across the table, to allow his guest to feel more comfortable.

Napoleon's forces pressed only fifteen miles behind the fleeing British along the road to Astorga. But Moore's columns were converging. Then came another setback: they would now have to use the same route as retreating Spanish forces, remnants of Romana's army scattered by Soult near Leon on 30 December. Provisions would be even less adequate. Moore reached Astorga on the 30th to find no stores: they had been eaten by Spanish troops, local civilians, or Baird's men on the outward march. 'I have no option now but to push down to the coast as fast as I am able,' wrote Moore to Castlereagh on the last day of 1808. 'There is not two days' bread to carry the army to Villafranca... There is no means of carriage, the people run away, the villages are deserted, and I have been obliged to destroy great parts of the ammunition and military stores. For the same reason I am obliged to leave the sick. In short, my sole object is to save the army.' He added: 'I hope to find on the coast, transports for the embarkation of the troops. If not, I hope to be able to take up some position, which I can sustain until they arrive.' At this stage Moore still hoped to be able to choose either Vigo or Corunna as a departure port.

In Astorga horrors began to multiply. Outside Moore's rough headquarters all seemed chaotic: the confusion was increased by thick fog filtering through the narrow crowded alleys. Miserable Spanish troops from Romana's defeated army served to demoralize British soldiers even further – these survivors were half-naked and disease-ridden. Rioters scattered the contents of houses, and passageways became jammed with baggage wagons, horses, bullock carts, cattle, once elegant carriages, and sobbing Spanish citizens. Many of the troops were already without boots; women and children who had accompanied the march wore clothes which were already tattered and totally unsuited to a harsh Spanish winter. Houses were ripped open in the search for fuel, and men and women huddled round the fires, wiping their eyes and averting their faces from the stinking fumes. Some fires were unattended, or too large, and started others, and the acrid smoke swirled through the streets with the fog. French advance detachments could be seen on the outskirts of the town when the fog lifted, small black groups against the white countryside. 'The chatter of the muskets in the distance,' wrote one eye-witness, 'and the monotonous staccato calls of the bugles, mustering the scattered rearguard together, mingled with the cries of the women praying to the Virgin and the uproar created by the cursing of the military . . .' A captain in a detachment which had already moved forward described the destruction soon to become commonplace. 'About five o'clock we reached a few miserable dwellings inhabited by horror-struck and famished peasantry. Close to them we halted, and piled our arms in the snow. There appeared neither wood nor water near us to cook our scanty morsel. Impatient to satisfy the urgent demands of nature, the men pulled down doors, carried away chairs, carts etc. from the isolated houses of the helpless natives.' The first regiments systematically stripped bare the countryside, leaving nothing for those behind. Many troops in Astorga became insensible with drink, and when the main body of the army pushed forward from the town on 1 and 2 January 1809, groaning soldiers and women lay sprawled about the streets in a drunken stupor, easy prey for the first French cavalrymen.

Moore knew he could do nothing with his army except urge and prod it through to the coast. Only there would the men find safety. Yet for a commander such as Sir John Moore, always so attentive to the well-being of those under him, the situation held especial torment. He knew the promise of battle might bring his regiments together again, and he was also aware that many had believed he would fight at Astorga; but the countryside around offered no defensive positions, and the Spanish rout had precipitated confusion. Moore's decision to

The retreat: Moore's army winds up into the harsh mountains; soon those baggage carts had to be abandoned in the face of the terrible Spanish winter.

210

press on fanned the discontent in his army and led to further deadening demoralization. Helpless, he could only retreat and watch with anguish the hell his men had now to suffer. He chose to march at the rear to supervise the rearguard actions and to keep his experienced eye on the French; in this position he had also to witness the worst of the agony and destruction. Always he tried to inspire confidence. 'During all this retreat Moore accompanied the reserve,' wrote one officer in the Rifle Brigade, 'and rode besides his friend General Paget, their chief. His cheerful demeanour sustained the spirits of the wayworn, suffering soldiers.' But even Moore could not be everywhere to cheer his troops, and his aides saw the other side: his face suddenly lined and worn, and tears in his eyes, as he slumped in the privacy of his own quarters at night. And now the mountains of Galicia loomed ahead, glaring white in the occasional sharp shafts of sunlight, more often dark and bleak and shrouded in boiling black clouds. Up stretched the road, thick with ice, winding and twisting towards the open jaws of death.

'The English are running away as fast as they can,' boasted Napoleon in Benavente. He decided it was safe to leave the scene and departed for Paris on 2 January, ordering Soult to complete the destruction. French forces were reorganized, leaving Soult with 25,000 infantry and 6,000 cavalry, with 16,000 men under Ney within supporting distance. Moore had about 25,000 soldiers still under arms, but this outnumbered total dropped daily. Morale had slumped even lower as the long line clawed up the mountain ridges like some monstrous mangled centipede. 'The silence was only interrupted by the groans of the men,' remembered one Highlander, 'who, unable to proceed farther, laid themselves down in despair to perish in the snow.' Survivors broke the arms and legs of fallen comrades as they stripped the clothes from the stiffened corpses.

By nightfall on New Year's Day, Moore and the rearguard reached Bembibre. Over a thousand men from the regiments in front had been left behind too drunk to move after wine-vaults had been smashed open. Moore watched from his horse as men of the reserve tried to force the stupefied men to move, kicking them and poking them with their bayonets. Most remained unconscious. The reserve moved on, with Paget's cavalrymen picking their way through the bodies: many were women, with wine dribbling from mouths and nostrils and freezing on their faces. And then came the French, trotting through the grey snow for the slaughter, hacking the backs of the prostrate men and women or climbing from their saddles to exercise themselves by raping the women or mutilating the men. One British straggler survived his treatment by the enemy and crawled back to the British lines, his blood-soaked shirt pulled over his head to keep the biting air from his wounds. 'It was impossible to distinguish a single feature,' wrote one officer. 'The flesh of his cheeks and lips was hanging in dollops, his nose was split, and his ears, I think, were cut off. In addition to his wounds, it is probable that his limbs were frost-bitten.' He staggered sobbing to a fire, knelt, and raked the burning embers to him with his bare fingers.

Moore tried to prevent further straggling by parading such victims before their regiments, as an example of what might happen to others. General 'Black Bob' Craufurd, who had been told to take his Light Brigade along the southern road from Astorga to Vigo, both to help protect the British flank and to ease congestion on the more northerly route, employed even stricter discipline. Two men were caught straying from their regiment: Craufurd immediately ordered a drum-head court-martial which sentenced the culprits to a hundred lashes each. The fiery commander heard another man muttering 'Damn his eyes!' and he too was ordered to be flogged – three hundred lashes. The rest of the men had to watch the first sentence being carried out, some of them with 'tears falling down their cheeks from the agony of their feet, and many were ill with dysentery'. First to be flogged was the man sentenced to three hundred lashes; his Irish wife, watching with the troops, stepped forward to cover the bloody mess which had been his back. Enemy troops were about to attack. The brigade shuffled on.

*   *   *

Behind the clerk on his high stool in the Downing Street office flickered a newly fed fire. The clerk rubbed his warmed hands, picked up his quill and proceeded to write orders for Sir John Moore. His elegant handwriting covered the page with tragic, bureaucratic nonsense. 'Sir. I am directed by Lord Castlereagh to desire you will direct the Chief Officer of the Commissariat Department under your order to have weekly returns made up of the supplies sent from England which are consumed, with a statement of the remainder left unconsumed and the period for which the consumable articles are calculated to be sufficient – and you will be pleased to order that a copy of such returns be transmitted to me by every opportunity...'

On the afternoon of 3 January the starving British rearguard turned to snap back at their pursuers. French troops led by General Colbert had become over-confident, thrusting onwards to force the defile before Villafranca and sweeping a squadron of the 15th Light Dragoons away from the vital bridge over the Cua. Moore hastily directed defensive action; a bombardment from the Horse Artillery and rolling musket volleys forced Colbert's men back from the bridge, and British detachments clung to the western bank to gain retreating time for the remainder of the army.

But at 4 p.m. came the steady beat of approaching French drums; leading battalions of additional French infantry struck at the defences just before dusk. French troops filtered forward and hand-to-hand fighting broke out in the houses and among the smoking rubble. General Colbert fell with a shot in his head; his aide-de-camp crumpled beside him. Still the enemy pressed on, and the cold night air was rent with shrieks and strangled sobs. Moore held to the last moment, then skilfully drew off his troops at 10 p.m. and the retreat continued throughout the wild windy hours of darkness. Sleet hissed and spat in the faces of the soldiers; men and carts slipped into the black chasms on either side of the track; horses' hooves, now unshod, spurted blood; men sucked leather for want of food. Lord Paget had ordered horses to be destroyed as soon as they were unable to keep up, and the hills echoed with shots as weeping troops slaughtered their mounts: if the enemy seemed too near the animals had to be despatched with knives or blows from hammers or stones.

The sixty miles from Villafranca up the sullen mountain spurs to the barren Lugo plateau proved the worst of the retreat. Blasts of icy wind punched men to the ground, and they crawled instead. Scores were now collapsing. 'The road was one line of bloody footmarks from the sore feet of the men,' wrote one veteran of the 71st, 'and on its sides were the dead and dying. Human nature could do no more.' He himself had almost given in and had only struggled forward after being encouraged by a comrade. But now his friend faltered. 'He as well as myself had long been bare-footed and lame; he that encouraged me to proceed, now himself lay down to die. For two days he had been almost blind ... We sat down together; not a word escaped our lips. We looked round – then at each other, and closed our eyes.' Fire from French advance dragoons drove him on again; his friend remained.

Some women and children had so far managed to survive, mothers carrying or dragging their infants and all with bare bleeding legs. They looked, commented one rifleman, 'like a tribe of travelling beggars'. A few women were pregnant; one slipped to the rear of her husband's straggling column, gave birth in a ditch, and caught up again carrying the baby – and both survived. The wife of a soldier of the 92nd took up another baby, born a few moments before his mother had died in a bloody snow-drift. A veteran of the 71st found the stiffened corpse of a young woman with a whimpering child still clinging to the mother's icy neck. 'One of General Moore's staff officers came up and desired the infant to be brought to him. He rolled it in his cloak, amidst the blessing of every spectator.'

But pity had become a rare emotion. A German commissary officer, Augustus Schaumann, saw a woman fall up to her waist in a sucking bog, and as she slid down through the slimy, freezing muck, the men behind her walked over her head. He described the scene on the 5th: 'Every minute a horse would collapse beneath its rider, and be shot dead. The road was strewn with dead horses, bloodstained snow, broken carts, scrapped ammunition, boxes, cases, spiked guns, dead mules, donkeys and dogs, starved and frozen soldiers, women and children ... The road frequently followed a zigzag course along the very edge of a precipice ... We waded through snow and mud over the bodies of dead men and horses. The howling wind, as it whistled past the ledges of rock and through the bare trees, sounded to the ear like the groaning of the damned ...'

Until now Moore still believed that he might cut south for embarkation at Vigo; the navy favoured this port. He preferred

Corunna because it gave better defensive positions from which to cover the departure, but he had deferred his final decision until he received the report of his engineer, Fletcher. The latter reported on the night of 5 January and agreed with Moore. Early next morning the British commander issued instructions for the army to make for Corunna. George Napier galloped off to take the order to the leading divisions, whose existing instructions were to branch onto the Vigo road at Lugo. The first division Napier met was Sir David Baird's, now at Nogales, and Baird, suffering from exhaustion, now made a terrible mistake. Napier's horse was blown; Baird would not give him another, but said he would see that the message continued forward. Reluctantly, Napier agreed and returned to the reserve. Baird sent on a drunken dragoon who lost the order. The leading regiment of Fraser's division had struggled nearly ten miles down the road from Lugo to Vigo before it could be recalled, and over 400 men perished during this useless exertion.

Sir John still struggled to keep his army together and moving at maximum pace: he tried coercion, exhortation and plain speaking: a General Order issued at the ramshackle town of Lugo on 6 January declared: 'Generals and commanding officers of Corps must be as sensible as the Commander of the Forces, of the complete disorganisation of the army... The Commander of the forces is tired of giving orders which are never attended to: he therefore appeals to the honour and feelings of the army he commands; and if those are not sufficient to induce them to do their duty, he must despair of succeeding by any other means.'

But Moore knew that only the prospect of battle would unite his men, and now, at Lugo, came such a possibility. Moore decided to defend the hills around the town, using the excellent positions provided by dry stone walls and winding hedges sloping down into the valley; to the right lay the unfordable Minho river and to the left spread inaccessible hills. The men were issued with pipe clay from the Lugo stores and ordered to whiten their belts, to be smart for battle, and they obeyed with typical grumbling – but as Moore had hoped and expected, they began to rally. Moore's personal magnetism could be seen in the way these troops, so dejected and exhausted, suddenly revived. Even though they now numbered no more than eigh-

teen thousand they remained superbly confident that under
Moore they would beat the French: at last the 'Duke of Damnation' could be dealt with.

Soult probed forward on the morning of the 7th, believing
he had once again run into Paget's heroic rearguard; French
guns were brought forward to batter a gap in the centre of the
British position, through which Soult intended to pierce four
squadrons of cavalry. But the first explosions on the hillsides
before him brought a jolting reply: fifteen British guns blazed
and blasted the French artillery into silence. Soult tried to
sweep round to the left, and managed to drive back outposts
of Leith's brigade. But Moore came up and rode in the midst
of his men, shouting encouragement, waving his hat and urging
the troops to use their bayonets. And so they did, cheering as
they stabbed into the French column and hurtling back the
enemy. Soult's men pulled back leaving four hundred
behind.

The French commander waited for reinforcements and
ordered Ney to detach a division to outflank the English on
the right – a move which Moore constantly feared though the
difficult country would delay the French attempt. The nervous
wait continued throughout the 8th, with the armies standing
to their arms beneath a slate-coloured sky; guns remained
silent. Moore knew it would be foolish to venture from his defensive positions and had to rely on Soult moving first – Soult
refused to oblige until his outflanking attempt had been
accomplished. At 10 p.m. Moore ordered the retreat; he could
delay no longer; his troops filed wearily from their defensive
positions and took to the road. Grumbling immediately increased, with troops cursing the enemy, the foul weather, their
ill-fortune, and even their commander.

But one wise sergeant had the sense to understand Moore's
reasons for avoiding further conflict. 'This was a season of singular and almost unexampled peril,' he wrote in his memoirs. The
British army 'was not in a condition to fight more than one
battle. It was unprovided with draught cattle, had no means
of transporting reserve ammunition, no magazines, no hospitals, no second line, no provisions ... The state of the magazines decided the matter; for there was not bread for another
day's consumption in the stores at Lugo.' And in Napier's

Eye-witness painting by a captain in the 88th of part of the British rearguard crossing the Constantine bridge, on the way down to Corunna.

words: 'A defeat would have been ruin, a victory useless.'

Moore's temporary stand had in fact been extremely valuable: Soult now knew his opponent could still bite; his own men were suffering from exhaustion, the weather and lack of supplies. From Lugo onwards the pressure on the British rearguard lessened, and Moore had gained time which he would use to excellent advantage at Corunna.

Nevertheless, fresh terrors lay ahead for Moore's army. A vicious storm of howling wind and sleet-thickened rain burst upon the British as they retired from Lugo; lamps set to mark the line of march were blown or washed out, and guides lost their way. Men stumbled through the night, falling into ditches where many were so weak that they drowned, unable to summon the strength to climb out. Only one division gained the main road, the other two split apart, and the rear columns were still near Lugo when pale daylight came. Fortunately the enemy could not begin to advance until late on the 9th, and even then at a slower pace.

Food again proved scarce, although some salt fish and rum rations were handed out during the day – with unfortunate effect. 'As we had neither fires nor kettles,' wrote Schaumann, 'the salt fish was eagerly swallowed raw, while the rum ... was poured down afterwards. The combination of the two in empty stomachs resulted in the death of many of the men on the spot, while several others went mad. One of them took up a defiant attitude ... in the middle of the road, and with fixed bayonet shouted that he was General Moore, that the army was to halt, turn and give battle, and the first man who dared to pass him by and disobey his orders he would kill outright.' Cavalry rode over him and left his mangled body in the mud.

Men hobbled on, clutching their rags around them, lifting flayed feet for one tortured step after another, no longer conscious of companions who suddenly collapsed besides them, no longer caring or hoping for an end to their agony. Napier believed that the march from Lugo to Betanzos cost the army in stragglers more than double the men lost so far in the retreat. Casualties came from the weather and from exhaustion: Moore had eased the French pressure, but could do nothing to save his men from the greater enemy. 'We came down from the hills more dead than alive,' remembered one foot soldier. 'If it had not been for the promise of food when we got down to the sea, we would never have done it.' But the army struggled through Betanzos on 10 January, and beyond the next hill the road wound down to Corunna and the coast. Retreat had almost ended.

The heights had been crossed. Winds became more gentle, and the men stumbled down past fields which began to show green. They came to the plain and the clouds parted, and around them the orange trees were already in flower and the rye in ear. They felt soft grass beneath their raw naked feet. Stores had been hurried out from Corunna. Soon they would sail from cursed Spain. 'Whenever we gained the summit of a hill,' wrote a captain, 'all eyes were on the watch to catch a glimpse of the ships.' And then they saw masts, and an officer with a spy-glass shouted that from the riggings fluttered the flags of the Royal Navy.

Soldiers straightened their backs, picked up their feet, and on 11 January marched down to the bridge across the tidal Mero at Burgo. Sir John Moore waited for them beside the road to see them come. 'Every commanding officer headed his regiment, and every captain and subaltern flanked his regularly formed section. Not a man was allowed to leave the ranks until a regular halt took place. But the evil attending irregular marching was past and irreparable; unfortunately this soldier-like manner of marching was resorted too late to be of much effect.' One by one the regiments passed their commanding general. He spoke to their officers, congratulating some, casti-gating others. At 3 p.m. he saw one of the last brigades coming towards him, the smartest he had yet inspected: these soldiers were marching in column of sections, drums rattling, shoulders back, with the drum-major twirling and throwing his staff. 'These must be the Guards,' commented Moore correctly. Then came General Paget with his indefatigable rearguard.

Engineers ran forward to blow up the bridge after them. Only the day before these engineers had failed in their attempt to destroy the bridge at Betanzos, and Paget had bawled at the officer in charge: 'What, Sir! What! Another abortion!' This time the engineers made sure, using such a massive charge that huge chunks of masonry were sent hurtling through the air and a tremendous noise echoed round the Corunna hills. One man was killed by a rock which almost sliced him in half, and accord-ing to one eye-witness the flying debris 'caused what the whole of Soult's cavalry could not effect during the retreat. The light company of the 28th and Captain Cameron's company of the 95th broke their ranks and ran like turkeys.' But at least the French would now be checked.

Moore rode into Corunna and to his balconied headquarters on the Canton Grande. From there he could see the bay – but insufficient ships. Those in the harbour were mainly hospital and store vessels: the main transport fleet had still to arrive. The French would reach Corunna before embarkation could be completed. A battle would have to be fought.

*   *   *

Moore left his quarters soon after dawn on the 12th to spend a hard day organizing his men into immediate defences and studying positions for the coming clash. He disliked what he discovered. The town itself was weakly fortified, though suffi-ciently strong to oblige an enemy to break ground before it, and to the south the area would be commanded by heights close

220

to the walls. Nor did the surrounding countryside offer much satisfaction. A chain of rocky hills, running from the coast north-west of Corunna to the Mero mountain, offered a good defensive line, but Moore had too few troops to hold such an extended range, and if not wholly occupied the French might turn it to the right. Moore had no choice but to use a lower and smaller range, almost encircled by the other and within cannon range of the higher hills. The British left flank would be protected by the Mero estuary, but inland the ground levelled, making the army vulnerable to a turning movement which could cut the British off from Corunna. Moore therefore decided to deploy more than a third of his force to serve as a flank-guard on his right, initially positioned close to the town.

Corunna – a sketch found tucked in a copy of *Moore's Campaign in Spain*, written by his brother James.

Preparations for battle and for embarkation continued. During the night of the 12th and in daylight on the 13th a series of explosions thundered through the air and shattered windows, blasts of hot air knocking men backwards: magazines were

221

A sketch by Sir Robert Kerr Porter: the magazines outside Corunna are blown up to prevent their falling into French hands.

being blown up, including a huge reserve of powder sent by the British to help the Spaniards. Corunna itself had become 'one uninterrupted bustle'. According to one officer: 'Whole troops of young and beautiful girls go in procession with baskets on their heads, carrying ammunition to forts and to batteries, and it looks wonderfully fine.'

The bulk of naval transports had begun to arrive, and initial embarkation started – the sick, dismounted cavalrymen, the best of the surviving horses and fifty-two pieces of artillery. Moore intended to fight the battle virtually without cavalry, which would anyway be of limited value in the broken terrain, and without artillery, except for eight British and four Spanish guns: there might not be time to load the rest after the battle. Horses were dragged unwillingly to the boats; others, less fit but equally loved by their riders, many of whom owed their lives to their horses, were being slaughtered or turned loose. One trooper unsaddled his mount for the last time, slapped the animal's haunches to send him away, and turned to his boat, only to find his horse plunging into the water like a dog behind him. Twice the animal struggled to the transport vessel, but could not be taken on board. 'All those who witnessed this incident had tears in their eyes.' Men could feel pity again.

Moore closeted himself in his quarters on the morning of the 13th, while the tumult continued around him. He sat to write

222

a despatch to Castlereagh, his first since 31 December, and his words made sad reading. 'Situated as this army is at present, it is impossible for me to detail to your Lordship the events which have taken place since I had the honour to address you . . . Your Lordship knows that had I followed my experience as a military man, I should have retired with the army from Salamanca . . . I was sensible however that the apathy and indifference of the Spaniards would never have been believed, that had the British been withdrawn, the loss of the cause would have been imputed to their retreat, and it was necessary to risk the army, to convince the people of England, as well as the rest of Europe, that the Spaniards had neither the power nor the inclination to make any efforts for themselves.'

He had harsh words to say about his soldiers, whom he loved so much. 'I am sorry to say that the army, whose conduct I had such reason to extol in its march through Portugal and in its arrival in Spain, has totally changed its character since it began to retreat. I would not have believed, had I not witnessed it, that a British army would in so short a time, have been completely disorganised. Its conduct during the late marches has been infamous beyond belief. I can say nothing in its favour, but that when there was a prospect of fighting the enemy, the men were then orderly, and seemed pleased, and determined to do their duty.'

Moore wrote under great strain; his eyes were ringed with weariness. His exhaustion showed in his letter: some words were omitted, others misspelt, and his writing was even more illegible than usual. Sentences were smudged and the ink ran blotchy. He assured Castlereagh that he would refuse terms dishonourable to Britain, but he warned that 'my position in front of this place is a very bad one' and described the situation as critical. He added: 'I have written under interruption and with my mind much occupied with other matters – my letter written so carelessly, can only be considered as private – when I have more leisure I shall write more correctly . . .' Moore scrawled his signature across the bottom of the third page, the nib spluttering ink in his haste. He threw down his pen and hurried from his table. This letter would be his last communication with Castlereagh; those scribbled words were probably the last he ever wrote.

Now battle would bring a chance of redemption for the British troops. Moore seemed inexhaustible, riding from one defensive position to another, talking to his men and cheering them up, issuing orders, correcting dispositions; or he supervised the embarkation of all available men from the harbour, returning to his room only to snatch meals or brief his officers. He remained cheerful. One officer who had come in with the fleet described him during these tense days: this newcomer had presented himself to Moore, 'who received me most kindly, and notwithstanding the cruel anxiety he must have suffered, still supported that most engaging exterior so endearing to his friends, and so prepossessing to strangers on whom he did not think it proper to frown'.

Hectic activity continued throughout the 14th and 15th; agents brought in reports of increased enemy preparations on the Mero mountain, and fresh columns moving towards the front. Moore slumped on his couch late on the 15th, leaving orders that he should be woken as soon as his military secretary, thirty-year-old John Colborne, returned from a reconnaissance mission. The young officer returned at three o'clock next morning and struggled to rouse his general. 'It's Colborne, Sir. Colborne.' The words had to be repeated before Moore stirred, but when he did so it took him only a moment to be fully awake. He plied Colborne with questions as he pulled on his boots and crammed food into his mouth. He walked to the door and turned back to Colborne. 'Now, if there's no bungling,' he declared, 'I don't see why we should not all be off safely tomorrow.'

Dawn broke as Moore visited the forward outposts along the ridge below Monte Mero. The ground was hard under his horse's hooves, and breath from the animal's nostrils almost froze in the keen air. Mists swirled from the enemy positions in front as Moore scanned the hillside for signs of enemy activity. He snapped his telescope shut: the French were motionless. Embarkation could continue. Moore stayed in the front lines until 10 a.m., talking to his men, then rode back down to the harbour leaving orders for three guns to be fired if the enemy appeared about to move forward. At the sea-front Moore gave instructions for the final retirement of the main army to the hundred transports now riding the swell in the sparkling bay; this last withdrawal would take place during the night. But at noon the reserve received orders to march for the harbour: as they had distinguished themselves during the retreat, Moore had decided to reward them by giving them the chance to choose the most comfortable berths on board. The men sang as they marched.

Just before 2 p.m. Moore mounted his cream and black stallion to ride back to the lines before Monte Mero; he was about to put spurs to his horse when three guns boomed from the slopes beyond Corunna. The French were moving. Moore and his staff galloped through the reserve units, which had already been turned from their march to the harbour and were now being hurried back to battle. One of the staff officers noted Moore's face, and could hardly believe it possible 'for a man so worn down with fatigue and anxiety to have been so transformed. It was a transition from fixed gloom bordering almost on despair, to a state of exaltation.' Only the previous day another officer had seen him staring 'wistfully at the enemy, apparently wishing with painful eagerness for a battle'. Now a messenger on a lathered horse brought a report from General Hope: 'The enemy's lines are getting under arms.' But the report had already been rendered out of date. French *tirailleurs* – light troops – had swarmed down onto the lower slopes to surge about the British advance picquets, and these forward posts had begun to fall back. Behind the *tirailleurs* three dense columns of enemy infantry could be seen, and the noise of rattling drums was abruptly drowned by the thunder from French supporting guns.

Both sides had about the same number of men, 15,000, but the French had greater artillery strength, and Soult clearly intended to make full use of this superiority. Cannons belched at the British lines, with salvo after salvo of round-shot screaming into the waiting ranks of British troops. One enemy column pushed towards the left, another towards the centre, and the third and strongest in the direction of the British right, where Moore had expected the main attack to be concentrated. The British commander had confidence in the ability of the extra men on the right, commanded by Fraser and covered by Paget, so he galloped towards the village of Elvina in the centre. He

Corunna: the battle in the broken ground by the vital village of Elvina.

judged correctly that Elvina would be the pivot of the battle, and the place where he would be most needed.

Even before he reached the conflict he had examined enemy movements, guessed Soult's intentions, and issued the requisite orders. He could see eight regiments of French cavalry trotting from behind the infantry stumbling towards Elvina; these horsemen seemed to be moving towards the British right, as if to sweep behind the line and severe communications with Corunna. Moore immediately despatched an officer with orders for Fraser and Paget: the first should check the turning movement by advancing out of the Corunna suburbs into prepared positions on the heights of Santa Margarita, while Paget should move up towards San Cristobal, to attack the enemy flank when he judged a suitable moment had arrived. Then Moore spurred his horse on again.

The General was indeed sorely needed in the centre. French infantry had pushed down the steep slope before Elvina, and

226

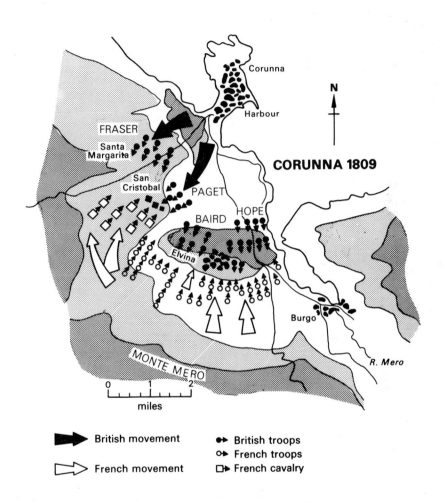

CORUNNA 1809

British movement

French movement

British troops
French troops
French cavalry

Corunna – British troops begin the counter-attack just before Moore falls. British defenders could hear excited French voices – '*En avant! En avant!*' and even more shrill: '*Tuez! Tuez! Tuez!*' Round-shot continued to batter the British defences, until the cannon-ade suddenly died, to be replaced by myriads of musket bullets humming and hissing among the stone walls, ricocheting from the rocks, thudding into wood and turf. British soldiers tried not to cower before the fusillade, but more and more threw up their arms and dropped to the ground. First one house on the outskirts of the village fell, then another, and it seemed the British line might crumble before the French advance. And then Moore arrived.

Charles Napier described the scene. 'All were anxious for the appearance of Sir John Moore. There was a feeling that under

228

him we could not be beaten, and this was so strong at all times as to be a great cause of discontent during the retreat wherever he was not. "Where is the General?" was now heard along that part of the line where I was...Suddenly I heard the gallop of horses, and turning, saw Moore. He came at speed, and pulled up so sharp and close, he seemed to have alighted from the air; man and horse looking at the approaching foe with an intenseness that seemed to concentrate all feelings in their eyes...Thrown on its haunches, the animal came sliding and dashing dirt up with its forefeet, thus bending the General forward almost to its neck; but his head was thrown back, and his look more keenly piercing than I ever before saw. He glanced to the right and left, and then fixed his eyes intently on the enemy's advancing column, at the same time grasping the reins with both his hands, and pressing the horse firmly with his knees. His body thus seemed to deal with the animal while his mind was intent on the enemy, and his aspect was one of searching intenseness beyond the power of words to express. For a while he looked, and then galloped to the left, without uttering a word.'

But after Moore's temporary departure the French came on and threw the British from Elvina. The General rode back and Napier sought permission for his Grenadiers to advance. 'No,' said Moore, 'they will fire on our own picquets in the village.' 'Sir, our picquets, and those of the 4th regiment also, were driven from thence, when you went to the left.' 'Were they! Then you are right. Send out your Grenadiers.' Napier turned to a waiting officer. 'Clunes, take your men and open the ball.' And the British began to strike back. Moore slipped away again, to reappear almost immediately – in his usual fashion he seemed to be everywhere. The ground near him was churned by French shells; a round-shot struck the soil between Napier and Moore, and the General was still controlling his shying horse when another shot ripped off the leg of a nearby soldier. The man screamed horribly, wrote Napier, 'and rolled about so as to excite agitation and alarm with others. The General said, "This is nothing, my lads. Keep your ranks. Take that man away. My good fellow, don't make such a noise; we must bear these things better." He spoke sharply, but it had good effect, for this man's cries had made an opening in the ranks, and the men shrunk from the spot... But again Moore went off, and I saw him no more...'

One regiment, the 4th, seemed in danger of being outflanked, and these men formed the end of the whole line. Paget had still to move up in support. Moore immediately directed the 4th to throw back its right wing at right angles to its front, thus protecting the flank. Despite artillery and incessant musket shot, the 4th executed the movement with perfect parade-ground precision. Moore stood in his stirrups and yelled: 'Well done! That's exactly how it should be done!' Then he cantered back to the centre to organize a counter-attack by the 50th and 42nd against the enemy in Elvina. He placed himself at the head of the 42nd and called the advance. 'My brave Highlanders!' he shouted. 'Remember Egypt! Think on Scotland!' The Highlanders formed line, raised muskets, spewed a devastating volley into the French; then they charged. Over the field they went and through the houses, lunging with their bayonets, disembowelling all who stood before them and driving the French back until checked by a high stone wall. Men from the 50th also plunged forward, with similar slaughter. 'Well done 50th!' exclaimed Moore from the thick of the fight. But the British troops were winded and scattered, and back came the French with reinforcements. Elvina fell again; the 42nd and 50th were spent and the bodies of Highlanders lay heaped behind the walls and houses; Moore sent a staff officer rushing for support.

Above, the sun started to sink on this winter's afternoon, shining through the smoke; down in the harbour troops in the naval transports crowded the gunwales to see the battle on the slopes above them: thin skeins of men, blue and red, running and advancing and criss-crossing through the murk to the sound of shrill bugles and crashing cannon. Minute by minute the French bombardment continued, and the sky seemed thick with shot and shell. Moore ordered a diversion by Guardsmen to ease pressure on the 42nd until help came, but then disaster almost struck. Some of the 42nd began to pull back, believing the Guardsmen had come to relieve them, and a crack appeared in the thin British line. Moore, as always, was there to repair the flaw. 'My brave 42nd. Join your comrades. Ammunition is coming, and you still have your bayonets.' Back they went,

Corunna – the
French lines
advance against
Moore's positions.

Moore raising his hat to them as they returned; the line held.
At the same time tumult increased on the right: Paget had
begun his counter-attack. A staff officer found Moore 'in the
best of spirits, as the troops everywhere stood firm'. The commander and the soldiers had achieved the apparently impossible: the army which had degenerated into almost a rabble on
the road to Corunna now fought courageously and calmly with
peak efficiency.

But British losses increased at each enemy artillery salvo.
Men lay strewn in the reeds and amongst the rocks, and severed
limbs marked the bloody spots where French fire had ruptured
the British positions. Out in front the wounded screamed for
help, and the men in the rigid British lines had to stand and
watch them. Always the French guns boomed; Napier tried to
cheer his men: 'Don't duck,' he told them. 'The ball has passed
before you hear the whizz.' Still the soldiers instinctively
lowered their heads – except for one man, so short he only came
to his comrades' shoulders. Napier promised to make him a sergeant after the battle but never saw him again. Musket fire continued, and round-shot skimmed the crest of the ridge and
bounced across the torn turf to roll red-hot against the tight

Moore receives his
fatal wound. British ranks. General Sir David Baird, second-in-command, quit the battlefield supported in his bloody saddle and with his right arm mangled by grape-shot. And now General Sir John Moore was suddenly flung from his shrieking horse.

He fell heavily on his side. For a second he lay there, then struggled to raise himself. He uttered no cry, and not a muscle on his face altered. Officers hurried from their horses and clustered round. At first they believed him unhurt; Colonel Graham, kneeling beside him, noticed how composed his features were. And then they turned him on his back and saw the mess spurting through the scarlet uniform on his left breast and shoulder. The whole of his side was already saturated with blood. A round-shot had punched a hole so deep that the lung lay exposed; a thick piece of uniform had been driven far into the gaping wound still with two buttons attached, the ribs over the heart and part of the collar-bone had been splintered, his chest muscles had been torn into long strips, which had sprung apart and then tangled together with the force of the blow; the left arm only remained linked to his body by the sleeve of his coat and thin shreds of skin. Moore, fully conscious, squeezed his aide's hand as he tried to turn to see the Highlanders. The 42nd were advancing. Moore said nothing, but smiled gently with satisfaction. Officers and men dragged him to the shelter of a bank, where a surgeon examined his wound and muttered 'hopeless'. Moore knew it. 'My good man,' he whispered, 'you can do me no good, it is too high up.'

He agreed to be taken to the rear and chose to be carried on a blanket, perhaps not as jolting as a waggon. 'We shall keep step and carry you easy,' said a huge Highlander. As they lifted him his sword jabbed up into the wound, and an aide started to unbuckle the belt. Moore stopped him. 'It is as well as it is. I'd rather it should go out of the field with me.' He told surgeons to leave him. 'You can be of no service to me. Go to the wounded soldiers to whom you may be useful.' As the soldiers carried him away from the battle he kept asking them to stop and turn him round to face the front, so that he could listen to the firing. All seemed to be well; the British were advancing. Moore's bearers continued, tears streaming down their grimy cheeks. Schaumann witnessed the scene in Corunna. 'Among many wounded men who were borne past us into the town there appeared at about 4 o'clock a party of several *aides-de-camp* and officers, marching very slowly and sadly behind six soldiers bearing a wounded man in a blood-stained blanket slung upon two poles . . .' Moore was lifted carefully into a darkened headquarters room, now deserted, all belongings having already been taken on board including the General's personal items.

His pain had intensified and he could scarcely speak, though he whispered to his shocked servant: 'My friend, this is nothing.' But to his faithful companion he gasped: 'Anderson – don't leave me.' Paul Anderson knelt beside his mattress on the floor, holding his hand tight. The spasm eased and Moore muttered: 'You know, Anderson, I have always wished to die this way.' His face remained calm, but had turned pale as marble; his eyes stayed bright and his mind alert. To everyone who crept into the room he asked: 'Are the French beaten? Are they beat?' The enemy had indeed begun to pull back; fighting had dwindled into desultory artillery fire with the French unable to batter the British into submission. Back in the headquarters room, heavy with the sickly scent of blood, Moore croaked again; Anderson had to bend low to catch the words. 'You will see my friends as soon as you possibly can. Tell them everything. Say to my mother . . .' His head fell back; a clergyman dropped on his knees opposite Anderson and began to mumble prayers. But Moore began to whisper once more, his mind at last beginning to wander. 'Is Paget in the room?' 'No', answered Anderson. 'Remember me to him. It's General Paget I mean. He's a fine fellow.' Then came a further terrible pause before the soft voice added, as if in apology: 'I feel myself so strong. I fear I shall be a long time in dying.' Another pause; then another whisper: 'It is great uneasiness. It is great pain.' At about 8 p.m. he uttered his last words. 'Stanhope,' he said to Lady Hester's brother. 'Remember me to your sister.' He pressed Anderson's hand tight to his body, and died. His young staff officers, faces white beneath the stains of cannon powder and sweat, covered their eyes and sobbed aloud.

* * *

General Hope, commander after the departure of Moore and Baird, considered the embarkation of the army his first responsibility, and undertook no offensive movement after the retiring French. The Battle of Corunna closed with both sides occupying their original positions. But Moore's purpose had been achieved: the remaining British troops were taken on board during the night and throughout the next day, 17 January. Exhausted soldiers moved back, still in good order but with uniforms in rags, covered with blood and filth, and their faces gaunt. Citizens made the sign of the cross as they passed. The French were too weakened to follow, although a few detachments moved cautiously forward on the 17th; at 8 p.m. one or two guns bombarded the fleet. Soon after, Sir John Moore's body was carried to the landward bastion of Corunna citadel and buried in a shallow grave. No coffin could be prepared, and the tall figure was merely wrapped in the General's soiled military cloak. Later, when the French occupied

Corunna, Soult ordered guns to be fired over Moore's grave in honour of his opponent.

Within a week the fleet had brought the British army home. Up to 6,000 men had perished in the retreat to Corunna and a further 600 had fallen during the final battle. Some of Moore's troops were landed in English ports during the hours of darkness to avoid alarming local inhabitants by their fearful appearance; most received a joyful welcome. With them came news of the death of Sir John Moore.

Immediate controversy arose, with Whigs championing Moore against the Tory ministry, and the Tories attacking the fallen general in return. The outcry continued despite a glowing General Order issued from the War Office on 1 February: 'The benefits derived to an army from the example of a distinguished Commander do not terminate at his death; his virtues live in the recollections of his associates, and his fame remains the strongest incentive to great and glorious action.' Moore had declared in his last despatch: 'I cannot think, after what has happened, that there can be any intention of sending a British force again into Spain.' On 22 April the arrival of Sir Arthur Wellesley in the Peninsula proved Moore incorrect.

Yet Sir John paved the way for this second, and ultimately triumphant, attempt. Wellesley's orders benefited from mistakes made with Sir John Moore: no more would British forces be sent on an ill-prepared mission over the Portuguese frontier. Further, Moore's desperate decision to strike north from Salamanca, despite the terrible dangers, rather than retiring as his military wisdom cried out for him to do, gave the Spaniards in the south valuable breathing time. Even more important, the move helped stimulate Spanish resistance, and left a legacy of British willingness to support her ally. If Napoleon had overrun the entire country at that time, the Spanish will to resist might have collapsed – and Wellington could not have succeeded without the assistance of the guerrillas. Years later Wellington admitted: 'D'you know, Fitzroy, we'd not have won, I think, without him.'

On 24 February 1809 George Ponsonby failed in his attempt to force a House of Commons inquiry into the decision to send an army into Spain. His motion was defeated by ninety-three votes. It would perhaps have been better for Sir John

Sashes used to lower Moore's body into the hastily-dug grave; buttons and a piece of cloth from his uniform; the sword worn by Moore at the Battle of Corunna.

Burial of Sir John Moore by Thomas Ballard, depicted with the help of a description given to the artist by the Reverend H. J. Symons who officiated at the hurried ceremony.

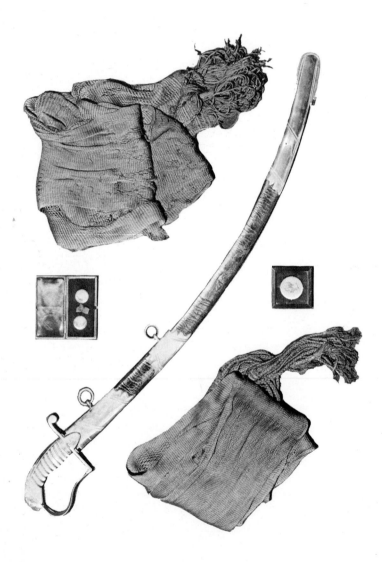

236

Moore's reputation if Ponsonby had won: at least the facts surrounding the whole sad and hopeless situation in which Moore had been placed might then have been revealed. Instead, his brilliant skills were eclipsed. His very character attracted ill-feeling from jealous individuals who could not match his virtues: not until 140 years later, with General Harold Alexander, would Britain have a military leader so completely uncorrupt and incorruptible. And Moore, perhaps the greatest tactical commander in the history of the British army, who had begun to display strategic ability at least on a level with Wellington, became chiefly remembered in history through poetic verse.

Within days of his death poems were appearing in print to honour his name. By and large these elegiac efforts were as sentimental and unrealistic as the monument later erected in St Paul's Cathedral. The first appeared in the February issue of *The Gentleman's Magazine*: 'In length of days, and life's enjoyments, poor/Yet rich in highest honours – here lies Moore ...' Another came in March: 'How are the mighty fallen! how sunk the brave!/In haste committed to a foreign grave ...' Fortunately these soon disappeared. Then, eight years after Corunna, an obscure Irish curate named Charles Wolfe succeeded in having eight stanzas published anonymously in *The Newry Telegraph*. Despite inaccuracies, the atmospheric flavour of the poem makes it a fitting memorial to Sir John Moore. Later it would be chanted by hundreds of boys and girls performing their party pieces in Victorian and Edwardian parlours. The poem became far better known than the general.

> Not a drum was heard, not a funeral note,
> As his corse to the rampart we hurried;
> Not a soldier discharged his farewell shot
> O'er the grave where our hero was buried ...

ACKNOWLEDGEMENTS

The photographs and illustrations in this book are reproduced by kind permission of the following. Those on pages 91, 97 and 98, by gracious permission of Her Majesty the Queen; pages 25, 43, 79, 96, 112, 130, 132, 164, 199, 218, 228, 231 and 232, National Army Museum; pages 12, 14, 28–9, 32, 53, 64, 76–7, 92–3, 110–11, 136 and 145, National Maritime Museum; pages 18–19, 60, 66, 120, 123, 129, 134, 154, 186 and 189, National Portrait Gallery; pages 41, 57, 148, 163, 166, 171, 177, 181 and 222, Trustees of the British Museum; pages 8–9, 82, 102, 142, 204 and 226, Radio Times Hulton Picture Library; pages 131, 206 and 236, The Royal Greenjackets; pages 221 and 237, Junior Infantrymen's Battalion, Shorncliffe; pages ii and 119, Scottish National Portrait Gallery; pages 210–11, J. S. Dickinson; page 2, from *Glasgow Memorials* by Robert Renwick; page 3, Victoria and Albert Museum; page 5, photo: Country Life; page 22, Colonel C. B. C. Anderson; page 36, Shorncliffe Military Library; page 46, Bibliothèque Nationale, Paris; page 118, Black Watch Museum; page 123, from *Travels in Turkey, Asia Minor and across the Desert into Egypt* by W. Wittman; page 133, courtesy of the Trustees of the Chevening Estate; page 140, courtesy of Mrs Morris Waddington; page 169, His Grace the Duke of Wellington, MVO, OBE, MC; page 174, Trustees of the Wallace Collection; and on page 183, Colonel B. A. Fargus. Illustration Research Service and Celia Dearing supplied the pictures. The maps were drawn by Bucken Limited.

SELECT BIBLIOGRAPHY

Anon, 'Journal of T.S. of the 71st Highland L.I.' in *Memorials of the Late Wars*, Edinburgh, 1828.

Brownrigg, B., *Life and Letters of Sir John Moore*, London, 1921.

Bruce, H. A., *The Life of General Sir William Napier*, London, 1864.

Bunbury, Sir Henry, *Narrative of Certain Passages in the Late War with France*, London, 1852.

Fortescue, Sir John, *A History of the British Army*, 13 vols., London, 1899–1930.

Fuller, J. F. C., *Sir John Moore's System of Training*, London, 1925.

Glover, Richard, *Peninsular Preparations*, Cambridge, 1963.

Hibbert, Christopher, *Corunna*, London, 1961.

Maurice, Major-General Sir J. F., *The Diary of Sir John Moore*, 2 vols., London, 1904.

Meryon, C. L., *Memoirs of Lady Hester Stanhope*, London, 1845.

Moore, James Carrick, *The Life of Lieutenant-General Sir John Moore*, 2 vols., London, 1834.

Moore, James Carrick, *A Narrative of the Campaign of the British Army in Spain Commanded by His Excellency Lieutenant-General Sir John Moore*, London, 1809.

Napier, General Sir William, *The Life and Opinions of General Sir Charles Napier*, London, 1857.

Napier, W. F. P., *History of the War in the Peninsula*, vol. 1, London, 1835.

Oman, Carola, *Sir John Moore*, London, 1953.

Oman, Charles, *A History of the Peninsular War*, vol. 1, Oxford, 1902.

Paget, Sir A. (Ed.), *The Paget Papers*, 2 vols., London, 1896.
Public Record Office: Documents Relating to Sir John Moore.
Schaumann, August, *On the Road with Wellington*, London, 1924.
Weller, Jac, *Wellington in the Peninsula*, London, 1962.

INDEX

Abercrombie, General Sir Ralph, in West Indies, 65, 66, 67, 69, 70, 71, 72, 73; in Ireland, 75, 77; in Holland, 89, 92, 94, 95, 97, 98, 100, 101; in Mediterranean, 103, 104; campaign in Egypt, 105, 106, 107, 108, 113, 114, 115, 116, 117, 118; death of, 121, 122; 139

Aboukir, 105, 106, 107, 108, 109, 121, 122

Alexander, General Harold, 238

Alexandria, 105, 106, 112, 113, 114, 115, 116, 117, 118, 119, 120, 121, 122, 124, 143, 144

Alkmaar, 93, 94, 100; convention of, 101

American Revolution, the, 1, 5, 8, 9, 10, 11, 12, 13, 14, 15, 16, 125

American War of Independence – see American Revolution

Anderson, Paul, 21, 22, 71, 74, 75, 81, 84, 95, 97, 100, 101, 108, 120, 121, 145, 233, 234

Argyll, Elizabeth, Duchess of, 4, 5, 6

Astorga, 207, 208, 209

Baird, Sir David, 175, 179, 182, 184, 185, 187, 188, 189, 190, 191, 193, 195, 196, 198, 199, 200; and retreat to Corunna, 203, 204, 206, 208, 216, 232, 234

Bembibre, 212, 213

Benavente, 204, 205, 206, 207, 208, 212

Bentinck, Lord William, 178, 179, 180, 181, 184

Bergen, 96, 97, 98, 100

Berthier, Marshal Louis Alexandre, 196

Blake, General Joachim, 180, 187, 191

Boyd, Sir Robert, 25

Brownrigg, Sir Robert, 101, 126, 128, 143, 144, 150, 156

Bueno, Brigadier-General Don Augustin, 192, 194

Burgoyne, General John, 8, 9

Burrard, General Sir Harry, 97, 157, 158, 159, 161, 162, 163, 165, 168, 172, 173

Calvi, 28, 29, 30, 49, 50, 51, 52, 53, 54, 55

Camden, Lord John, 135, 138

Campbell, General Alexander, 65

Castaños, General Francisco, 163, 180, 182, 184, 187, 190, 192

Castlereagh, Lord Robert, 138, 144, 146, 147, 152, 153, 154, 155, 156, 158, 159, 160, 162, 169, 172, 173, 175, 178, 181, 185, 191, 193, 194, 195, 198, 206, 214, 223

Charmilly, Colonel Venault de, 192, 193, 194

Cintra, convention of, 167, 168, 172

Clinton, General Sir George, 13, 14

Cochrane, Captain Alexander, 108

Cochrane, Admiral Thomas, 135, 136, 137

Colborne, John, 207, 224

Coote, General Sir Eyre, 107, 109

Cornwallis, General Charles, 1st Marquis of, 14, 15, 83, 84, 85, 86, 87, 88

Corsica, 27–42, 44–59, 61, 62, 63, 87, 125, 137, 157

Corunna, 162, 173, 175, 179, 180, 184, 186, 187, 188, 191, 198; British retreat to, 202–19; preparations for battle at, 219, 220, 221, 222, 223, 224; battle of, 225–35, 238

Cradock, General John, 113, 114, 196

Craufurd, General Robert, 205, 206, 213

Cuesta, General, 180

Dalrymple, Sir Hew, 157, 159, 161, 164, 165, 167, 168, 169, 170, 172

D'Aubant, Colonel Abraham, 42, 44, 45, 47, 48, 49

242

Dickson, Captain, 26
Drummond, Colonel James, 70
Drummond, William, 141, 142, 144
Duckworth, Admiral Sir John, 143, 144
Dundas, General Sir David, 21, 31, 33, 34, 35, 36, 37, 38, 40, 41, 42, 43, 97, 127, 128
Dundas, Henry, 1st Viscount Melville, 63, 135
Dunlop, Captain, 11, 12, 71
Dupont, General Pierre, 163

Egypt, campaign in *1801*, 104, 105, 106, 107, 108, 109, 112, 113, 114, 115, 116, 117, 118, 119, 120, 121, 122, 124, 157
Elliot, Sir Gilbert, 28, 30, 31, 36, 40, 45, 49, 55, 56, 57, 58, 59, 61, 62, 63, 64, 72
Englefield, Captain, 41, 42
Erskine, Sir James, 55
Escalante, Captain-General Don Ventura, 192
Esla, river, crossing of, 204, 205, 207, 208

Ferrol, 134, 135, 136
Fox, Caroline, 139, 140, 143, 145, 146
Fox, Charles James, 138, 139, 141
Fox, General Henry, 138, 139, 140, 141, 143, 144, 145
Fraser, General Mackenzie, 144, 157, 203, 216, 225, 226
Frere, John Hookham, 185, 186, 187, 188, 190, 191, 192, 193, 194, 195, 200, 201
Friant, General Comte Louis, 115

George III, 5, 16, 59, 128, 137, 158, 160
Gustavus IV, King of Sweden, 147, 148, 149, 150, 151, 152, 153, 154, 155, 156, 157, 158

Hamilton, Douglas, Duke of, 4, 5, 10, 16, 58
Hay, Major Lewis, 74
Helder, the, 91, 92, 93, 94, 101
Hillows, William, 54, 55
Holland, allied expedition in *1799*, 89, 91, 92, 93, 94, 95, 96, 97, 98, 99, 100, 101, 157
Hood, Admiral Sir Samuel, 24, 25, 26, 27, 31, 33, 34, 39, 41, 42, 44, 45, 46, 47, 49, 50, 51, 61
Hope, General Sir John, 67, 68, 69, 70, 114, 155, 157, 179, 180, 182, 184, 185, 187, 191, 192; and retreat to Corunna, 203, 225, 234

Howe, General Sir William, 8, 9
Howick, Lord, 141
Hutchinson, General Hely, 113, 114, 122, 124

Ireland, Moore's service in *1790*, 17, 20, 21; Moore's service *1797-9*, 75, 76, 77, 78, 80, 81, 82, 83, 84, 85, 86, 87, 88, 125

Jaffa, 104, 105
Jaques, Colonel John, 20
Johnson, General Henry, 83
Jourdan, Marshal Jean Baptiste, 179
Junot, General Jean Andoche, 146, 150, 162, 163, 165, 166, 167, 198

Keith, Admiral Lord George Elphinstone, 103, 104, 106
Keogh, Matthew, 81, 83
Koehler, Major (later General) George, 27, 31, 33, 34, 35, 38, 39, 44, 45, 104, 105

Lake, General Sir Gerard, 77, 78, 83, 84, 85, 86
Leger, Colonel Barry St, 8
Leith, General John, 187, 217
Lisbon, 162, 163, 165, 168, 170, 172, 175, 176, 178, 179, 180, 181, 185, 190, 196
Ludlow, General George, 107
Lugo, 214, 216, 217, 218, 219

Macdonald, General Jacques, 89
Mackenzie, General Sir Kenneth, 157
Madrid, 178, 180, 182, 183, 185, 186, 188, 190, 191, 192, 193, 195, 196, 201
Maria Carolina, Queen of Naples, 103, 139, 140, 141, 142, 143, 144, 145
Masséna, Marshal André, 91, 102, 137
McLean, General Francis, 10, 11, 13
Melville, Lord – *see* Dundas, Henry
Menou, General Jacques, 116, 124
Minorca, 1, 7, 8, 9, 10, 87, 103
Moore, Charles, 1
Moore, Francis (Frank), 1, 20, 160
Moore, Admiral Sir Graham, 1, 6, 15, 83, 87, 133, 135, 136, 146
Moore, James, 1, 11, 14, 15, 17, 21, 58, 84, 85, 86, 102
Moore, Jane, 1, 160
Moore, Jeannie (Sir John's mother), 1, 4, 6, 15, 21, 24, 25, 58, 73, 74, 101, 129, 133, 138, 147, 160, 234

Moore, Dr John (Sir John's father), 1, 4, 5, 6, 9, 10, 12, 13, 15, 17, 20, 21, 23, 25, 73, 83, 101, 102, 116, 121, 124; death of, 124

Moore, General Sir John, character and ability, 1, 3, 13, 14, 17, 21, 40, 63, 72, 73, 76, 77, 78, 80, 84, 85, 86, 87, 88, 102, 113, 125–8, 151, 157, 209, 231, 235, 236; training methods, 78, 87, 88, 125, 126, 127, 128; early life, 1, 4, 5, 6; with 51st Regt., 1, 6, 7, 9, 10; service in America, 10, 11, 12, 13, 14, 15; in Parliament, 16, 17; service in Ireland 1790, 17, 20, 21; attitude to French Revolution, 22, 23, 24; moves to Gibraltar 1791, 23, 24, 25; moves to Corsica 1794, 26–30; and attack on San Fiorenzo, 31–9; attack on Bastia, 40–42, 44, 45, 47–50; attack on Calvi, 49–55; as Adjutant-General in Corsica, 55–61; return to London, 61–3; service in West Indies 1796, 63–73; ill with fever, 73–4; return to England, 74–5; service in Ireland 1797–9, 75–88; in Holland 1799, 88–102, 157; in Mediterranean 1800, 102–4, 157; in Egypt 1801, 104–8, 109, 112–22, 124, 157; at Chatham, Shorncliffe and Sandgate, 1802–5, 125–30, 132, 137, 138; receives knighthood, 130; and Lady Hester Stanhope, 130–32, 138, 156, 178, 195; expedition to Spain in 1804, 132–7; and Caroline Fox, 139, 143, 145, 146; service in Sicily 1806–7, 138–46; mission to Sweden in 1808, 146–59, 170; moves to Portugal, 158–63, 165, 167–70; meets Wellesley, 170, 171; receives command of British forces, 172, 173; prepares for invasion of Spain, 173–6, 178–80; invades, 180–84; at Salamanca, 184–90; first plans for retreat, 190–92; moves north against Soult, 193–6, 198–201; orders retreat, 201, 202; during retreat, 203–9, 212–15; decides on Corunna as embarkation port, 215, 216; in final stage of retreat, 217–20; preparations for battle at Corunna, 220–24; in battle of Corunna, 225, 226, 228–31; wounded, 232, 233; death of, 234

Morshead, General William, 65, 68

Murat, Joachim, 149, 150

Murray, Colonel (later General) George, 149, 153, 154, 155

Murray, General James, 7, 8, 10

Napier, General Sir Charles, 228, 229, 230, 231

Napier, George, 216

Napoleon, (Bonaparte), 24, 25, 74, 75, 102, 103, 105, 106, 121, 128, 129, 132, 133, 137, 143; invades Portugal, 146; joins army in Spain, 183, 196; moves against Moore, 201, 203, 204, 205, 206, 208, 212; leaves for Paris, 212; 235

Nelson, Viscount Horatio, 45, 46, 47, 48, 50, 51; wounded at Calvi, 52; Nile victory, 86; Moore's description of, 103, 104; victory at Trafalgar, 137

Ney, Marshal Michel, 212, 217

Oakes, General Hildebrand, 109, 117, 120

Paget, Sir Henry, 1st Marquis of Anglesey, 117, 123, 124, 157, 200, 201, 203, 205, 206, 207, 208, 212, 213, 214, 217, 220, 225, 226, 230, 231, 234

Palafox y Melzi, José de, 180

Paoli, Pasquale di, 28, 29, 30, 31, 33, 34, 40, 57, 58

Pellew, Admiral Sir Edward, 135

Penobscot Bay, 10, 11, 12, 13

Pitt, William, 16, 17, 23, 59, 60, 61, 62, 63, 130, 131, 134, 135, 137; death of, 138

Portland, Duke of, 62, 63, 147

Portugal, 75, 103, 146, 150; Moore proceeds to, 157, 158; campaign begins in, 162; Vimeiro, 165; 167, 168, 169, 175, 184, 189, 196

Pringle, Colonel, 7

Pulteney, Sir James, 134

Quelus, Moore's HQ at, 170, 172, 175, 176, 180, 181

Rifle Corps, the, 125, 126, 127

Roche, Philip, 83

Romana, General La, 187, 191, 195, 198, 201, 208

Sahagun, 200, 201, 203

St Lucia, 63, 64, 65, 66–74, 76

Salamanca, 179, 182, 184, 185, 187, 188, 191, 193, 196, 223, 235

San Fiorenzo, Corsica, 30–42

Schaumann, Augustus, 215, 218, 219, 233

Shorncliffe, 126, 127, 137

Sicily, 138–46, 157

Smith, Admiral Sir Sidney, 137, 138, 139, 140, 141, 143

Soult, Marshal Nicolas Jean de, 196, 198, 200, 203, 204, 206, 208, 212, 217, 218, 220, 225, 226, 235

Spain, 132; Moore's expedition to *1804*, 133–7; French invasion of, 149–50; 157, 158, 159; campaign in, 163; plans for British advance into, 168–70, 172–6, 178–80; British invasion of, 180–93, 196, 198, 199; retreat from, 201 ff

Spencer, General Brent, 150, 157, 163

Stanhope, Charles, 132, 234

Stanhope, Lady Hester, 130, 131, 132, 138, 156, 178, 195, 234

Steuart, General Sir James, 75, 77

Stewart, Colonel William, 125, 126

Stuart, General Sir Charles, 47, 48, 49, 50, 51, 52, 54, 55, 56, 63, 87, 103

Stuart, Charles, 190, 191

Stuart, General Sir John, 119, 139, 140, 141

Suvorov, Marshal Count Alexander, 89, 90, 102

Sweden, 146, 147, 148, 149, 150, 151, 152, 153, 154, 155, 156, 157, 158, 159, 165, 170

Thornton, Edward, 151, 155, 156

Toulon, 24, 25, 26, 27, 28, 34, 42, 50

Trigge, General Sir Thomas, 56, 58, 59, 63

Villafranca, 207, 208, 214

Villettes, Colonel William, 42

Vimeiro, battle of, 165, 167, 175

Warren, Admiral Sir John Borlasse, 86, 87

Washington, George, 9, 14

Wellesley, Sir Arthur (later Duke of Wellington), 150, 157, 158, 159, 162, 163; at Vimeiro, 165; 167, 168, 169; meets Moore, 170–71; 200, 235, 238

Wellington, Duke of – *see* Wellesley

West Indies, 63, 65, 66, 67, 68, 69, 70, 71, 72, 73, 74, 75, 87

Wexford, 80, 81, 82, 83

Wolfe, Charles, 238

York, Frederick Augustus, Duke of, 63, 87, 95, 100, 101, 124, 127, 129, 138, 143, 147, 156, 157, 158